# The Film Legacy of Edgar Allan Poe

*by Bruce G. Hallenbeck*

First published in 2020 by

Tomahawk Press
sales@tomahawkpress.com
www.tomahawkpress.com

ISBN 13: 978-0-9557670-6-7

Edited by Bruce Sachs

Designed by Steve Kirkham – Tree Frog Communication www.treefrogcommunication.co.uk

Printed by Gutenberg Press, Malta

This book is dedicated with respect and love to the King of Poe Pictures, the legendary Roger Corman. In the spirit of Poe, who was heavily influenced by the women in his life, I also dedicate this book to three of my own *grande dames:* To the memory of my paternal grandmother, Martha Hallenbeck, whose favourite Poe picture was Roger Corman's *The Premature Burial*; to my sister Susan, whose favourite is Corman's *The Tomb of Ligeia*; and to my wife Rosa, who favours Stuart Gordon's *The Pit and the Pendulum.*

# ACKNOWLEDGEMENTS

This book would not have been possible without the help of the following individuals:

Sam Umland, for all of his hard work; Jonathan Rigby, author of the book *American Gothic: Sixty Years of Horror Cinema*; actor David Frankham, for his memories of appearing in *Tales of Terror*; the late Hazel Court, for her reminiscences of making *The Raven*; the late Adrienne Corri for sharing her recollections of co-starring in the 1960 version of *The Tell-Tale Heart*; Jeffrey Combs, for his memories of being directed by Stuart Gordon; writer/producer/director Ansel Faraj, for his fascinating stories concerning his web series *Theatre Fantastique*; my old friend Walter L. Gay, who helped me track down the 1966 version of *The Black Cat*; Jim Wynorski, for providing a splendid interview regarding his film *The Haunting of Morella*; triple-threat Mark Redfield, who gave me an extensive interview about the making of his film *The Death of Poe*; actor Kevin G Shinnick, for recounting his experience of playing Dr Moran in Redfield's film; Filmmaker Dave Hastings (*House of Screaming Death*) for his invaluable research on two rare screen versions of *The Tell-tale Heart*; Stephen Jacobs for alerting me to the 1928 version of *The Tell-Tale Heart*; Cynthia Brown, Roger Corman's incredibly helpful and generous Executive Assistant; Steve Kirkham for the wonderful design of this book; and of course, my peerless publisher, Bruce Sachs at Tomahawk Press.

*"(We) liked just any horror movie, but our faves were the string of American-International films, mostly directed by Roger Corman … (We)had our own name for these films, one that made them into a separate genre. There were westerns, there were love stories … and there were **Poepictures**"*

*Stephen King in his memoir ON WRITING (Scribner, 2000)*

# FOREWORD

**M**y first encounter with Poe was for a school assignment when I was twelve or thirteen and much too young to fully appreciate the masterfully macabre explorations of the human psyche that so epitomize his works. I was to read "The Fall of the House of Usher" and write an essay on it, an endeavor that proved so enthralling that I later asked my parents for Poe's complete works for Christmas.

Years later, while making a series of low budget films for Allied Artists and American International Pictures, Roderick Usher inhabited my thoughts

once more. I came to Jim Nicholson, the head of AIP, requesting a longer shooting schedule and twice the usual budget to make *House of Usher*. He agreed immediately. His partner, Sam Arkoff, was not so eager. "Roger, we have a problem," he said. "There are no monsters." Thinking quickly, I replied, "The house *is* the monster."

It had never been my intention to make a series of Poe Pictures. I had only wanted to do the one that had so captured my imagination all those years ago. But after the film became an incredible commercial and critical success, a sequel was only logical. And then another. And another.

It was the unconscious mind that guided me through all those "Poe Pictures." Not my own, but rather a conscious commitment to evoking the unconscious – the deepest, darkest pits of ourselves from which so many of Poe's greatest horrors emerge. We shot nearly ever scene in the confines of a sound studio. My theory, which I followed religiously, was that to reproduce Poe's unconscious, we had to sequester ourselves from the outside world. Then and only then could the full extent of the Poeian dread be felt. By the eighth and final film – *The Tomb of Ligeia* – I had become so weary of my own theory that I deliberately filmed it in the English countryside in broad daylight.

From the beginning, my first choice for Roderick Usher was Vincent Price. Like Usher, Vincent was highly intelligent, highly educated, and full of angst in the best possible way. No longer a young leading man, Vincent was not only of the age but of the mind for Poe's Usher. He became the incarnation of not only Roderick Usher but of Poe himself. He was as much an inhabitant of Poe's country of the mind as I was.

Keeping the unconscious mind in the back of our own, we tried to make each subsequent film unique from the last. In *The Raven*, for instance, screenwriter Dick Matheson and I introduced humor. In *The Tomb of Ligeia*, Bob Towne, who would go on to become the Academy Award-winning screenwriter of *Chinatown*, worked with me to make the film, in part, a love story. But from one Poe Picture to the next, it was always our hope that the film read as unequivocally Poeian. We wanted our audience to leave their seats newly and frightfully aware of their own subliminal selves.

*Roger Corman*

Roger Corman, 2020

# INTRODUCTION

**A** commemorative service marking the centenary of Edgar Allan Poe's birth was held in London, on 1 March 1909 at the Authors' Club. The service merited a brief report in the New York Times the next day. According to the *New York Times* article, presiding at the London event was celebrated author Sir Arthur Conan Doyle, who 'was supported by Ambassador [Whitelaw] Reid and Mrs. Humphry Ward, many leading British authors and a large number of American residents of London.' Among other luminaries in attendance were J. Ridgeley Carter, Secretary of the American Embassy, Professor George Grafton Brown of Brown University, and Mrs. Patsy Cornwallis-West, a beauty who was once the mistress of the then King of England, Edward VII. As one might expect, Sir Conan Doyle acknowledged Poe as the inspiration for his detective stories, saying, 'It is the irony of Fate that he, as he said, should have died in poverty, for if every man who wrote a story which was indirectly inspired by Poe were to pay a tithe toward a monument it would be such as would dwarf the pyramids.'

In America, Poe's grave went unmarked for twenty-six years. When a monument was finally erected, in November 1875, the one American author who attended the ceremony was Walt Whitman. The Raven Society (established 1904) at the University of Virginia held a centenary celebration with a small program on 19 January 1909 as indicated by a small notice in the *New York Times*, but otherwise, the centenary of Poe's birth went largely unobserved in his own country. Poe would finally attain a modicum of respectability on the centenary of his death, when, on 7 October 1949, a 3¢ U.S. postage stamp was issued with his picture on it. Ironically, he had been omitted from the "Famous Americans" stamp series issued a few years earlier, in 1940, comprised of 35 stamps honouring American authors, poets, educators, scientists, composers, artists, and inventors. The five poets included in the 1940 series (all born in the nineteenth century) more esteemed (and perhaps considered more wholesome) than Poe at the time were Henry Wadsworth Longfellow, John Greenleaf Whittier, Walt Whitman, James Russell Lowell, and James Whitcomb Riley. In 2009, Poe would be acknowledged again by a second postage stamp celebrating the bicentenary of his birth, by which time a professional American football team, the Baltimore Ravens, had been named after his most famous poem, the team located in the city where Poe died in 1849 and was subsequently buried.

In contrast, the tercentenary service of William Shakespeare's death was marked with great aplomb in America. Held in New York slightly over seven years after the Poe centenary, the commemorative service was presented at the Cathedral of St. John the Divine on Easter Sunday, 23 April 1916. Judith Buchanan indicates that two ennobled British actors, Herbert Beerbohm Tree and Johnston Forbes-Robertson, 'each gave an address and the eminent American actor Frederick Warde read the second lesson. The service closed with the singing of "America."'

The congregation then repaired to Central Park where, despite the rain, a floral wreath was laid on Shakespeare's statue. As part of the tribute, Tree placed a 'British flag over the bust of the statue.' Rather obviously, the ceremony served not only to recognize the prestige of Shakespeare, but also to reaffirm British and American unity during World War I, then raging in Europe.

Most certainly the cultural capital associated with Shakespeare in America helps to explain the pomp and circumstance accorded the Bard's tercentenary service in 1916, while Poe's lack of it helps to explain why there was no equivalent service held on his centenary in 1909. Between 1899 and the dawn of the sound era in 1927, Judith Buchanan reports there were between 250 and 300 motion picture adaptations of Shakespeare. In contrast, during the same period, there were a mere 12 adaptations of the works of Poe, of uneven quality. Some critics have argued that certain films of the period, such as D. W. Griffith's *The Sealed Room* (September 1909), may have been 'inspired by' the works of Poe (in this instance, 'The Cask of Amontillado'), thus adding to the overall number, but *The Sealed Room* could just as easily been inspired by Verdi's *Aida*, a revival of which opened at the New York Metropolitan Opera on 16 November 1908, featuring Enrico Caruso as Radamès and the Metro debut of conductor Arturo Toscanini, receiving thirteen performances during the 1908–09 season. In addition, some of the silent era adaptations of Poe are actually what we would now refer to as 'bio-pics,' loosely autobiographical films largely focused on Poe's writing of his most famous poem, 'The Raven.' One of these 'bio-pics,' the only known film to be released in America in 1909 in order to commemorate the centenary of Poe's birth, actually misspelled Poe's name—D. W. Griffith's *Edgar Allen* [sic] *Poe*. Poor Poe.

Griffith's Poe-inspired *The Sealed Room* opened the first week of September, 1909, coinciding with the arrival in New York of Sigmund Freud on his first and only trip to America. (He had been invited to deliver a series of lectures on psychoanalysis at Clark University in Worcester, Massachusetts.) As the ocean liner George Washington arrived in New York Harbour, Freud purportedly remarked to fellow passenger Carl Jung, "They don't realize that we are bringing them the plague." Indeed. Claudia C. Morrison states in *Freud and the Critic* that after 1909 "the number of articles and books on his [Freud's] ideas steadily increased until by the 1920's [sic] there were, according to one source, 'more than two hundred books dealing with Freudianism,'" and that A. A. Brill's English translations of Freud began appearing in 1910.

Neurotic artists such as Poe immediately became the favoured subject of psychoanalytic critics, and psychoanalytic readings of Poe's tales had a major influence on the reception of his tales in the years following—and, in turn, the film adaptations based on them.

With the exception of D. W. Griffith's silent era films *Edgar Allen Poe* (1909) and *The Avenging Conscience* (1914, loosely based on 'The Tell-Tale Heart'), there were no historically significant film adaptations made in America, or elsewhere, based on Poe's tales. By the late 1920s, however, after the rise of psychoanalysis and the cinematic avant-garde, certain of his tales became of interest to filmmakers. The subjective, distorted perception of a tortured narrator – widely popularized by the use of the delusional narrator, Francis, in *The Cabinet of Dr. Caligari* (1920) – conveniently meshed with the avant-garde cinema's preference to represent or approximate the Freudian dream state or dream world. Charles Klein's *The Telltale Heart* (1928), for instance, is clearly inspired by the German Expressionism of Caligari, as is Jean Epstein's *La Chute de la Maison Usher* (*The Fall of the House of Usher*, 1928), and James Sibley Watson and Melville Webber's *The Fall of the House of Usher* (1928). But the historic interest of these films resides in them being examples of the cinematic avant-garde; the fact they are Poe adaptations now seems incidental.

As it happened, a figure emerged from the avant-garde who went on to direct Hollywood's first Poe adaptation of the sound era, *The Murders in the Rue Morgue* (1932). This figure was Robert Florey, born in Paris in 1900. As Brian Taves has shown, Universal's decision to hire Florey as director of, first, *Frankenstein* (on which he was replaced by James Whale), and then *The Murders in the Rue Morgue*, was in large part due to his knowledge of the Grand Guignol Theatre, in which Florey had been involved before moving to America in 1921. Florey's avant-garde films include *The Life and Death of 9413: a Hollywood Extra* (1928), *The Love of Zero* (also 1928) and a film Taves describes as having a 'Poe-like' scenario, *Johann the Coffin Maker* (1928, believed lost). These films' expressionistic set design and lighting, avant-garde compositions and camera angles, as well as their exploration of subjective states, all foreshadow the visual style of Florey's later films. As Taves observes, with *Murders in the Rue Morgue* and his later thrillers, such as *The Florentine Dagger* (1935), *The Face Behind the Mask* (1941), and *The Beast With Five Fingers* (1946), Florey would prove to be gifted 'in both writing and directing stories imaginatively mediating elements of mystery and horror.' Most importantly, however, *Murders in the Rue Morgue* drew on elements taken from the plays of the Grand Guignol Theatre, or the "Théâtre des Horreurs," as it is named in Karl Freund's *Mad Love* (1935).

The central thrust of this book is that 'Poe Pictures', a term coined by famed horror author Stephen King, represent the irrevocable transformation of Poe's tales having been first adapted by writers in the Grand Guignol Theatre. As we shall see, this transformation must be understood as an adumbration, a 'faint outline,' a 'partial concealment' in the sense of 'overshadowing,' of Poe's source tales. Put in another way, Poe Pictures are Grand Guignol disguised as Poe adaptations. It has never been an uncommon occurrence that critics lament the fact that movie adaptations of Poe seldom adhere to their source texts. That is because they are not, strictly speaking, Poe adaptations at all, but Poe as filtered through the Grand Guignol.

By no means did Robert Florey alone bring a European sensibility to the horror films produced by Universal: that had been done by Paul Leni, the German expatriate who, as Thomas Schatz has observed, was an expert 'at translating expressionist style into the language of Hollywood.' Schatz asserts it was Leni's *The Cat and the Canary* (1927) that 'set the pattern' for Universal's 'old dark house' formula, and his direction of Conrad Veidt in *The Man Who Laughs* (1928), about a man whose face was distorted at birth into a grotesque grin, invoked Lon Chaney's performance in *The Phantom of the Opera* (1925). Florey's European training and his interest in the macabre made him a good fit at Universal, the one Hollywood studio that was very clearly, as Schatz writes, 'fascinated with the horrific.' Although studio politics led to Florey being replaced as director of *Frankenstein*, he had for that film's initial spectacle of monstrous creation turned for inspiration to German Expressionist films such as *The Golem* (1920) and to Fritz Lang's *Metropolis* (1927), but when reassigned to the adaptation of Poe's 'Murders in the Rue Morgue,' he turned for inspiration to the Grand Guignol, explaining why so very little of Poe's source material is used in the film. And so Robert Florey brought to Hollywood his first-hand knowledge of the Grand Guignol.

Universal's subsequent Poe adaptation, Edgar G. Ulmer's *The Black Cat* (1934) – featuring the historic first teaming of Karloff and Lugosi – is considered by Weaver and Brunas as 'one of the decade's most disturbing exercises in the Grand Guignol.' The subsequent Poe adaptation produced at Universal that also featured Karloff and Lugosi, *The Raven* (1935), 'owes little to its Poe sources,' in the words of Don G. Smith, but it does owe a great deal to the Grand Guignol: a mad doctor, an escaped criminal, blackmail, brutal mutilation under the pretext of plastic surgery, torture, murder, and pervasive sadism. The film would cause a major furore in England, where, again according to Smith, 'the X rating for horror films was soon established,' thus bringing an end to Universal's so-called 'golden age of horror.' Subsequently, no further Poe adaptations were produced by Universal for nearly six years.

The best-known and most popular of Edgar Allan Poe adaptations remain those directed by Roger Corman in the 1960s for American International Pictures. Between 1960 and 1965, Corman made a series of eight films based on Poe works, most of them starring Vincent Price: *House of Usher* (1960), *Pit and the Pendulum* (1961), *Tales of Terror* (1962), *Premature Burial* (1962), *The Raven* (1963), *The Haunted Palace* (1963), *Masque of the Red Death* (1964) and *Tomb of Ligeia* (1965). These films have become classics of their type and are still often seen today on Blu-ray disc and on classic movie channels. Their lush atmosphere, ripe performances and haunting musical scores set the gold standard for all Poe adaptations to follow.

Poe is still being adapted for the screen as these words are being written. A new version of *The Masque of the Red Death* is in production in Japan; actor/writer/director Sylvester Stallone is currently penning a screenplay about Poe himself; and enterprising independent filmmakers continue to mine the writer's short stories, novellas and poems for inspiration.

This book will explore how Poe and, indeed the Grand Guignol works of blood and terror he inspired, continue to be relevant in the 21st Century. In a world in which that century began with the real–life horrors of 9/11, Poe could never cease to be important to the human psyche.

**Notes**

"Honor Poe in London; Conan Doyle Acknowledges His Inspiration at Authors Club Dinner," New York Times, March 2, 1909, p. 4; "Raven Society Celebrates; Poe Centenary Is Appropriately Observed at University of Virginia, New York Times, January 19, 1909, p. 4; Judith Buchanan, Shakespeare on Silent Film: An Excellent Dumb Discourse, Cambridge: Cambridge University Press, 2009, pp. 1-2, 190; Claudia C. Morrison, Freud and the Critic: The Early Use of Depth Psychology in Literary Criticism, Chapel Hill: The University of North Carolina Press, 1968, pp. 11, 35; Brian Taves, Robert Florey: The French Expressionist, Metuchen: Scarecrow Press, 1987, pp. 39, 96, 124, 137; Thomas Schatz, The Genius of the System: Hollywood Filmmaking in the Studio Era, Minneapolis: The University of Minnesota Press, 2010, pp. 88, 89; Tom Weaver, Michael Brunas and John Brunas, Universal Horrors: The Studio's Classic Films, 1931-1946, 2nd Edition, Jefferson: McFarland, 2007, pp. 87; Don G. Smith, The Poe Cinema: A Critical Filmography of Theatrical Releases Based on the Works of Edgar Allan Poe, Jefferson: McFarland, 1998, pp. 57-58.

# CHAPTER ONE
# THE SILENT POE

*'Then I grew angry and cursed, with
the curse of silence, the river, and the wind, and the forest, and the
heavens, and the thunder, and the sighs of the water-lilies.'*

**Silence, a Fable**

The movies were born in the late 19th Century in the United States and France. Originally shown on 'peep show' devices called Kinetoscopes, films were ultimately screened on projectors for public exhibition; the first such film shown to an audience was Thomas Edison's *Blacksmith Scene* in 1893. French brothers August and Louis Lumière held their first screenings of projected motion pictures in 1895.

At the time, filmmaking was not referred to as an 'art form.' It was merely a new invention, a source of amusement much the same as video games were a hundred years later.

Fantasy quickly took hold in the nascent cinema however, and along with it came its twin, darkness. Frenchman Georges Méliès, a former stage magician, created the first special effects in such films as *A Trip to the Moon* (1902) and *The Impossible Voyage* (1904), perhaps his most famous works. Even earlier, however, he had made what some consider to be the first horror film, *La Manoir du Diable* (*The Haunted Castle*, 1896), featuring a bat flying into a medieval castle and transforming into the Devil (an unknown actor, probably magician Jules-Eugene Legris). It was a bit early in the game to attempt to actually horrify audiences, as the intention was to induce wonder and amusement rather than fear. Nevertheless, its visual trappings, themes and characters certainly evoke the yet-to-be-invented genre of the horror film, and with its transformation from bat to human, some have even called it the first vampire film.

Despite its popularity in the theatre of Grand Guignol and literature, horror was slow to gain a foothold in the new medium. The first adaptation of Mary Shelley's *Frankenstein* didn't arrive until 1910, courtesy of Thomas Edison's sixteen-minute version, which softened its horrific elements, reassuring its patrons that Edison and company had 'tried to eliminate all the actually repulsive situations and to concentrate on the mystic and psychological problems that are to be found in this weird tale.'

Yet, the year before, Edgar Allan Poe had made his first screen appearance. The earliest surviving film related to Poe is called simply, *Edgar Allen Poe*, which is also the first of many films in which the author's middle name is misspelled. Running a mere seven minutes, it purports to portray some of the important moments of Poe's life. Directed by D W Griffith for the American Mutoscope & Biograph Company, the film stars Herbert Yost (aka Barry O'Moore) as the destitute Poe, attempting to comfort his dying wife Virginia (Linda Arvidson), when, by a twist of fate, he spies a raven perched upon his bust of Pallas above the door of their dingy apartment. The rest, as they say, is history.

Griffith, of course, was one of the greatest American filmmakers of the silent era, notorious for his blatantly racist *The Birth of a Nation* (1914), yet progressive in his approach to the new medium of film, developing storytelling techniques that were revolutionary at the time and are still used today, After acting in some films for director Edwin S Porter at the Edison Company, Griffith was offered a job at the struggling American Mutoscope & Biograph Company, where he directed over 450 short films, pushing the envelope of what could be done with the medium with nearly each one. Along with his cinematographer G W Bitzer, Griffith created and developed such cinematic techniques as iris shots, cross-cutting, masking and the device of the flashback.

*Edgar Allen Poe* (1909)

Griffith had a fascination with Poe, and for Poe's centenary year of 1909, he got together with writer Frank E Woods to create the short film *Edgar Allen Poe.* It was one of many high-profile tributes to the author during that year. For example, the Poe centenary was celebrated at the University of Virginia, with Dr Herbert Nash of Norfolk (who, a local newspaper reported, 'had a brief acquaintance with Poe during the poet's last visit to Virginia') giving a reminiscence of the author and 'stereopticon views of the university during Poe's stay in the college were shown.'

The new medium of film, however, could accomplish much more, for Herbert Yost was the spitting, moving image of Poe in Griffith's seven-minute short, despite the wild overacting of the period. While not a strict biographical piece, *Edgar Allen Poe* is based on actual incidents from Poe's life.

As the film opens, the author is in a grief-stricken frenzy when he chances to see a raven perched on a bust of Pallas above the door of their cold, seedy apartment. Inspired by this vision, he takes off his coat and sets to work on what will be his masterpiece. He has thoughtfully placed his coat upon Virginia as she lies in bed, to ease her wracked body from the cold.

Finishing his narrative poem, Poe rushes, sans hat and coat, to a publisher, where he has difficulty attracting anyone's attention. One editor, however, peruses 'The Raven' and offers him a whopping ten dollars for it. Poe is delighted with his 'good fortune' and accepts the editor's offer. When he returns to his wife, she is dying, and the film ends on a tragic note as Virginia dies in Poe's arms.

As is the case with many of the early Biograph shorts, the title cards for *Edgar Allen Poe* have been lost over the years, but they're hardly needed: the story, such as it is, is told completely visually, with no need for dialogue or descriptive narrative cards. All of the information we need is there in the visuals – the dingy apartment, the mortally ill wife, the busy publishing house – all tell us exactly what is going on in Poe's life. Although the style of the film is still quite theatrical, it was another rung on the ladder of Griffith's burgeoning cinematic experiments, telling its tragic story economically and without a great deal of flourish.

While there are brief records (basically no more than the titles) of a French version of *The Gold Bug* and an Italian version of *The Pit and the Pendulum* for the year 1910, the films themselves appear to be hopelessly lost. The next major cinematic production having to do with Poe was again from D W Griffith, this time loosely based on 'The Tell Tale Heart' and the poem 'Annabel Lee.' And, on this occasion, it was a feature film that ran 78 minutes.

*The Avenging Conscience: or Thou Shalt Not Kill* was made for the Majestic Motion Picture Company in 1914. The film starred Henry B Walthall, an American stage and film actor who had worked with Griffith at Biograph (which was located in New York) and who followed the director to California's Reliance-Majestic Studios. He had appeared in Griffith's eleven-minute Poe-inspired short *The Sealed Room* (1909), which had been loosely based on 'The Cask of Amontillado' with a touch of Balzac's 'La Grande

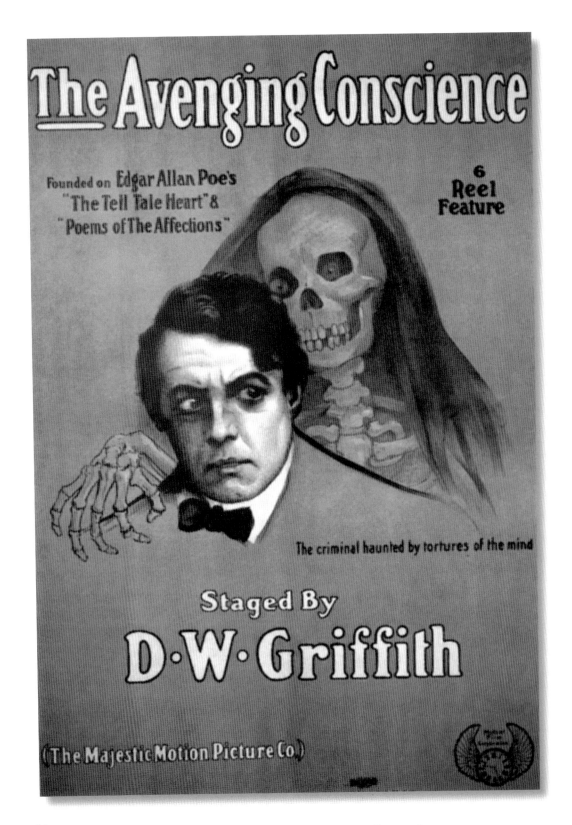

**This and Right:** *The Avenging Conscience* (1914)

Breteche' thrown in for good measure. In *The Avenging Conscience*, Walthall was cast as 'The Nephew,' the story's protagonist, who falls in love with a beautiful woman played by Blanche Sweet, an actress who had begun her career in the earliest days of the silent film industry and another veteran of Griffith's Biograph days.

In the film, The Nephew is prevented by his uncle (Spottiswoode Aitken) from wooing his sweetheart. As revenge, he kills his uncle and hides the body behind a wall he has built. He is tormented by guilt, however, and he becomes hyper-sensitive to sounds, such as the mere tapping of a shoe or the shriek of a bird. Finally, the ghost of his uncle appears while, at the same time, the police discover his crime. At the end of the film, in a touch that also marred Edison's adaptation of *Frankenstein*, it is revealed that it has all been a nightmare and that the young man's uncle is still alive.

Released by Mutual Film Corporation in August, 1914, *The Avenging Conscience* is the earliest and most important feature-length cinematic adaptation of Poe to have survived. Elegantly photographed by G W Bitzer, who would also shoot *The Birth of a Nation*, the 'third act' segment, which is closest to Poe's 'The Tell Tale Heart,' holds the most interest for viewers today, and certainly for Poe enthusiasts. The sounds that plague The Nephew's conscience have to be conveyed entirely visually, which, as photographed by Bitzer, work extremely well. The editing by James Smith and Rose Smith is highly sophisticated in this sequence and adds immeasurably to its power.

While *The Avenging Conscience* is nearly ruined by its happy ending – audiences were still not used to horror in the cinema – the murder scene and most of what follows is very effective for the time in which it was filmed. The climax goes off the rails into a flight of fantasy involving frolicking fairies and Grecian dancing, and one can only imagine what Poe would have thought of a happy ending to his 'Annabel Lee' and 'The Tell Tale Heart.' However, *The Avenging Conscience* is an important and memorable attempt to translate some of Poe's mood into a feature-length film; while not completely successful, it is a pivotal work from one of cinema's first great filmmakers.

Walthall went from playing a Poe protagonist to portraying Poe himself in *The Raven* (1915), a fictionalised and stylised 'biography' of the writer.

POE REINCARNATED
appears in the person of
Henry B. Walthall
The Living Image of America's Greatest Poet,
in
"THE RAVEN"
In 6 acts
A ROMANCE OF
EDGAR ALLAN POE
By George C. Hazelton
(founded upon Mr. Hazelton's widely known novel and play)
Directed by Charles J. Brabin
WARDA HOWARD
the great emotional actress, appears with Mr. Walthall in this, the most ethereally artistic, intensely fascinating and soul-stirring photodrama of the year.

Essanay
"FIRST TO STANDARDIZE PHOTOPLAYS"
1333 Argyle Street, Chicago, Ill.
George K. Spoor, President

Trademark Reg.
U. S. Pat. 1907.

*The Raven* (1915)

Based on a play by George Cochran Hazelton (which was in turn based on his novel), the feature was directed by Charles Brabin, a Liverpool-born filmmaker who had emigrated to New York in the early 1900s. There, he did some stage acting and joined the Edison Manufacturing Company in 1908, where he also did some acting, writing and directing. Brabin had a brief career in talkies, directing, among other films, *The Mask of Fu Manchu* (1932), starring Boris Karloff.

*The Raven* begins by addressing Poe's lineage, with Poe's parents (Hugh Thompson and Peggy Meredith) introduced in the opening scenes before the author is even born. After the loss of his parents, Poe is adopted by John and Francis Allan (Ernest Maupain and Eleanor Thompson), from whom he receives his middle name.

The film then fast-forwards in time to fifteen years later, when Poe is a student at the University of Virginia. Due to his gambling debts and his burgeoning drinking problem, Poe begins to have difficulties discerning fantasy from reality. In one vivid example of this growing problem, he hallucinates that he has killed a man in a duel.

Later, he meets Virginia Clemm (Warda Howard), whom he falls in love with and marries. His drinking and gambling continue, however, and his situation becomes more and more difficult. This plunges him into depression, and, in an alcohol-induced hallucination, while sitting alone and brooding, he experiences the basis for his most famous work, 'The Raven,' when he thinks he sees a raven – which, the intertitles tell us, croaks the word 'Nevermore' over and over again – enter his room and land on a bust of Pallas.

He attempts to make a living through his writing, but money is difficult to come by, and Virginia dies because he is unable to care for her. Toward the end of the film, Howard also plays Helen Whitman (as well as 'The Lost Lenore' and 'A Spirit') to whom Poe later becomes engaged, but never marries. The film as it survives today appears to be incomplete, with portions of the final reel missing, and, in what remains, Poe and Helen never meet.

*The Raven* still holds a fascination because of the central sequence in which Poe's poem is recreated onscreen for the first time. Because of his appearance in two Poe pictures, Walthall was dubbed 'the image of Poe' in the film's publicity.

As written by Brabin, *The Raven* seems to treat Poe as more of a mentally disturbed individual rather than as a brilliant writer. The sequence recreating the poem features some heavy-handed symbolism, with Poe stumbling outside while the word WINE appears on a rock against which he steadies himself. As he reaches for another glass of wine, the glass transforms into a human skull. There are moments when *The Raven* almost feels like a pro-Prohibition tract.

Despite these dated morality metaphors, however, Brabin's take on *The Raven* is an interesting one, and Walthall is very good as Poe, attempting to portray his genius as well as his demons. Having Howard playing Virginia, Helen and 'Lenore' is a nice touch. Although it seems to exist now only in 57 and 45-minute versions, what is left of *The Raven* is very tantalising indeed, and whets the appetite for more silent film adaptations of Poe to come.

World events intervened before the next cinematic Poe adaptation; the First World War, otherwise known as the War to End All Wars, began in Europe in July 1914 and raged on until November 1918. Over nine million combatants and seven million civilians died in one of the most horrific wars in history. It resulted in the fall of the German, Russian, Ottoman and Austro-Hungarian empires.

The defeat of Germany brought about a new wave of horror cinema in that nation. The most famous was *The Cabinet of Dr Caligari* (1919), directed by Robert Wiene, which some critics opine was an Expressionist view of the German government, with the 'somnambulist' Cesare (Conrad Veidt) representative of the ordinary German conditioned to be a soldier. At least that was the way that author Siegfried Kracauer saw it in his book *From Caligari to Hitler: a Psychological History of the German Film* (1947).

*Caligari* may have been the quintessential German Expressionist film, but the next Poe film, also German, took its cue from another source: the French theatre of Grand Guignol. In 1919, the same year that *Caligari* was unleashed to a startled yet war-weary world, the horror anthology film was born in Germany as a 112-minute feature – an epic by the standards of the day – called *Unheimliche Geschicten (Eerie Tales)*. The film incorporated no less than five stories into its considerable running time, including one by Robert Louis Stevenson and one by Poe. The framing story took place in an antique bookshop in which the characters of Death, the Devil and a Strumpet amused each other at closing time by reading the tales to each other out of books.

Directed by Richard Oswald, an Austrian director/producer/screenwriter, and written by Anselma Heine, Robert Liebmann and Oswald, *Eerie Tales* was not only the first horror anthology film, it was also one of the most ambitious. It starred Conrad Veidt from *Caligari*, Reinhold Schunzel and Anita Berber in each of the five segments, which included Poe's 'The Black Cat' and Stevenson's 'The Suicide Club.'

*Eerie Tales* was no Expressionist film, however. Unlike *Caligari*, whose every frame dripped with symbolism, *Eerie Tales* went for a more visceral approach, one of the first films to present horror in a physical way rather than in a psychological, dreamlike fashion a la *The Avenging Conscience*. There was no heavy-handed moralising here: after the real horrors of the War to End All Wars (which, of course, it didn't), *Eerie Tales* went straight for the jugular, one of the first films to present horror in a straightforward, realistic fashion.

Le Theatre du Grand-Guignol had been founded in Paris in 1894 and had been an almost immediate sensation. In a sense, it was anthology theatre, as patrons would see five or six short plays in one evening, with the most popular by far being horror plays. There were several adaptations of Poe, who was very highly regarded in France, including 'The System of Dr Tarr and Professor Fether' and 'The Tell Tale Heart.' The plays were known and loved for their gory special effects and their infamously bloody endings; ironic indeed that the theatre itself had formerly been a chapel.

*Eerie Tales* is constructed very much like an evening at the Grand Guignol, with its opening tale, 'The Apparition,' concerning a man and a woman who check into a hotel; the man goes out for a walk in the evening, but when he returns, his wife has vanished. He is told by the *concierge* that he had checked in alone. What transpires ends with a shock when we discover that the Black Plague is involved. This is essentially the same story that Alfred Hitchcock would film in 1938 as *The Lady Vanishes* and Terence Fisher and Antony Darnborough would co-direct in 1949 as *So Long at the Fair*, and it is fascinating to observe how the same tale served several different filmmakers in various ways.

The second story, 'The Hand,' involves a love triangle in which Schunzel murders Veidt and is haunted by the 'ghosts' of his hands. It is one of the most atmospheric of all the *Eerie Tales* and very well acted by Veidt, Schunzel and Berber.

Next up is the first cinematic adaptation of 'The Black Cat,' which also concerns a love triangle in which Schunzel finds to his horror that he has walled up his black cat along with his adulterous wife (Berber). The horror is muted somewhat as we never see what is behind the wall, except for the cat crawling out. There was, however, still no horror genre in the cinema of

1919 –so we are spared the sight of his wife's dead body. But the elements of Grand Guignol are certainly present, even if the visuals are depicted somewhat timidly,

The fourth tale is Stevenson's 'Suicide Club,' which generates considerable suspense when Schunzel discovers that the exclusive club to which he now belongs engages in a sinister ritual: its president (Veidt) brings out a deck of cards as the final order of business every evening, and whoever draws the Ace of Spades must die that night. The story is well told, with Schunzel ultimately turning the tables on Veidt as Oswald turns the screws of tension.

The final segment, 'The Spectre,' is an original story by Oswald and easily the weakest of the five. It's a whimsical tale, perhaps intended to relieve the viewer from the horrors of the other stories, but it merely seems out of place. 'The Spectre' involves a nobleman (Schunzel) who makes a play for the wife (Berber) of a baron (Veidt); the latter then contrives a 'haunting' to scare the would-be seducer out of his wits.

Overall, *Eerie Tales* is highly sophisticated in both concept and execution and it managed to establish both the horror anthology, and, to a certain extent, the horror genre itself, at least in the silent era, in a single stroke. It was also one of the first –if not *the* first – straightforward adaptations of a Poe story on film, even if it changed some of the details, which would happen repeatedly with Poe adaptations.

It would be nine years before the next major cinematic Poe adaptation, and this one would have more to do with the world of surrealism and the avant-garde than with Grand Guignol. Jean Epstein's *The Fall of the House of Usher* (French: *La Chute de la maison Usher*, 1928) is important for a number of reasons. Although based on a short story (albeit a somewhat lengthy one) it is feature length, with a running time of 63 minutes. Epstein was not only a filmmaker, he was a film theorist, literary critic and novelist who was associated with French Impressionist Cinema, otherwise known as the 'first avant-garde' or 'narrative avant-garde.' Films that fall into this category include Abel Gance's *Napoleon* (1927), Marcel L'Herbler's *El*

This Page & Opposite: Epstein's
*The Fall of the House of Usher*
(1928)

*Dorado* (1921) and Jean Renoir's *Nana* (1926). Epstein's Poe adaptation falls firmly into this category.

It is also important to note that the screenplay for *Usher* was co-written by Luis Buñuel, who would shock the world a year later with his 16-minute short *Un Chien Andalou*, co-written by Salvador Dali. The short was Buñuel's first film as director, had no plot in the usual meaning of the word, and was full of shocking images, opening with a scene of an eye being slit by a razor. *Usher* was Buñuel's second film credit; he had previously worked as assistant director on Epstein's film *Mauprat* (1926).

Epstein's *Usher* follows the Poe story fairly closely, but with one important difference: Madeleine Usher (Marguerite Gance) is now Roderick Usher's (Jean Debucourt) wife rather than his sister, which changes the family dynamics of the story considerably. Epstein's film is more about mood than plot, however, and it has atmosphere in spades. The cinematography by Georges Lucas and Jean Lucas is lush and sumptuous, with a good deal of camera movement (somewhat unusual for the period) and a plethora of location work.

A visual feast, the 1928 *Usher* is a masterpiece of art direction (by Pierre Kefer) and surprising images. Although the exterior of the house is a rather small and none too convincing model, the interior is a riot of dreamlike imagery, with billowing curtains, long dark corridors, a fireplace with flames as big as a bonfire and plenty of cold, unfriendly spaces.

Mixed in with this extraordinary atmosphere is the story of Allan (Charles Lamy), a friend of Usher's who rides his horse through desolate terrain to reach Roderick's house, where his friend lives with his ill wife Madeleine. Interestingly, before Allan sets out on his journey, he stops at a local inn, where the villagers express horror that he is going to the 'cursed' house of Usher. This trope was already a cliché by then, repeated dozens if not hundreds of times in horror films over the years, probably originating with a similar scene in F W Murnau's seminal *Nosferatu* (1922).

A doctor (Fournez Goffard) also lives in Usher's house, where he constantly attends Madeleine. Although she is ill and quite frail, Usher's wife is also

**Scenes from the short *The Fall of the House of Usher* (1928)**

his muse; he is painting a portrait of her, as all of the Usher men seem to have done with their wives over the centuries. This is where Epstein's *Usher* departs the most from Poe: rather than some sort of strange malady (most likely catalepsy) that affects the Usher bloodline, the curse that befalls Madeleine has something to do with the painting that Roderick is slaving over, although it is never made clear exactly what that connection is.

The ending, too, veers wildly from Poe: after Madeleine returns from the grave, Roderick manages to escape the crumbling house with her in tow. This 'happy' ending seems quite jarring, although it is beautifully shot and composed, with a sky full of stars (obviously lights strung up on a backdrop) looming over the Usher manse as it is destroyed.

Obviously, Epstein's film is not a commercial one; Buñuel didn't care for it, as he felt it deviated too much from the source material, and he quit the film before it was completed. Viewed today, however, this first feature-length adaptation of Poe's story is something of a cinematic marvel, far ahead of its time, surprising us with editorial and directorial choices repeatedly; a scene of copulating toads, for example, is dropped in sometime after Madeleine is buried. To show that life goes on, perhaps?

Coincidentally, another unusual version of *The Fall of the House of Usher* was made in America in the same year as Epstein's. This, however, was a short film, running only thirteen minutes, and so avant-garde it made Epstein's adaptation look completely linear by comparison. The short *The Fall of the House of Usher* is an experimental film directed by James Sibley Watson and Melville Webber. Watson was a medical doctor, a publisher, editor, photographer and filmmaker who was fascinated by the dreamlike power of film. Webber was a director and actor who would later work with Watson on *Lot in Sodom* (1933).

Their version of *Usher* doesn't even attempt to tell a coherent story; like *Un Chien Andalou*, the film is a series of disconnected, sometimes jarring images,

although none of them is as shocking as anything in Bunuel's film. The image is all, including shots filmed through prisms to create optical distortions; one of the first experimental films to be made in the US, it was heavily influenced by *The Cabinet of Dr Caligari* in its bizarre use of odd, off-kilter camera angles and heavily stylised sets.

The story is essentially the same: a traveller (Melville Webber himself) arrives at the Usher home to find that Roderick (Herbert Stern) and Madeleine (Hildegard Watson, James Sibley's wife) are living with a serious family malady. Roderick's senses have become overly acute, while Madeleine wanders about in a nearly somnambulistic state. Ultimately, the story ends tragically, as in Poe's original tale.

Nothing more and nothing less than a Gothic mood piece, Watson's and Webber's *Usher* is intriguing to view today. It is something of a tribute to German Expressionism at a time when German filmmakers themselves were abandoning the form. It captures the feeling of a nightmare quite effectively and was hailed at the time as the best film of its kind since *Caligari*.

It is interesting to note that, time after time, screen adaptations of Poe have been surrealistic in nature. His writings lend themselves to Grand Guignol because of their physical horror, while surrealists have found that they can be just as frightening as terrors of the psyche,

One final silent postscript: also in 1928, a 24-minute 'picturisation,' of Poe's work – as it is referred to in the credits of *The Tell Tale Heart* – was produced by German filmmaker Charles Klein. A belated *Caligari*-inspired expressionist horror film, it was the first 'official' version of the Poe story – notwithstanding the elements taken from it in *The Avenging Conscience* – to be adapted for the cinema.

Starring Otto Matiesen as The Insane and William Harford as The Old Man, it is a highly faithful version of Poe's story, even to the point of featuring Poe's opening words from the story scrolling up the screen immediately after the opening credits. It quickly becomes obvious that the

This and Left:
*The Tell Tale Heart* (1928)

highly stylised set design is heavily inspired by *Caligari*, complete with crooked, angled doors and windows. Unlike the recent American version of *Usher*, however, this short, experimental film has a strong narrative drive and an excellent performance by Matiesen, who is made up to resemble Poe himself.

Poe's 'Imp of the Perverse' is prominent here, as The Insane practically begs the detectives (Hans Fuerberg and Charles Darvas) to discover his heinous crime. The beating of The Old Man's 'hideous heart' is nicely represented by the image of a pounding hammer, and Leon Shamroy's shadowy camerawork creates a mood of madness and paranoia that is pure Poe.

By 1928, the cinema had found its voice. Along with the likes of Al Jolson and Lon Chaney, films based on the works of Edgar Allan Poe would start to speak.

*Chapter One – THE SILENT POE*

# CHAPTER TWO
# THE UNIVERSAL POE

*'Sound loves to revel in a summer night.'*

*Al Aaraaf*

The stock market crash in October 1929 and the wave of human misery that resulted during the Great Depression coincided, ironically, with the birth of the American horror film. As is so often the case, human nature seemed to demand a safety valve for its anxieties and the 1930s saw the full flowering of the genre. Despite the fact that money was scarce, to say the least, and every penny in a family's budget was like gold, people flocked to see the 'talkies' in tremendous numbers. And where horror rose, Poe, who filmmakers loved to adapt because of his inherent surrealism and Grand Guignol physical horror, was not far behind.

When movies found their voice, that voice was punctuated by screams. Early talkies reveled in music, to be sure; *The Jazz Singer* (1927) was the first 'all-talking, all-singing' musical, after all. But the music of horror was quick to arrive with Tod Browning's *Dracula* (1931), followed in rapid succession by James Whale's *Frankenstein* (1931), and the horror film, which had only whispered in the dark during the silent era, came into its own with creaking doors, howling wolves and screaming maidens.

Universal, the company that had released both *Dracula* and *Frankenstein*, quickly became the home of horror, and it took them no time at all to adapt Poe for the screen, starting with *Murders in the Rue Morgue* (1932), very loosely based on Poe's short story. The film came about because *Frankenstein's* director, Robert Florey, and its star, Bela Lugosi, had been dropped from *Frankenstein*. Florey had originally intended to have helmed that project, having developed it for some time, but producer Carl Laemmle, Jr was unhappy with Florey's work on it and Lugosi supposedly (although this point is controversial) turned down playing Frankenstein's Monster because the role contained no dialogue.

In compensation, both men were handed by Laemmle, *Murders in the Rue Morgue* (which itself had been intended for George Melford, the director of Universal's Spanish-language *Dracula*, 1931). Born in Paris, Florey had written articles about film for several French magazines before he set sail for the United States in the early twenties. Sent to Hollywood as a correspondent for a French publication, Florey decided to settle there and work in the film industry, starting as a gag writer, working as a foreign publicity agent for Douglas Fairbanks, Mary Pickford and Rudolph Valentino, and ultimately signed (in 1924) as an assistant director at MGM. His on-the-job training led to him directing two short avant-garde films, *The Life and Death of 9413, a Hollywood Extra* (1928) and *Skyscraper Symphony* (1929), both of which were highly acclaimed and both strongly influenced by German expressionist techniques. Florey was given the assignment of co-directing (with Joseph Santley) the first talkie comedy from the Marx Brothers, *The Coconuts* (1929), filmed at Paramount's Astoria Studios in New York.

After directing some films in France (*The Road is Fine* and *Love Songs*, both 1930, and *Black and White*, 1931), Florey returned to Hollywood where he was asked by Universal to develop *Frankenstein* after the unexpectedly huge success of *Dracula*. Florey and screenwriter Garret Fort came up

**Bela Lugosi as Dr Mirakle in**
***Murders in the Rue Morgue* (1932)**

with a screen treatment for *Frankenstein* and recent evidence reveals that Florey was kicked off the project largely because of the fact that James Whale, who had just completed production on *Waterloo Bridge*, was offered the pick of the properties on Universal's upcoming schedule, and he chose *Frankenstein*, also casting in doubt Lugosi's claim of turning down the role because it had no dialogue.

Whatever the case, Florey and Lugosi eagerly teamed up for *Murders in the Rue Morgue* and the director was keen to adapt his love for German expressionist cinema for a Hollywood oeuvre. Aided and abetted by German-born cinematographer Karl Freund (who had photographed *Dracula*), Florey set to work to create a dark and disturbing vision.

Lugosi had been a distinguished stage and film actor in his native Hungary, and in 1920 he emigrated to the US. In 1927, his fate was sealed when he was cast as Count Dracula in the 1927 Broadway stage adaptation of Bram Stoker's novel. He became Universal's first talkie 'horror star' in the 1931 film adaptation, which became both a blessing and a curse in his later career.

Unusually for the period, the leading lady got top billing over the leading actor in *Murders*: Sidney Fox had made her Broadway debut in 1929 in the comedy *It Never Rains*, quickly following that up with another smash, *Lost Sheep*, in which she was spotted by Universal's Carl Laemmle Jr. who cast her opposite Bette Davis in *The Bad Sister* (1931), ultimately leading to *Murders in the Rue Morgue*.

Cast as Pierre Dupin, Leon Wycoff was a veteran of the stage, and *Murders* was his first feature film. This was definitely not the case with Bert Roach, who had been highly acclaimed in King Vidor's *The Crowd* (1928). He was cast in *Murders* as Pierre's roommate, Paul.

Brandon Hurst (Prefect of Police) had previously appeared in John S Robertson's *Dr Jekyll and Mr Hyde* (1920) alongside John Barrymore, while Irish-born actor D'arcy Corrigan (Morgue Keeper) had appeared in such silent classics as Erich von Stroheim's *The Merry Widow* (1925). Rounding out the cast, African-American actor Noble Johnson (Janos, the Black One) had appeared in everything from Cecil B DeMille's *The Ten Commandments* (1923) to *The Mysterious Dr Fu Manchu* (1929) and would soon achieve genre immortality for his appearances in *The Mummy* (1932) and *King Kong* (1933). Far down the cast list for *Murders* was Arlene Francis (Woman of the Streets), whose film career never really took off, and who is remembered today for her long stint on the television game show *What's My Line?*, which debuted in 1950.

Filmed between 10 October and 13 November 1931, *Murders in the Rue Morgue* may not be pure Poe – few films are – but it is pure Grand Guignol. One cannot get much more Grand Guignol in fact, than the film's most notorious scene, which fell victim to many local censor boards in the States. In this scene, Lugosi's Dr Mirakle, whose 'mad' plan is to mate a human woman with his ape, Erik, has a prostitute (Arlene Francis) tied to cruciform-shaped beams in his basement. He attempts to transfuse Erik's blood into

*Murders in the Rue Morgue*(1932)

her, with disastrous results. She perishes and he flies into a rage: 'Your blood is rotten! Black as your sins! You cheated me! Your beauty was a lie.' Then, unceremoniously, his servant, Janos 'the Black One,' pulls a lever which drops her body into the Seine, which runs beneath the basement.

The sequence is disturbing even by today's standards. Although nothing graphic is actually seen, the prostitute's screams and whimpers are harrowing, as is Lugosi's unhinged demeanour. 'If you only last one more minute,' he tells her, 'then we shall see… We shall know if you are to be the bride of science!'

With a rather bizarre 'unibrow,' Dr Mirakle is not quite the suave creature of night that Lugosi's Dracula was, but he dominates the film as a doctor who is every bit as mad as Colin Clive's Dr Frankenstein. He also savages the beliefs of anti-evolutionists, who were still very much a part of the American scene, with the famous 'Scopes Monkey Trial' having been decided as recently as 21 July, 1925.

Set in 1845 Paris, the time period of the film predates Darwin, but Dr Mirakle was nothing if not prophetic. Presiding over his carnival sideshow which highlights Erik, Mirakle responds to a member of the audience who has accused him of heresy with biting, sarcastic bombast: 'Heresy? Do they still burn men for heresy? Then burn me, monsieur, light the fire! Do you think your little candle will outshine the flame of truth?'

In an interview many years later, Robert Florey recalled: 'I wrote the *Rue Morgue* adaptation in a week… I used the same device I employed in my *Frankenstein* adaptation. Bela Lugosi became Dr Mirakle – a mad scientist desirous of creating a human being – not with body parts stolen from a graveyard and a brain from a lab, but by the mating of an ape with a woman.'

Indeed, Mirakle is 'mad' from the get-go. In another scene, he pronounces: 'My life is consecrated to a great experiment. I tell you I will prove your kinship with the ape. Erik's blood will be mixed with the blood of man!'

Aside from Lugosi, there are no truly memorable performances in the film (with the possible exception of Corrigan as a suitably mordant morgue keeper). Sidney Fox is a typically insipid early thirties heroine, although she figures in what is perhaps the most impressively shot scene in the film, in which she swings back and forth on a large swing hanging from a tree, the camera attached to the swing, creating a dizzying effect.

Indeed, to Florey, visuals were all, and the film succeeds on a primal level, dovetailing nicely with its bestial subtext. The streets of this 'Paris that never was' are filled with tottering buildings standing up or leaning over at all sorts of odd angles, with Charles D Hall's (*Dracula*) art direction bringing Caligariesque Expressionism to a mass audience. Although the French milieu mixed with the German is a trifle confused, the atmosphere created by Hall and Freund is the best thing about the film after Lugosi's performance.

As medical student Pierre Dupin, Waycoff (later to be known as Leon Ames) is but a pale shadow of Poe's master detective C August Dupin and not a patch on that character intellectually. Bert Roach as Pierre's roommate

Paul comes across as the stereotyped 'sissy' from early thirties cinema, while Johnson merely gets to leer and menace as Janos.

The real star of the film is, in a certain sense, the ape. In fact, the ape may have been the reason this particular Poe story was chosen for production, as apes were incredibly popular 'heavies' for horror films during the late silent and early sound era. From Richard Rosson's *The Wizard* (1927), a remake of the French film *Balaoo the Demon Baboon* (1913) through Alfred Santell's *The Gorilla* (1927, of which *The New York Times* opined, was '…as if…Mack Sennett in a restrained mood had turned to Edgar Allan Poe's *The Murders in the Rue Morgue…*') to Rupert Julian's *The Leopard Lady* (1928), the ape was the go-to 'monster' of the period, with the latter film owing a special debt to Poe and featuring the very first appearance of 25-year-old Filipino make-up artist Charles Gemora as the ape, a role he would return to again and again.

Known as 'the King of the Gorilla Men,' Gemora had arrived in San Francisco as a stowaway, later moving to Los Angeles and earning money making portrait sketches near the gates of Universal Studios, where the company rewarded him by putting him to work in the sculpture department for William Worsley's *The Hunchback of Notre Dame* (1923), starring Lon Chaney in the title role. Ultimately, Gemora's five-foot four-inch stature made him a natural to don a gorilla suit, and he ended up so attired in *Murders in the Rue Morgue* as Erik.

Gorilla suits were still rather primitive in those days, and Gemora's was no exception. The killer in Poe's story was an 'Ourang-Outang,' but in the Florey film it is obviously a gorilla… except for the close-ups in which it is a rather over-the-hill chimpanzee from the Selig Zoo, which, by its rapid hand movements, occasionally appears to be masturbating.

Whatever the case, this rather ill-conceived double act doesn't really work; it's well-nigh impossible to 'match' a chimpanzee with a man in a gorilla suit. To make matters even worse, Paul, a medical student with no apparent knowledge of zoology, mistakes the beast for a baboon.

The film's climax, in which Gemora carries Fox over the Paris rooftops, is nicely staged, but Gemora's gorilla suit is too obviously just that. The combination of Caligaresque sets and a man in a gorilla suit straight out of an *Our Gang* comedy (which Gemora had also appeared in) makes for a bizarre juxtaposition, and the climax is not what it should have been.

Apparently, audiences of the time thought so too, as *Murders in the Rue Morgue*, released on 21 February 1932, was not the box office success that *Dracula* and *Frankenstein* had been. Its lack of financial success meant that Lugosi would not receive the types of leading roles that Universal would give to Karloff, and the heavily-accented Hungarian's long career decline began.

Viewed today, *Murders in the Rue Morgue* has some good moments mixed in with some rather dreadful ones; one of the weaker films of Universal's horror pantheon of the early thirties, it has the power to charm mainly because of Lugosi's performance and the unusual, dreamlike atmosphere created by its sets and cinematography. As a horror classic, however, it cannot compare to *Dracula*, *Frankenstein*, *The Mummy* (1932) or *The Invisible Man* (1933). And as an adaptation of Poe, it is an utter failure: C Auguste Dupin, one of Poe's greatest and most intelligent characters, becomes a love-smitten buffoon. Such is Hollywood.

Hollywood had nothing to do with *Unheimliche Geschilchten* (aka *The Living Dead*, 1932), essentially Richard Oswald's talkie remake of his own silent anthology film of the same German title from 1919. This time, the stories dovetail into each other, without the framing story of the antique bookshop from the original. Starring Paul Wegener, Maria Koppenhofer and Blandine Ebinger, *The Living Dead* is technically superior to the silent version and features a powerful performance by Wegener.

Wegener was probably best known for his spectacular 1920 film *The Golem: How He Came into the World*, which he wrote, directed and starred in. One of the classics of German cinema, the film was one of many in which Wegener indulged his personal interests in the supernatural and mysticism. An actor with a powerful screen presence, he frequently found himself typecast as villains, and *The Living Dead* was no exception.

Wegener plays Morder, a rather warped scientist who murders his wife (Koppenhofer) and walls her up in his basement. Based on Poe's 'The Black Cat,' this version of the tale is nearly identical to the one Oswald made in 1919, but when the police uncover his crimes, Morder escapes and hides in a wax museum filed with figures of murderers and torture devices. He is followed by a reporter (Harold Paulsen), who tails him from the wax museum into an asylum (in a sequence based on Poe's 1845 tale 'The System of Dr Tarr and Professor Fether'). After some darkly comic incidents there, Morder escapes yet again to a house that just happens to be the home of Stevenson's 'The Suicide Club.' While Morder may have been good at escaping, his luck was extremely bad when it came to what he was getting into!

Wegener's screen presence dominates the film, which is directed for maximum atmosphere and suspense by Oswald. *The Living Dead* was released at the time that Hitler was coming to power, and Oswald saw the writing on the wall. He fled his native land after the Nazi takeover and emigrated to the United States. There, he continued to make films, such as *Isle of Missing Men* (1942) and *I Was a Criminal* (1945). His son, Gerd Oswald, who also became

**This & Right: *The Living Dead* (1932)**

a director of such films as *A Kiss Before Dying* (1956) and *Brainwashed (1960)*, was also known for directing several classic episodes of the TV series *The Outer Limits* (1963-1965).

Although *The Living Dead* didn't set the world on fire in 1932 (it wasn't even released in the United States until 1940) there are two interesting postscripts regarding the film: It was one of over 200 film titles in the list of independent feature films made available for television transmission in the US that were announced in the 4 April 1942 issue of *Motion Picture Herald*. At that time, television broadcasting was just being pioneered and didn't really get off the ground until the end of World War II. Although there is no documentation to show when it was originally broadcast, *The Living Dead* appears to have been one of the first feature films shown on American television.

In addition to that singular honour, the *Black Cat* and *Dr Tarr and Professor Fether* sequences were part of the omnibus film *Dr Terror's House of Horrors*, released independently as a 'roadshow attraction' in 1943. The feature-length film was composed of scenes from such European horror classics as Carl Dreyer's *Vampyr* (1932), and Wegener's *The Golem: How He Came Into the World*, among others. The project was tied together by a 'wraparound' story involving a mysterious occult investigator called Dr Terror, who proceeds to introduce seven tales from his personal casebook of supernatural encounters. The title *Dr Terror's House of Horrors* was later used for the first Amicus anthology horror film, released in 1964.

The earliest known 'talkie' adaptation of 'The Tell-Tale Heart' appeared in Britain in 1934, which turned out to be a busy year for Poe pictures. Directed by Brian Desmond Hurst, who would later helm what many consider the definitive version of Charles Dickens' *A Christmas Carol*, aka *Scrooge* (1951), starring Alastair Sim in the title role. Hurst, who was born in Northern Ireland, learned the art of filmmaking from none other than John Ford – claimed by some to have been his cousin – when he went to Hollywood in the twenties. In 1933, he returned to the UK, and the following year he directed his first feature, *The Tell-Tale Heart* (US: *Bucket of Blood*), a 55-minute adaptation of Poe's story.

Filmed at the Blattner Studios in Elstree, *The Tell-Tale Heart* featured a mostly amateur cast, although actor John Kelt (The Old Man) had appeared in several silent films, including *Pillars of Society* (1920) and *The Adventures of Mr Pickwick* (1921). Yolande Terrell (The Girl) later appeared in *They Drive by Night* and *Night Journey* (1938), while the other actors, Norman Dryden (The Boy), Thomas Shenton (First Investigator), James Fleck (Second Investigator) and Colonel Cameron (Doctor) never made any other screen appearances.

In the book *Re-viewing British Cinema, 1900-1992* by Wheeler W. Dixon, Hurst was quoted as recalling, 'At the big Elstree studios nearby they said, "There's a fellow over at Blattner's studio who's making practically a silent picture."' Indeed, following in the tradition of some of the silent Poe pictures, Hurst's *The Tell-Tale Heart* is a somewhat experimental, avant-garde film, and, despite it being a talkie, the dialogue is very sparse.

Thought to be a 'lost' film for many years, *The Tell-Tale Heart* is now available for viewing at the British Film Institute website. It's well worth a look, as Hurst's direction is quite stylish for the time, opening up with The Boy in his prison cell, where he has drawn a myriad of "eyes" on the wall. The story then unfolds in flashback, using a fair amount of actual wordage from Poe's story in his narration. Although the film runs under an hour, padding is still necessary to achieve even that length, and some dreamy, romantic scenes of Dryden and Terrell walking hand in hand through fields and woodlands are added, although admittedly they're very well photographed by Walter Blakeley and Hurst himself.

The build-up to the murder is slow and methodical and it must be said that the make-up on Kelt's eye is especially repellent, especially for the early sound era. The murder itself is not as gruesome as one might envisage, but it works in the dark, moody context of the film. Sound is used especially well in the denouement, with the steady 'beat-beat-beat' of the heart gradually building up to a faster and faster rhythm, until The Boy (and the film itself) tips over into madness. Much of the promise that Hurst fulfilled with his great version of A Christmas Carol is on display here, and, despite the often amateurish acting, the film captures much of the shadowy mood and all of the obsessive plot of Poe's familiar story.

After this detour to Germany and England, it was back to Hollywood and Universal for the next major Poe adaptation, *The Black Cat* (1934). It

Bela Lugosi and Harry Cording in
*The Black Cat* (1934)

was to be the first of eight horror films co-starring the studio's two titans of terror, Karloff and Lugosi. Helmed by Czech-born director Edgar G Ulmer, *The Black Cat* may have little to do with Poe – its screenplay by Peter Ruric (aka Paul Cain) merely uses ailurophobia (the fear of cats) as a jumping-off point for the action – but it is one of the finest horror films that Universal ever produced, and one of the darkest.

Ulmer was an interesting character. He lived in Vienna as a youth, where he worked in theatre while studying philosophy and architecture. While learning his craft in set design for Max Reinhardt's theatre, he apprenticed under F W Murnau and worked alongside directors Billy Wilder, Robert Siodmak and Fred Zinnemann. Ulmer left with Murnau to go to Hollywood in 1926, where he was assistant art director on Murnau's masterful *Sunrise*. The first feature he directed in the United States was *Damaged Lives* (1933), a low-budget exploitation 'shocker' that dealt with venereal disease. His next feature was *The Black Cat*, a major leap forward in his career, but ironically one that also sowed the seeds of his self-destruction. He had an affair with Shirley Beatrice Kassler, who had been married since the previous year to producer Max Alexander, who just happened to be the nephew of Universal head honcho Carl Laemmle. Her divorce from Alexander in 1936 and her marriage to Ulmer that year led to his being blacklisted from major Hollywood studios, and he would spend the rest of his career making 'B' films for various independent companies.

*The Black Cat* was Ulmer's one opportunity to show what he could do with an 'A' budget, and he obviously relished the chance. In addition to Karloff and Lugosi, the cast included David Manners, of *Dracula* and *The Mummy* fame, as Peter Alison, the closest the film has to a hero. As his new bride Joan, Jacqueline Wells (later known as Julie Bishop), a veteran of Laurel and Hardy comedies and early talkies such as *Tarzan the Fearless* (1933), made her one and only appearance in a horror film.

Austro-Hungarian Egon Brecher, who would soon be seen in many horror films including Universal's *Werewolf of London* and *The Black Room* (both 1935), was cast as the Majordomo. British actor Harry Cording, who would end up doing character work in dozens of Universal horrors, including *Son of Frankenstein* (1939), *The Wolf Man* (1941) and *The Mummy's Tomb* (1942), was chosen for the enigmatic role of Thamal, the manservant of Vitus Werdegast (Lugosi), who seems to switch allegiances to Hjalmar Poelzig (Karloff) during the course of the proceedings. Universal contract player Lucille Lund portrayed two roles, those of Karen Verdegast and her daughter. A young John Carradine, soon to be a mainstay of horror films, has an uncredited role as an organist in a Satanic ritual.

Cinematographer for *The Black Cat* was the great John J Mescall, who had photographed such silent classics as Ernst Lubitsch's *The Student Prince in Old Heidelberg* (1927), but really came into his own working for James Whale in such films as *Bride of Frankenstein* (1935) and *Show Boat* (1936). The music score for *The Black Cat* is especially interesting: it consists of various classical pieces compiled by music director Heinz Eric Roemheld and was one of the first feature films to have an almost continuous musical score, with pieces by Liszt, Schumann, Tchaikovsky, Bach, Beethoven and Brahms used to maximum effect.

The story, credited to Ruric and Ulmer, concerns the Alisons, American honeymooners traveling in Hungary, who share a train compartment with Dr Vitus Werdegast (Lugosi), a gentleman with an air of melancholy about him; he is returning to visit what's left of the town he defended before he became a prisoner of war, 'rotting away' in a gaol cell for fifteen years. He is also returning to even the score with Hjalmar Poelzig (Karloff), who is his arch-enemy.

When their bus crashes during a thunderstorm and Joan is slightly injured, the Alisons, Poelzig and his servant Thamal are taken into Poelzig's home, which was built upon the site of an especially bloody World War battle. Werdegast, who has an overpowering fear of cats, finds himself playing a game of chess for Alison's life, while grieving over his lost daughter, who, unbeknownst to him, is still alive in the house. We also discover that Poelzig is a Satanist who is hoping to sacrifice Joan at a ceremony in the dark of the moon.

According to Ulmer, the character of Poelzig was inspired by real-life occultist Aleister Crowley, while the name was inspired by architect Hans Poelzig, with whom Ulmer claimed to have worked on the sets of Wegener's *The Golem: How He Came Into the World* – although no record of Ulmer's involvement on that film exists.

Other sources indicate that Poelzig's mannerisms and characteristics were based on those of director Fritz Lang (*Metropolis*, 1926). While Ulmer admired Lang's films, he found him to be sadistic as a director and as a human being. The likelihood is that Poelzig was an amalgamation of Crowley and Lang, which made him a formidable character indeed.

Originally released in the UK under the rather generic title *The House of Doom*, *The Black Cat* is a delirious Gothic masterpiece under any moniker. It's safe to say that in many ways, the film was ahead of its time. Its subtext of Satanism, necrophilia, torture and sadism would not be echoed in horror cinema until the early 1960's. Censors in such far-flung countries as Italy, Austria and Finland banned the film, while others – such as the UK censor – trimmed some of the more gruesome scenes, such as the climax in which Werdegast flays Poelzig alive.

The nearly continuous musical score makes *The Black Cat* seem like a literal symphony of horror, with Schumann's 'Opus 44' especially well used as Poelzig's leitmotif. Mescall's camerawork is fluid and brilliant, prowling the halls of Poelzig's Frank Lloyd Wright-styled mansion like a voyeur who is peering at something that he shouldn't be seeing.

In their first cinema outing together, Karloff and Lugosi give restrained, top-notch performances. Karloff, with a severe, shockingly white close-cropped haircut that makes him look vaguely like a Nazi, strides about the film like a harbinger of doom. There's one remarkable shot in which his lust for Joan is visually realised in a close-up of his hand squeezing the torso of a nude female statue as he eyes the heroine.

Poelzig is totally evil, and yet when Werdegast flays the flesh from his body at the climax, we feel that not even he deserves such a horrible fate. Werdegast leers at him as he intones: 'Do you know what I am going to do to you now? No? Did you ever see an animal skinned, Hjalmar? That's what I'm going to do to you now…flay the skin from your body… slowly… bit by bit."

Werdegast has much to repay Poelzig for: As he tells the Alisons in the train compartment, where he first meets then, "Have you ever heard of Kurgaal? It is a prison below Omsk. Many men have gone there. Few have returned. I have returned. After fifteen years, I have returned.'

During that fifteen years, Werdegast has had plenty of time to think about revenge. When Werdegast discovers that Poelzig has kept the body of

*Chapter Two – THE UNIVERSAL POE*

his (Werdegast's) late wife in an upright glass coffin, while sleeping with his daughter – thus, Poelzig's own stepdaughter, a very kinky arrangement indeed – he goes nearly mad with hatred for his old enemy. The film becomes a deadly game of chess between the two of them – in one scene quite literally – and when Werdegast discovers that Poelzig has murdered his daughter, he goes completely off the rails, ties him to his own embalming rack and 'skins' him.

Lugosi gives one of his best performances as Werdegast. He presents us with a tortured, sympathetic character and his delivery of some classic lines is second to none. 'The phone is dead,' he says to Poelzig during their chess match. 'Do you hear that, Vitus? Even the phone is dead.'

Earlier, another remarkable sequence occurs with a masterful, subjective-camera voyage through the cellars of the mansion, with Poelzig intoning in voice-over:' 'Come, Vitus, are we men or are we children? Of what use are all these melodramatic gestures? You say your soul was killed and that you have been dead all these years. And what of me? Did we not both die here in Marmorus fifteen years ago? Are we any the less victims of the war than those whose bodies were torn asunder? Are we not both the living dead? And now you come to me, playing at being an avenging angel – childishly thirsty for my blood. We understand each other too well. We know too much of life. We shall play a little game, Vitus. A game of death, if you like.'

At the film's truly Grand Guignol climax, it is perhaps understandable that in the melee, Alison thinks Werdegast is trying to harm Joan and shoots him. As he prepares to die from his wounds, he is able to say, 'It's the red switch, isn't it, Hjalmar? The red switch ignites the dynamite. Five minutes and Marmorus, you and I, and your rotten cult will be no more… It has been a good game.'

Years later, Ulmer admitted that Poe's name was used mainly to bring in the patrons, to give the film some gravitas beyond the teaming of the horror titans. Indeed, Werdegast's ailurophibia is not even a particularly important plot point, and is explained by Poelzig with the statement: 'You must be indulgent of Dr Werdegast's weakness. He is the unfortunate victim of one of the commoner phobias, but in an extreme form. He has an intense and all-consuming horror of cats.' After that speech, Werdegast's 'phobia' is only alluded to once more.

Whether or not Ulmer's *The Black Cat* owes much to Poe, it owes much to Grand Guignol and the Gothic tradition. The film is a nightmarish tour-de-force of both psychological and physical horror; as critic Philip French has said, 'This bizarre, utterly irrational masterpiece, lasting little more than an hour, has images that bury themselves in the mind.'

When it was released in the spring of 1934, *The Black Cat* became Universal's biggest hit of the year. And just in time, too: in the US, the Production Code became strictly enforced a couple of months later, in response to many such 'graphic' pre-Code films. If *The Black Cat* had been released a few months later, it probably would have been shorn of its most memorable sequences, and we would have been deprived of much of its hallucinatory power.

Far, far away, at the opposite end of the spectrum, an independently produced adaptation of 'The Black Cat' called *Maniac* (aka *Sex Maniac*) was also released in 1934. Advertised with the come-on, 'He menaced women with his weird desires,' *Maniac* was directed by exploitation specialist Dwain Esper from a script by his wife, Hildegarde Stadie.

Esper is now known for such low-budget exploitation fare as *Marihuana* (1936) and *How to Undress in Front of Your Husband* (1937), made for a company called Roadshow Attractions, an American indie outfit that ignored the Production Code and were thus able to include scenes featuring nudity and violence, which led to Esper being given the nickname 'the father of modern exploitation.' The films were promoted as 'cautionary tales' to prevent the filmmakers from being arrested for obscenity, although that did sometimes occur.

As far as modern standards are concerned, the only thing obscene about *Maniac* is its ineptitude, from abominable acting to shoddy sets to grainy cinematography. The plot, such as it is, has something to do with a former vaudeville star (Bill Woods) who has a talent for impersonation. As vaudeville is dead, he finds himself assisting a mad scientist (Horace Carpenter) in attempting to reanimate corpses and, ultimately, he ends up going mad himself.

Mixed in with all this nonsense is a subplot about a 'cat farmer' which leads to a scene in which a cat's head is squeezed and his eyeball pops out. Fortunately, the cat in question only had one eye and a glass eye was inserted into the empty socket before filming, and then popped out in front of the camera.

Made on a shoestring for $5,000 and running only 51 minutes, *Maniac* is certainly one of the weirdest Poe adaptations ever made, and that's saying something. Filled with intertitles about 'dementia praecox' and other mental illnesses, with scenes superimposed from Benjamin Christensen's silent film *Haxan* (aka *Witchcraft Through the Ages*, 1920) and Fritz Lang's *Siegfried* (1923), and with some of the most unforgettably awful performances ever committed to celluloid, *Maniac* is listed as one of "the 100 most amusingly bad films ever made" in the book *The Official Razzies Movie Guide* by John Wilson. And rightfully so.

The year 1935 brought a far more interesting Poe-related indie called *The Crime of Dr Crespi*, which had the distinction of starring no less a luminary than Erich von Stroheim. The actor/director was currently working primarily as an actor again after being dismissed from directing *Queen Kelly* and *Walking Down Broadway*. He has the title role in *Dr Crespi* as a sort of mad scientist who has created a serum that brings about a catatonic stupor to whoever is injected with it. He uses this serum against Dr Stephen Ross

(John Bohn), a man who has married Crespi's former love, Estelle (Harriet Russell). The drug places Ross in a catatonic state, but leaves him aware of his surroundings, which brings about the only part of the film based on Poe, in which Ross is buried alive a la Poe's 'The Premature Burial.' After Ross has been buried, his colleagues Dr Arnold (Paul Guilfoyle) and Dr Thomas (Dwight Frye) suspect foul play and exhume his body, finding Ross very much alive and out for revenge.

Billed in its advertising as "The screen's super-thriller...an epic of horror,' *The Crime of Dr Crespi* is actually a very cheap 63-minute thriller, although compared to *Maniac* its budget was probably quite generous. The acting is also very good, with von Stroheim underplaying a role that could easily have been portrayed as an over-the-top, cackling maniac. Instead, von Stroheim utters his lines in a very matter of fact fashion, as author Jonathan Rigby noted in his book "American Gothic: Sixty Years of Horror Cinema": '...Von Stroheim is at the top of his form when he visits the morgue and lifts the sheet over his rival's inert body, crooning juicy lines like, "I hoped and prayed for the chance to pay you back some day, with compound interest," as cinematographer Larry Williams shoots up at his gloating face from a low angle.'

The finest moments of cinematography occur during the burial sequence, which obviously quotes from the very similar scene in Carl

     *Chapter Two – THE UNIVERSAL POE*

Dreyer's *Vampyr* (1932) in its harrowing subjective camera approach to the grim proceedings. The camera cascades down into the grave, soil covers the camera lens, a bell tolls and tight close ups of all the principal actors are edited for maximum effect.

Frye, in an unusual bit of casting, actually gets to play a straight non-maniacal role for a change; he is, in fact, an almost heroic character. Although he was a highly respected and versatile stage actor, *Dr Crespi* gave him the highest billing of his screen career and he carries off the role very well indeed, giving the second best performance in the film after von Stroheim.

For an independent production shot in eight days, *The Crime of Dr Crespi* is surprisingly good under the direction of Hungarian-born John H Auer, another actor turned director. Filmed at the old Biograph Studios in The Bronx, it has a completely different atmosphere from the studio–produced horror films of the time, and even though it was released (on 24 September 1935) after the enforcement of the Production Code, it remains a very strong and claustrophobic horror film.

Critics of the time had mixed feelings about *Dr Crespi*. 'BRC', writing in the 13 January 1936 edition of *The New York Times* opined, 'The picture… is based on a story by Mr Auer, "suggested" by Edgar Allan Poe's story, "The Premature Burial…" The only redeeming presence in the picture is that of Dwight Frye, as Dr Crespi's assistant. Mr Frye, once chosen as one of the ten best legitimate actors on Broadway, makes the best of a bad situation which, of course, is not very good.'

*The New York Sunday News* was more generous, its anonymous reviewer noting, '…The film develops a real atmosphere of horror that is dramatically effective.' Distributed by Republic Pictures in the US and British Lion Films in the UK, *The Crime of Dr Crespi* has since fallen into the public domain and has been unjustly forgotten. It is ripe for rediscovery.

That same year, it was back to Universal for the next big-screen Poe adaptation, *The Raven*, teaming Karloff and Lugosi together for the second time. Unlike the 1915 film of that title, Universal's *The Raven* was not a Poe biopic, but rather an original horror tale in which Lugosi's character, Dr Vollin, is obsessed by the writings of Poe. He saves the life of a beautiful dancer (Irene Ware) with whom he also becomes obsessed, imagining her to be his 'Lenore.' When she rejects his advances, he completely loses his grip on reality. One of the world's greatest plastic surgeons, Vollin agrees to alter the appearance of Edmond Bateman, a wanted criminal, transforming him into a travesty of a human being to guarantee his obedience. Then he invites the dancer and her father to his home, in which he has installed a Poe-inspired dungeon complete with pendulum, to fulfil his desire to torture.

The screenplay by David Boehm, a veteran dialogue scribe of musicals such as *Gold Diggers of 1933*, is over the top, to say the least, and it gives Lugosi licence to chew the scenery to bits. The actor is aided and abetted in this by director Louis Friedlander, aka Lew Landers, who cut his teeth on serials such as *The Vanishing Shadow* (1934). *The Raven* often feels like

Boris Karloff as Edmond Bateman in *The Raven* (1935)

Bela Lugosi as Dr. Richard Vollin in *The Raven* (1935)

Lugosi and Karloff together in a scene from *The Raven* (1935)

a serial, with one cliffhanger topping another, gimmicks such as revolving rooms, walls that slowly close in and of course the pendulum itself (although no pit is in evidence).

Boehm's script gives Lugosi some memorable lines he can gloat over, such as 'Torture waiting... waiting. It will be sweet, Judge Thatcher!' and the penultimate scene in which he goes completely insane, shouting, 'Poe, you are avenged!' Dr Vollin is a complete egomaniac, something that is apparent from an earlier scene with Judge Thatcher (Samuel S Hinds) to whom he announces, 'I am a law unto myself.'

If *The Black Cat* features one of Lugosi's finest performances, *The Raven* features one of his worst. The epithet 'ham' has frequently been applied to the actor, and nowhere else in his cinematic oeuvre is it more applicable than here. Mind you, he is fun to watch in *The Raven*, but his performance is so flamboyant that it is impossible to take him seriously.

Karloff's performance is a study in contrast. Understated, sympathetic (even if he is a murderer), he quietly steals the picture from Lugosi. When he first comes to see Dr Vollin, he hopes to have his looks changed for the better. 'I'm saying, doc,' he tells Vollin, 'maybe because I look ugly...maybe if a man looks ugly, he does ugly things.' Vollin, of course, makes him look even uglier, more grotesque, so that he will more likely do the 'ugly' things he commands him to do,

Shot in only fifteen days on a budget of $109,750, *The Raven* is a completely different animal from *The Black Cat*. Although it runs a brisk 61 minutes and there are rarely any slow spots, it completely lacks the atmosphere and depth of characterisation that distinguished Ulmer's masterpiece. *The Raven* is fun, even amusing, but its horror is so overstated that it becomes an unintentional parody, with the exception of Karloff's performance.

Oddly enough, in 1935 it was considered very strong stuff; its themes of gruesome revenge by means of torture, not to mention Vollin's intentional disfigurement of Bateman, mitigated against the film's box office success at the time. The fact that the Production Code was now fully in force may have had something to do with that, as the public's mind was more on wholesome family entertainment (Shirley Temple was Hollywood's biggest star of the time) than it was on horror. *The Raven* caused something of a scandal in the UK, which led to a temporary ban on horror films in Great Britain. As a result, Universal made no horror films at all in 1937 and 1938, which was difficult for Karloff, the more versatile actor, and devastating to Lugosi, for whom horror was his bread and butter. When Universal started making horror films again in 1939, however, Lugosi returned in one of his greatest roles, that of Ygor in Rowland V Lee's *Son of Frankenstein*.

Poe did not return to the cinema until 1941, and then it was in a short film, only twenty minutes long, called *The Tell-Tale Heart*. The film was a featurette from MGM designed to precede the main attraction, a common practise during the 1930s and 1940s. Although two-reel comedies such as

The Three Stooges shorts were more ubiquitous, short literary adaptations were favoured by MGM.

*The Tell-Tale Heart* was the very first directorial effort from Jules Dassin, who had worked as an assistant to Alfred Hitchcock and Garson Kanin. Later known for his *film noirs* such as *Brute Force* (1947) and *The Naked City* (1948), it is easy to see, upon viewing *The Tell-Tale Heart*, from where those shadowy, atmospheric visuals arose.

Photographed by Paul Vogel, who also shot Tod Browning's *Freaks* (1932), *The Tell-Tale Heart* is far more faithful to Poe's short story than was Griffith's *The Avenging Conscience*. The fact that the film was a short meant that no padding was necessary, although a back story was given to the unnamed weaver (Joseph Schildkraut) who is the main protagonist. He is dominated, humiliated, and physically and verbally abused by an older man (Roman Bohnen) with whom he shares lodgings. Able to bear his constant mistreatment no longer, the young man enters the old man's room and murders him. He buries the body beneath the floorboards and ultimately becomes convinced that he can hear his victim's heart beating. When two policemen (Oscar O'Shea and Will Wright) visit the house to inquire about the whereabouts of the old man, the young weaver confesses his crime.

Dassin accentuates the sound effects in the climactic sequence to the nth degree, turning the screws of tension. It is a bravura sequence, and Vogel's camerawork is black and white cinematography at its most stylish, all shadows and light, again presaging the film noir mood in which Dassin would later specialize.

The acting is first-rate. Austrian-born Schildkraut had previously won an Oscar for his portrayal of Captain Alfred Dreyfus in *The Life of Emile Zola* (1937) and he shines here as the put-upon young man who finally snaps. Bohnen, as the old man, is every bit the unpleasant character he was in Poe's story, and then some. In the original tale, the narrator kills the old man because of his clouded, 'vulture-like' eye which offends the younger man so much that he murders him on that basis alone. The only addition to the story made by screenwriter Doane Hoag in Dassin's version is the fact that the old man is an abusive, downright nasty individual, which probably made his murder more 'understandable' to a 1940s audience used to black and white characters.

Dassin's *The Tell-Tale Heart* is a masterful telling of the tale, one of the finest adaptations of a Poe story ever put on the screen. In *Time* Magazine's 6 April 2008 issue, film critic Richard Corliss, writing on the occasion of Dassin's death a couple of weeks previously, pointed out that *The Tell-Tale Heart* was 'possibly the very first movie to be influenced by *Citizen Kane*... positively a-swill in Orson

The Tell-Tale Heart (1941)

Wellesian tropes: the crouching camera, the chiaroscuro lighting, the mood-deepening use of silences and sound effects.'

Corliss could indeed be correct; *The Tell-Tale Heart* was released on 25 October 1941 – just in time for Halloween – while *Citizen Kane* had premiered on 1 May. Whatever the case, Jules Dassin's *The Tell-Tale Heart* is a tiny, bewitching masterpiece.

In that same year of 1941, for no particular reason, Universal decided to film *The Black Cat* again, this time, as a comedy. With more than a touch of irony, intended or not, the writing credits for the film read: 'Screenplay by Robert Lees, Robert Neville, Fredric I Rinaldo and Eric Taylor…. Story by Edgar Allan Poe.' It is extremely doubtful that Poe would have recognised his tale in this creaky 'old dark house' yarn of dark and stormy nights, the reading of a will and a houseful of cats. It is more likely that the author would have revolved in his grave at immense speed.

The story concocted by those four screenwriters – four times as derivative as one screenwriter could make it – concerned the elderly and eccentric Henrietta Winslow (Cecilia Loftus) who lives in an old mansion with her housekeeper (Gale Sondergaard) and her myriad of cats. As her health fails, she is visited and surrounded by her greedy would-be heirs who gather to await her impending death. Needless to say, the heirs are picked off one by one. Whodunit?

Director Albert S Rogell, whose feature immediately preceding *The Black Cat* was an adaptation of *L'il Abner* (1940), assembled an all-star cast for his Poe picture: Basil Rathbone, Broderick Crawford, Bela Lugosi, Anne Gwynne, Gladys Cooper, Claire Dodd and a very young Alan Ladd are among those trapped at the Winslow Estate during a raging thunderstorm. Boarded in with them, much to their consternation, is a perpetually befuddled Hugh Herbert as an antiques dealer called Mr Penny.

The typical old dark house plot sees Henrietta murdered by someone from her own clan. According to her will, all of her worldly goods go to her feline friends and none of her relatives will receive a penny until all of the cats are deceased. Despite that codicil, however, it is the relatives themselves who end up dying.

We are quickly introduced to the usual suspects: Rathbone as Mr Hartley, housemaid Abigail played by the ever-sinister Sondergaard, and Lugosi as an obvious red herring. Crawford plays the overly eager real estate agent while Herbert is the buffoon to Crawford's straight man, but his exaggerated antics and mannerisms wear thin before long.

There are some mildly amusing lines here and there, such as when Crawford meets Ladd and observes, 'So you're the guy that slugged me.' The slightly-built Ladd replies to the much-larger Crawford, 'Yeah, and I'll do it again anytime you train down to my weight.'

Most of *The Black Cat*, however, is a waste of formidable talent. Rathbone and Lugosi have little to do; their roles could have been played by almost anyone. The film really rests on the shoulders of Crawford, Herbert,

Chapter Two – THE UNIVERSAL POE

Sondergaard, Cooper and Gwynne. They all do what is required of them, with Crawford providing many of the bright spots and demonstrating the comedic talent that he would ultimately hone to perfection in such films as George Cukor's *Born Yesterday* (1950). Herbert is very much an acquired taste, his trademark line of 'Woo-hoo' wearing on the audience after a while.

As with most Universal films of the period, *The Black Cat* looks terrific, fluidly photographed by Stanley Cortez, who also shot Orson Welles' *The Magnificent Ambersons* (1942). As a Poe picture, however, it's mildly entertaining at best, witless at worst and not the least bit frightening.

Meanwhile, the real world was at war and the United States was forced to enter it in December 1941 after the bombing of Pearl Harbour. By that time, Hitler and his madmen had already marched across Europe and it must have seemed to some that the apocalypse was at hand. Strangely, though, the human taste for fictional horror often seems to be at its height when conditions in the world are at their worst, and not only did Universal horror flourish, the genre blossomed at other studios as well, including RKO, where Val Lewton's unit was assigned to make horror films from particular titles such as *Cat People* (1942); and 20th Century-Fox, where German-born director John Brahm made such elegant horror films as *The Undying Monster* (1942), *The Lodger* (1944) and *Hangover Square* (1945).

Poe's popularity waxed and waned over the years, both critically and commercially. By the 1940s his stories and poems were commonly taught in most American schools; 'The Raven' was especially well known to nearly all high school students. Although some critics of Poe, such as Aldous Huxley, felt that his writing 'falls into vulgarity,' Poe's place in American letters was assured, not just in his native country, but all over the world; French literary critics were especially fond of him.

In 1942, 20th Century-Fox felt that Poe's reputation was solid enough to give him his own biopic entitled *The Loves of Edgar Allan Poe*, which, as the title suggested, concentrated on his love life. With a screenplay written by Samuel Hoffenstein and Arthur Caesar (with additional dialogue by Bryan Foy), the film was directed by Harry Lachman, who had helmed another sort of 'literary' film, *Dante's Inferno* (1935) as well as routine programmers such as *Charlie Chan in Rio* (1941).

Sultry young actress Linda Darnell was given top billing in the film as Virginia Clemm, Poe's greatest love. Only nineteen years old when she played the role, she had already made her film debut in 1939 in *Hotel for Women*. From age sixteen on, Darnell quickly climbed the ladder of stardom, and was Tyrone Power's leading lady in *The Mark of Zorro* (1940). She co-starred with Power again in *Blood and Sand* (1941) and, by the time she made *The Loves of Edgar Allan Poe* she was a bona-fide movie star, hence her billing over the actor who played the title role.

That actor was John Shepperd (later known as Shepperd Strudwick), a North Carolina native with extensive stage experience. Upon arriving in Hollywood, he tested for the role of Ashley Wilkes in *Gone with the Wind*

(1939) but lost the role to Leslie Howard. MGM didn't seem to know what to do with the actor, but when he moved to Fox, he was given his best shot at stardom with *The Loves of Edgar Allan Poe*. Stardom, however, eluded him, although he ended up having a long and distinguished second-tier career mainly on stage and television.

Jane Darwell, who played Mariah Clemm in the film, had just won an Academy Award for her performance in John Ford's *The Grapes of Wrath* (1940) and had also received excellent notices for her role in William Dieterle's *The Devil and Daniel Webster* (1941). Fox was eager to capitalise on her success as a character actress, and her performance is one of the best things about *The Loves of Edgar Allan Poe*.

Two actors who would later achieve fame appear in small roles in the film. Harry Morgan, later known to generations of American TV viewers as Colonel Sherman T Potter on *M*A*S*H* (1972-1983), was known as 'Henry Morgan' at the time and essayed the role of Poe's friend Ebenezer Burling. Morris Ankrum, a character actor who later specialised in some of the best-remembered science fiction films of the 1950s such as *Invaders from Mars* (1953), pops up in the small role of Mr Graham, one of Poe's employers.

Portraying Poe's other great love in the film, (Sarah) Elmira Royster, was Virginia Gilmore, a discovery of Samuel Goldwyn who had made her screen debut in *Winter Carnival* (1939). An up and coming young actress, Gilmore's

*Chapter Two – THE UNIVERSAL POE*

career soon faded and she ended up appearing in a number of B-movies before she retired from films in 1952.

Released on 28 August 1942, *The Loves of Edgar Allan Poe* has a running time of only 67 minutes, very short for a biopic. Indeed, the film glosses over and romanticises many aspects of Poe's life, beginning with his rather melancholy childhood and the devotion of his foster mother Frances Allan (Mary Howard), who is in direct contrast to his domineering and difficult foster father (Frank Conroy). Frances' love and support encourages Poe to fulfil his dream of writing, while his father wants him to go into the legal profession.

We follow Poe through the pangs of his first love, Elmira, who ends up marrying another while he is at university. Disowned by his foster father and drummed out of West Point, Poe finally finds someone to help him forget Elmira: Virginia Clemm, his cousin. When they marry, he creates his greatest works, such as 'The Raven.' Happiness, however, is shattered when Virginia becomes seriously ill.

There are two interesting age discrepancies in the casting: Howard seems far too young to be Poe's foster mother. The actress was in fact seven years younger than the actor who portrayed her foster son!

Although Darnell was nineteen at the time, Virginia Clemm was actually only thirteen when Poe, aged 26, obtained their marriage licence. These discrepancies mar the film somewhat, although it probably would have made audiences uncomfortable to see Sheppard waxing romantic to an actress who actually looked thirteen.

The most interesting aspect of the film, in many respects, deals with Poe's attempts to bring about fair and equal protection under copyright laws, which was a constant source of conflict between him and his employers. In real life, he and Charles Dickens battled against the established norms to bring about laws that would protect authors from having their work plagiarised. This is reflected in the film in which there is a scene in which Dickens (Morton Lowry) shows up to chat with Poe about their shared passion. In real life, the two actually did meet; in fact, some say that Dickens' pet raven, Grip, inspired Poe to write his famous poem. Although the raven doesn't appear in the film, the scene rings true and is well acted by both participants.

In fact, the acting in *The Loves of Edgar Allan Poe* is good to excellent across the board, with Shepperd especially fine as Poe, aging from his twenties to his forties, turning into a world-weary alcoholic before our eyes. If Fox and the other major studios had only come to realise what a special talent they had in Shepperd, he could have been a major star. He had the talent and the charisma; he just didn't fit into the cookie-cutter mould of what movie stardom was in the forties. Had he come along in the sixties, he might have fared better during that non-conformist decade, in which many moulds were broken.

Darnell is also excellent, especially once the character has reached the actress's own age; her utter devotion to her husband through his bouts of drunkenness and bad behaviour seems a little too saintly at times, although by all accounts the real-life Virginia was just as enamoured of Poe.

*The Loves of Edgar Allan Poe* is a good film that could have been something more. It is held together almost entirely by the performances of the two leads – along with Darwell and Howard – but a top-flight director such as, say, John Ford or Michael Curtiz could have made it into a more compelling film. One scene lingers in the memory: when Poe is asked by a potential publisher to read 'The Raven' to a group of printers, supposedly representing the 'man in the street.' Poe reads his poem to them with considerable theatrical power, and, after he is finished, the printers, who include one little boy (Leon Tyler), seem mostly unmoved, if not downright baffled. Once they have shuffled away, the little boy walks over to Poe, who is feeling dejected, and says to him: 'Mr. Poe, I thought your poem was *wonderful.*'

It is an emotionally moving scene, extremely well handled by all involved. It could easily have tripped over into the maudlin, but never quite crosses that threshold. And, in one fell swoop, the sequence made sport of Poe's critics and revealed why Poe has remained popular through the centuries: he appeals to the wide-eyed, childlike wonder in all of us.

In 1942, with its horror line booming under such titles as *The Ghost of Frankenstein* and *The Mummy's Tomb*, Universal decided to return to Poe one last time, although the result was a gothic mystery rather than an out and

out horror film. Poe's 'The Mystery of Marie Roget' was a sequel to 'Murders in the Rue Morgue,' bringing back detective C August Dupin from that tale. Written in 1842, 'The Mystery of Marie Roget' was then celebrating its centennial, which may have been one reason that Universal decided to dust it off and film it that year.

Poe's tale was the first murder mystery based upon the details of an actual crime. Poe called it 'one of his tales of ratiocination' rather than one of his horror stories. In the tale, Dupin takes on the case of perfume shop employee Marie Roget, whose body is found in the Seine. The plot is based upon the real-life murder of Mary Cecilia Rogers, a New York City woman whose corpse was found floating in the Hudson River. Months later, her fiancé was found dead, having committed suicide. The case remained an enigma and Poe attempted to solve it in fictional form with his story, which appeared in "Snowden's Ladies' Companion" in three instalments in November and December 1842 and February 1843.

Universal handed directorial duties for their film version to Phil Rosen, a prolific director who made over 142 films between 1915 and 1949. Rosen seemed to place quantity over quality, as few of his films were actually distinguished. In 1933, he had directed *The Sphinx*, a modest mystery/horror thriller starring Lionel Atwill for Monogram Pictures – and little of note since then. In 1941, he had directed the comedy-horror film *Spooks Run Wild*, starring Bela Lugosi and the East Side Kids, also for Monogram.

Universal's choice to put a director of programmers in charge of a period piece such as *The Mystery of Marie Roget* is something of a mystery in itself; suffice it to say that the company was going through something of an economy drive during the war and was mainly grinding out B-movies such as their horror product and the Sherlock Holmes series starring Basil Rathbone and Nigel Bruce.

In any case, Peggy Moran from Christy Cabanne's *The Mummy's Hand* (1940) was chosen to play the title role of Marie Roget, but, for whatever reason, she left the picture and was replaced by up and coming actress Maria Montez, a Dominican actress whose exotic beauty led to her being cast in a plethora of costume pictures such as Universal's prestige production *Arabian Nights* (1942), their first three-strip Technicolor production. With her unusual accent and stunning appearance, Montez was a natural to play the mysterious Marie Roget.

Top billing in the film is given to British-born film actor Patric Knowles, best known at the time for playing Will Scarlet to Errol Flynn's Robin Hood in Michael Curtiz's *The Adventures of Robin Hood* (1938). In the 1940s, he did a lot of work for Universal, mainly in their horror films such as *The Wolf Man* (1941) and its sequel, *Frankenstein Meets the Wolf Man* (1943). He was cast as Dr Paul Dupin in *The Mystery of Marie Roget*.

Other performers in the film included Maria Ouspenskaya (*The Wolf Man*) as Cecile Roget, John Litel (*They Died with Their Boots On*, 1941) as Henri Beauvais and Frank Reicher (*King Kong*, 1933) as a magistrate. Screenwriter

Michel Jacoby eliminated nearly everything from the Poe story except for its Paris setting and its title; he also moved up the timeline by 47 years, to 1889.

In a sense, however, Universal's *The Mystery of Marie Roget* is a sequel to their own film version of *Murders in the Rue Morgue*, with Knowles apparently playing the same character that was played by Leon Wycoff in that film, although the first name has been changed from Pierre to Paul. In *Murders*, he was a young medical student, and in *Mystery*, he is a full-fledged doctor. References are made to the previous film in dialogue exchanges such as when Beauvais says to him: 'Dupin? You had something to do with those murders in the Rue Morgue, didn't you?' and is answered by Prefect Gobelin (Lloyd Corrigan): 'Something to do? Monsieur, Dr Dupin practically solved those murders single-handed.'

Again, the basic plot is the same as Poe's story, but the devil is in the details: a doctor (rather than a detective) attempts to unravel the bizarre circumstances that led to a young actress (rather than a perfume shop employee) being found in the Seine. In standard and stereotyped fashion a la the Sherlock Holmes films, Dupin is the brilliant one, while the policeman (Corrigan) is an utter dolt as was Dennis Hoey's Inspector Lestrade in the Holmes series.

Although it looks great, especially for a B-picture (shot by Elwood Bredel, who had also photographed *The Ghost of Frankenstein*), *The Mystery of Marie Roget* is not nearly as interesting as it would have been had the script adhered more faithfully to Poe's story. Montez gets little screen time (although her character is perhaps the most intriguing in the film), so it's Knowles' movie all the way, and he runs away with it. Always a sincere and capable actor, Knowles shines as the clever doctor-cum-detective and the actor could have easily played the role in a series of films. Universal, however, was committed to their Holmes franchise, and *The Mystery of Marie Roget* turned out to be not just a rather tepidly-received one-off, but the final Universal Poe film of their classic horror period. After the war, it seemed as though the audience appetite for fictional horror was on the wane once they had seen the real horrors unleashed by World War II.

Nevertheless, as we shall see in the next chapter, there were definite signs of new blood.

# CHAPTER THREE
# THE POSTWAR POE

*'This – all this – was in the olden
Time long ago.'*

**The Haunted Palace**

**D**uring the postwar years, particularly in the United States, there was more prosperity than the world had ever seen before. There was a postwar baby boom, people saw the USA in their Chevrolets and everyone in America and around the world should have been living at the peak of optimism. But life is seldom so simple.

The postwar world was also highlighted by more anxiety than ever before. In the United States and throughout the world, the unleashing of the real-life horrors of World War II, from the unimaginable nightmare of the Nazi concentration camps to the equally unimaginable destructive power of the atomic bombs that were dropped on Hiroshima and Nagasaki, brought about new fears, new terrors about just what type of evil had been unleashed upon humanity. Added to this devil's brew, in the US at least, was the fear of communism, the paranoid anxiety that your neighbor might be a 'red' or that a communist was hiding behind every bush or under every bed. There was a new witch hunt abroad in the land, and it was called McCarthyism.

This postwar darkness was reflected in the new genre of film noir, an American style of crime drama that emphasised world-weary cynicism and sexual subtext. The visual look of film noir was influenced by German Expressionism and later, by Orson Welles' *Citizen Kane.* The first major film noir of the classic black and white era is generally considered to be John Huston's *The Maltese Falcon* (1941), photographed by Arthur Edeson, who had also shot Whale's *Frankenstein* and *The Invisible Man.*

In Britain, postwar cinema also tended towards the dark, but in a different way. The anthology film *Dead of Night* (1945) paved the way for horror-hungry audiences after the ban on such films during the war, while

**Scenes from *The Fall of the House of Usher* (1950)**

in America the horror genre went into a period of quiescence, temporarily replaced by film noir and horror comedies such as *Abbott and Costello Meet Frankenstein* (1948). Meanwhile, British cinema began its golden age, hitting new heights with such films as David Lean's *Great Expectations* (1946) and Carol Reed's noirish thrillers *Odd Man Out* (1947) and *The Third Man* (1949).

There had not been a major Poe feature in either country since 1942's *The Mystery of Marie Roget*, although the spirit of Poe still popped up occasionally in the titles of such B-movies as PRC's *The Black Raven* (1943), a routine 'old dark house' mystery. It wasn't until 1950 that another proper Poe adaptation was produced: Ivan Barnett's *The Fall of the House of Usher*, released in June of that year in the United Kingdom. *Usher* was filmed in Hastings by GIB Films, a low-budget outfit that produced second features. Barnett produced, directed and photographed the film; his only previous film work had been a documentary short called *Down to the Sea in Trucks* (1947).

Barnett began work on *Usher* shortly after completing his documentary, casting mostly amateur actors in the lead roles. The exception was Gwendoline Watford (later known as Gwen Watford), who was cast as Lady Usher. It was her film debut, but the actress was professionally trained and a veteran of the theatre, and later appeared in such films as Hammer's *Never Take Sweets from a Stranger* (US: *Candy from a Stranger*, 1960) and *Taste the Blood of Dracula* (1969), as well as such 'prestige' productions as *Cleopatra* (1963), before returning to the horror genre once more in the Tyburn Film Production *The Ghoul* (1975).

The other actors included Kaye Tendeter (Lord Roderick Usher), Irving Steen (Jonathan) and Vernon Charles (Dr Cordwell), none of whom ever appeared in another feature. The acting in the film is predictably stilted, not helped by an overabundance of post-dubbing.

The screenplay by Dorothy Cott and Kenneth Thompson is occasionally faithful to its source, but it goes off on some weird tangents: A traveller named Jonathan arrives at the Usher house to visit his old friend Roderick.

*Chapter Three – THE POSTWAR POE*

Upon his arrival, he finds that Roderick and his sister Madeline are in the grips of some strange malady. Roderick's senses have become overly attuned to the slightest sound or touch, while Madeline seems to be in a nearly catatonic state. It transpires that the Usher matriarch (Lucy Pavey), who has gone mad after a murder was committed, is living in a disused temple on the estate. All of the Ushers have been the victims of some terrible curse, and Roderick and Madeline are the latest to succumb to it.

When the film was released in June, it received a rare 'H' Certificate, to alert parents that the film was 'horror.' Apparently, the 'H' served as a come-on, as the British horror-starved audience made the low-budget feature into a 'sleeper' success as a second feature, and in some venues, it was even exhibited as 'top of the bill.' Although it is rarely seen today, Barnett's little Poe adaptation was reissued in 1955 and once more in 1961. Steve Chibnall and Brian McFarlane, in their book *The British 'B' Film* (Palgrave MacMillan, 2009) even posited that it may have been an influence in the development of Hammer horror.

While that theory may or may not be true, *The Fall of the House of Usher* has much to recommend it. The film is more linear and accessible than either of the silent versions, yet is as visually striking as either of them. Barnett was a better cinematographer than he was a director, and some of the shots of the wintry East Sussex countryside do indeed presage the look of many of the later Hammer horrors, with the forest and moorland settings for which Hammer became known. The wanderings of Lady Madeline through this country of the mind are exceptionally moody and dreamlike, and there are some dialogue-free passages that also presage Corman's psychological approach to Poe.

The acting, unfortunately, brings the film down a notch. Although Watford is fine in her film debut, it's easy to see why the other actors, amateurs all, made no further film appearances. They are as wooden as can be, and the film is further hindered by a needless wraparound story that takes place in a modern-day English gentlemen's club, illustrating, perhaps, the timidity of the British cinema of the time in its attitude toward horror.

Viewed today, Barnett's *The Fall of the House of Usher* is an interesting curiosity, a sometimes faithful, sometimes bizarre (Pavey as The Hag is merely distracting) version of Poe's story that arrived at a time when horror in the cinema was at a low ebb. Barnett's first feature was successful enough to win him a brief career as a director, ending with a short film called *Meet Mr Beat* in 1961, although he lived until 2013, passing away at the ripe old age of 88.

The year 1951 saw a most unusual Poe-related feature called *The Man with a Cloak*, adapted from a short story by John Dickson Carr called 'The Gentleman from Paris.' The film was directed by Fletcher Markle, a multi-talented Canadian screenwriter/producer/director/actor. He had previously directed and co-written a thriller called *Jigsaw* (1949) starring Franchot Tone and Jean Wallace, and had later helmed *Night into Morning* (1951), a drama

starring Ray Milland and Nancy Reagan. During the 1950s, he became a very active television producer/director, and he produced the first eight episodes of NBC-TV's *Thriller* hosted by Karloff.

Markle had originally hoped to cast Marlene Dietrich and Lionel Barrymore in *The Man with a Cloak*, but Dietrich turned down the role of the scheming maid and Barrymore was too ill to work. Barbara Stanwyck was then cast in the Dietrich role and Louis Calhern took the part of the ailing millionaire that had been intended for Barrymore.

The story takes place in New York City in the year 1848, when a Frenchwoman (Leslie Caron) visits exiled (and dissipated) former French diplomat Charles Thevenet (Calhern), who is the grandfather of her fiancé. The old man lives in a mansion with a housekeeper and a butler who are eager for him to kick the bucket so they can inherit his considerable fortune. Seeing the Frenchwoman as a threat to their future, the two scheme to get rid of her as well, but she is aided by a mysterious man in a cloak who calls himself Dupin (Joseph Cotten).

Cotten was a veteran of Orson Welles' Mercury Theatre, and, as was the case with many of those esteemed radio players, had a role in *Citizen Kane* (1941), his Hollywood debut. His star rose very quickly and he received rave reviews for his roles in Alfred Hitchcock's *Shadow of a Doubt* (1943), William Dieterle's *Portrait of Jennie* (1948) and Carol Reed's *The Third Man*

(1949). *The Man with a Cloak* was Cotten's first film at MGM since the classic thriller *Gaslight* (1944).

*The Man with a Cloak* is very well acted, but it's more of a straight drama than a thriller. Although there is intrigue, there is no real mystery: we know that the butler (Joe De Santis in a sly performance) and the maid are plotting Thevenet's demise from the get-go; the only question is how and when they're going to do it. As for the 'mystery' identity of Dupin, the man in the cloak himself, anyone who knows anything about Poe (spoiler alert!) will guess who he is from the outset. Not only is he named after a famous Poe character, he imbibes gallons of wine during the course of the film, runs up a huge tab that he can't pay (Jim Backus is amusing as the patient innkeeper), and, to top things off, there's a raven in Thevenet's house, kept as a pet.

As Dupin/Poe, Cotten is well cast. Like Poe, the actor was a southern gentleman and he has a lot of fun with the witty, cynical dialogue by screenwriter Frank Fenton. At one point, Thevenet's housekeeper (Margaret Wycherly) offers him some advice on his drinking. His response: 'Ma'am, I take advice as easily as I take a drink. The only trouble with me is I've never been able to make good use of either.'

In another scene, Dupin/Poe's landlady (Jean Inness) points out to him, 'You know, it's the first of the month.' He replies, 'I can understand your excitement; it only comes once every thirty days.'

The script is full of such banter, but the story unfolds slowly and the direction is sluggish. There is very little action, although Stanwyck is at her smouldering best as the duplicitous maid, another of her many femme fatale roles. She and Cotten have a good chemistry and, when they're onscreen, the movie crackles. Ultimately, however, it is a careful, pretty failure of a film (it lost $455,000 at the box office), but for true Poe enthusiasts, Cotten's performance alone makes it all worthwhile. It remains a handsomely mounted, at times intriguing curiosity.

The year 1953 was the height of the 3-D film craze. Three-dimensional stereoscopic film had been around in one form or another since 1915, but the lack of a standard system had delayed the format's development. The so-called 'golden era' of 3-D movies began in late 1952 with the release of the first stereoscopic feature in colour, Arch Oboler's *Bwana Devil*. The film was shot in

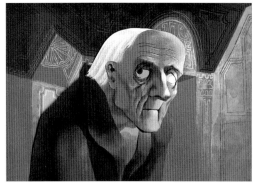

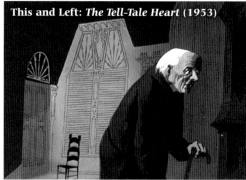

**This and Left: *The Tell-Tale Heart* (1953)**

'Natural Vision,' which became the standard for 3-D productions, and many 3-D films followed, including the Warner Bros blockbuster *House of Wax* (1953, starring Vincent Price, an actor who would soon loom large in Poe pictures.

In May 1953, production began in Hollywood on an animated version of *The Tell-Tale Heart*, which some sources claim was originally slated to be in 3-D. Although it is not known for certain whether or not the film was animated for 3-D, there was no reference to the format in a trade review of the time and the 'leaders' on the original prints make no mention of 3-D. In any case, the short film, running only a little over seven minutes, was released 'flat.'

*The Tell-Tale Heart* was produced by United Productions of America (UPA), an American animation studio that was founded as a result of the Walt Disney animators' strike of 1941, in which a number of long-time studio animators left Disney for greener pastures. UPA ultimately received a contract from Columbia Pictures to create animated shorts for that studio. They were known for their striking animation style and unique sense of design, winning the Academy Award in 1950 with their short *Gerald McBoing Boing*, based on a record by Dr Seuss.

The screenplay for UPA's *The Tell-Tale Heart* was co-written by Fred Grable and Bill Scott, the latter of whom became known as the co-creator and voice of the cartoon character Bullwinkle. The film was directed by Ted Parmelee, who later directed many episodes of *The Bullwinkle Show*. The artistic style of the film was derived from Eugene Berman, scenic and ballet designer of New York City's Metropolitan Opera. The official designer of the film was Paul Julian, one of the greatest background artists for the Looney Tunes and Merrie Melodies lines at Warner Bros. The musical score was composed by Boris Kremenliev, an American composer who specialised in eastern European folk music.

Narration for the film, which was very faithful to Poe, was provided by none other than James Mason, whose star was ascendant in Hollywood at the time, after making his mark in British films such as *The Wicked Lady* (1945) and *Odd Man Out* (1947). His starring role in *The Desert Fox: The Story of Rommel* (1951) had earned him such acclaim that a sequel of sorts, *The Desert Rats*, arrived from 20th Century-Fox in 1953.

Mason's urbane, smooth delivery is one of the greatest joys of Parmelee's *The Tell-Tale Heart*. The actor goes far above and beyond the call of his title of narrator; he gives a proper performance. A title card informs us of what we're in for: 'The film you are about to see is based on a story told a hundred years ago by American's greatest master of drama and suspense... The story is told through the eyes of a madman... who, like all of us, believed that he was sane.'

Then we are whisked into the world of Poe, with Mason portraying the unnamed narrator using Poe's prose, although condensed, almost word for word: 'True, I'm nervous. Very, very dreadfully nervous. But why would you say that I'm mad? See how calmly, how precisely I can tell the story to you. Listen. It starts with the old man...'

By the end of the film's seven minute and 24 seconds running time, we see that the narrator is, indeed, mad: 'Then I heard it. It might have been an ant, a clock… Louder, and still louder. They must hear it, and yet they sit and talk and talk. Of course they must! They know, they do! They're torturing me, watching me… Stop it! Stop it, you devils! Yes, yes, I did it! It's there, under the floor! Oh, stop it! It is the beating of his hideous heart!'

UPA created one of the most perfectly crafted Poe adaptations ever filmed. From the subdued light and shadow of its colour palette to its ground-breaking tone of dramatic tension (almost unheard of for an animated cartoon at the time) to Mason's spot-on portrayal of a madman trying desperately to cling to his reason, *The Tell-Tale Heart* is a mini-masterpiece of Poesque terror, and one not easily forgotten.

In Britain, the film was the first cartoon to be given the 'X' Certificate, which replaced the 'H' rating in 1951. Although it was nominated for the Academy Award for Best Short Film that year, it lost to Disney's *Toot, Whistle, Plunk and Boom*, perhaps because it was too strong in content for some members of the Academy. In 2001, Parmelee's *The Tell-Tale Heart* was named by the United States Library of Congress as a 'culturally significant' film and was selected for preservation in the National Film Registry – a rare honour for any film, but especially so for an animated short.

One often hears of a film that had been thought to have been lost being discovered in someone's attic. This literally occurred when, during the course of my writing this book, a second 1953 version of *The Tell Tale Heart* was discovered in the attic of a home in Scotland. The house's owner, Jeff Wells, had originally bought the 16mm film in 1984 when he was working in Brighton; after moving to Scotland, he stored the film in his attic and, in October of 2017, he cleaned out his attic and decided to sell the film.

After doing some online research, however, Wells discovered that it was worth quite a lot; it was, apparently, the sole copy of the twenty-minute version of Poe's story that had been produced by Adelphi Films, and directed by J B Williams, starring famed British actor Stanley Baker (*Zulu*, 1964).

Interviewed in the 23 October 2018 issue of *The Independent*, Wells said, 'I was stunned when I saw it was the same one I had. I really couldn't believe it. I thought that it can't possibly be the one I have they are looking for. Its discovery was a happy accident.'

Current Adelphi head Kate Lees said that the company had given up hope of ever finding a print of the film. She continued: 'It's a really good film. It's very spooky, gothic and scary and it's well directed. Stanley Baker is terrific.'

The British Film Institute has restored and digitized the film, which is now on their website. My UK correspondent, Dave Hastings, reviewed it for this book. Here is his complete review:

'After being missing for more than 50 years, this now rediscovered 1953 adaptation of Edgar Allan Poe's *Tell-Tale Heart*, is a remarkable and triumphant version of the infamous tale, one that parallels its author's own haunted fragile mentality.

'Unlike previous adaptations, such as Hurst's 1934 version, which relays the story as more of a flashback, or even the 1941 film that plays it safe in a more traditional linear storytelling form, here director J B Williams trusts the talents of his leading and only star, Stanley Baker, to tell the story as if you are watching a one-man stage play, as his character, actually depicting Edgar Allan Poe in a surprising twist, ceremoniously strides towards us encircled by shadow, breaking the fourth wall by addressing us himself, while simultaneously enacting the infamous tale he is currently writing and which we will come to know so very well.

'However, like the '34 version, there is an element of familiarity to the proceedings as notable connotations of German Expressionism still linger within the production design, wherein the aforementioned shadows cast their ever-increasing gloom over the tale being told as well as becoming synonymous with the Poe persona itself. Williams allows Baker free reign to portray Poe with enough faith that he seemingly pays more attention instead to how he can complement him visually. In a striking moment, Poe looks at himself in a mirror which has a large crack down the middle, metaphorically signaling the dual realm of the man's internal sanity and madness, while foreshadowing his story's ending in the process.

'Additionally, the set is a closed off affair, offered as a room out of which Baker seemingly reflects at the moon, as if not only engaging with us, his audience, but also our ally in the night sky. There are distinctive early Hammer horror vibes as well to the mise-en-scène with the design not unlike something one would find Peter Cushing's Baron Frankenstein sitting within, plotting his next body snatch. Yet while the likes of Terence Fisher would have allowed that space to stay open and work for the Baron's outwardly scheming persona, Williams does not give his Poe the same choice, as he frames the man sitting at tables or walking around maniacally through staircase spindles, as if behind a cell, trapped, tormented by the murderous actions he is concocting as well as agonising over to us, as if in confession.

'As this surprisingly effective short begins to reach its horrifying conclusion, it is clear why Williams has placed confidence in his sole character as Baker's dialogue and delivery of Poe all begin to punctuate faster and more feverishly. Additionally, the correct usage of sound plays ever greater into the account being told, as the beating heart, while previously subtle throughout, now begins to make itself known to the central narrative, tormenting Poe and his alternate persona he is currently creating while continuously reminding him of the crimes committed by their own fictional hands.

'While in previous adaptations (and arguably the majority since), Poe's alter ego/narrator would inevitably engage with and confess all to officers that are present in supporting roles, it is a testament to Baker's talents here that he presents an equally dramatic solo retelling and devastating conclusion, with the same amount of pathos and woe for his otherwise perfect crime as the closing moments develop.

'This newly discovered film is a wonderful and valuably restored contribution to the ever-popular retellings of Poe's notoriously gothic tale, one that, if summed up, could be described as a macabre and gothic version of the popular *Talking Heads* series by celebrated British writer Alan Bennett, whose solo creations within that context spoke directly to audiences as well, allowing their own sinister stories to unravel slowly but surely to those watching.

'Yet while there is a familiarity in Williams' vision that obviously predates Bennett's material, it is still unique and gorgeously gothic in tone, supported by an actor at the top of his game, complemented by strong visual direction and early postmodern narrative techniques which utilise darkness and explicit motifs to continuously remind us that all is not well with both Baker's Poe and the very world around him. Upon reflection, it is abundantly radiating the very essence of the real-life Poe himself.'

In the early fifties, two new attitudes toward popular culture led to the loosening of Hollywood's Production Code. The rise of television was first and foremost, and when sales of television sets started to go through the roof, cinema attendance decreased exponentially. Throughout the war years, the movies had had a virtual monopoly on what Americans spent for entertainment; radio was no competition. After the war, when televisions began to be sold *en masse*, the new medium took off like a rocket, and the audience appetite for this 'mixture of radio and pictures' became ravenous.

At the same time, the rigidity of the Production Code was starting to look very quaint indeed compared to such foreign imports as Giuseppe De Santis' *Bitter Rice* (1949) and Ingmar Bergman's *Summer With Monika* (1953), which dealt with adult themes that Hollywood productions wouldn't dare touch. The Code started to become unglued when, in 1952, Roberto Rosselini's *The Miracle* was released in the US. The very concept of the film seemed to be geared to courting controversy: It concerned a man, played by Italian director Federico Fellini, who deliberately impregnates an emotionally disturbed peasant woman (Anna Magnani) who believes herself to be the Virgin Mary.

*The Miracle* was one half of a portmanteau film called *L'Amore*; the other half, *The Human Voice* (based on a play by Jean Cocteau) was also directed by Fellini, but it was *The Miracle* that the State of New York sought to ban outright. The case went all the way to the Supreme Court, which overturned a 1915 decision that designated motion pictures as a commodity to be regulated and recognised film as an art form for the first time, protected under the First Amendment, which guarantees freedom of speech.

The Supreme Court decision opened the floodgates; although *The Miracle* was far from an exploitation film, it led to a decade that belonged to the likes of Marilyn Monroe and Jayne Mansfield, when sex sold and *Playboy* Magazine dominated the newsstands. By 1956, imported 'adult' films like Roger Vadim's *And God Created Woman* starring his then-wife, Brigitte Bardot, made millions by exploiting her fulsome form in various states of undress.

While motion pictures were finally recognised in the United States as the art form they had always been, comic books didn't fare so well. From the late forties onward, crime and horror comics became the scapegoat for all of society's ills, which came to a head when a controversial psychiatrist named Fredric Wertham published a tome called *Seduction of the Innocent*, postulating that horror and crime comic books were a direct cause of juvenile delinquency. The fact that the book's conclusions were based largely on undocumented anecdotes seemed to bother few at the time; the anti-comic book hysteria reached a fever pitch when the Senate Subcommittee on Juvenile Delinquency, led by anti-crime legislator Estes Kefauver, recommended that the comics industry tone down its violent and sexual content voluntarily. Thus, the Comics Code Authority was born, all horror titles were banned and comic books became blandly boring for a considerable length of time, forced to adhere to a code that was ten times stricter than the Hollywood Production Code had ever been.

Ironically, the furore over horror comics coincided with the rise of Poe within literary scholarship; the author's reputation had seen its ebbs and flows in the decades since his death, but in the post-war years, he became more highly regarded than ever, with many of his tales and poems becoming part of the curriculum in American schools. Perhaps the excesses of the horror comics – which often featured lurid covers depicting dismemberment and impalements – made Poe's stories such as 'The Tell-Tale Heart' and 'The Black Cat' more 'respectable'. Whatever the case, Poe's reputation was on the upswing again and Hollywood came calling.

One of the ways that Hollywood found to temporarily compete with television was 3-D. The other was to put more sex and violence into their pictures to compete with foreign imports. It was against this backdrop that the next major Poe adaptation, Warner Bros' *Phantom of the Rue Morgue* (1954), was produced. It was intended as a follow-up to their spectacularly successful *House of Wax*, the film that made Vincent Price a full-fledged horror star. As with that film, *Phantom* was shot in 3-D under the watchful eye of veteran director Roy Del Ruth, who had directed, among a myriad of films, the original version of *The Maltese Falcon* (1931).

This new version of *Murders in the Rue Morgue* was written by Harold Medford and James R Webb and it incorporated much more blood and thunder into the story than had the previous version in 1932. *House of Wax* had been a remake of Warner's own *Mystery of the Wax Museum* (1933) and had taken advantage of the relaxed Production Code to include such enticements as three-dimensional can-can dancers and a frightening make-up for Price's scarred face that outdid even the Pre-Code visage of Lionel Atwill in the same role.

The villain of *Phantom*, a character called Dr Marais, was played by Karl Malden, one of the new breed of 'method' actors, who was just about to receive his breakthrough role in Elia Kazan's *On the Waterfront*, released later in 1954. French actor Claude Dauphin (Inspector Bonnard) had made

Steve Forrest, Karl Malden and Claude Dauphin in
*Phantom of the Rue Morgue* (1954)

Steve Forrest, Anthony Caruso and Patricia Medina in
*Phantom of the Rue Morgue* (1954)

*Chapter Three – THE POSTWAR POE*

his American debut in David Butler's *April in Paris* (1952), in which he had co-starred with Doris Day and Ray Bolger. Patricia Medina, a sultry actress of English-Spanish heritage, was a veteran of such costume pictures as *Siren of Bagdad* and *Sangaree* (both 1953), while Dana Andrews' younger brother Steve Forrest (Professor Paul Dupin) had made his uncredited film debut in Mark Robson's thriller for producer Val Lewton, *The Ghost Ship* (1943). He had since distinguished himself in such films as Robert Wise's *So Big* and Richard Brooks' *Take the High Ground!* (both 1953). Interestingly, Charles Gemora, who had played the role of Erik the ape in the Lugosi version, assumed essentially the same role in *Phantom*, although his ill health required many of the scenes involving the gorilla to be performed by a stuntman.

Behind the scenes, cinematographer J Peverell Marley was brought back from *House of Wax* to photograph *Phantom*, and the previous film's composer David Buttolph returned to perform the same duties on the new production. As with *House of Wax*, the new production was photographed in 'WarnerColor'.

*House of Wax* had been kinetic, with several action set-pieces and a musical score that wouldn't quit. Although not as well-remembered, *Phantom* goes even further, its relatively lavish budget allowing for scenes involving scores of Can-Can dancers a la John Huston's recent *Moulin Rouge* (1952), with the 3-D effects giving the audience that 'in your face' quality. Filmed between September and November 1953 and released in March, 1954, *Phantom* anticipates the 'blood and thunder' approach that Hammer would become known for even more than *House of Wax* had done.

The story is fairly close to Poe: in 1870s France, a wave of gruesome murders occurs in the Rue Morgue district. Inspector Bonnard is getting nowhere with his investigation, but finds Professor Dupin to be a 'person of interest'. It transpires that Doctor Marais is engaged in some unusual animal experiments in which he trains mice to respond to the ringing of bells, a la Pavlov's dogs. It's pretty clear from the outset that Dupin is a Hitchcock-type 'wrong man' who is actually our hero, while Marais is established as the villain fairly early on, when we discover that he is training his ape to respond to the ringing of bells by killing the people who wear them.

The devil however, is in the details. Whereas the murders in the 1932 version had mostly occurred off-screen, the murders in *Phantom* take full advantage of the advances in sound, colour and 3-D to emphasize maximum shock. Indeed, there are sequences that are pretty strong stuff for the early fifties, as author Jonathan Rigby wrote in *The Fantastic Fifties #2*: 'For the time, these scenes really are eye-popping – brilliantly staged, executed with bags of kinetic energy and coming complete with a disturbingly eroticised undertow that in 1953 was quite new. Surprisingly bloody, they anticipate the gorier shockers that would come out of Britain at the end of the decade … The victims do an awful lot of high-decibel screaming and are subsequently discovered with ripped stockings and bloodily-lacerated legs provocatively

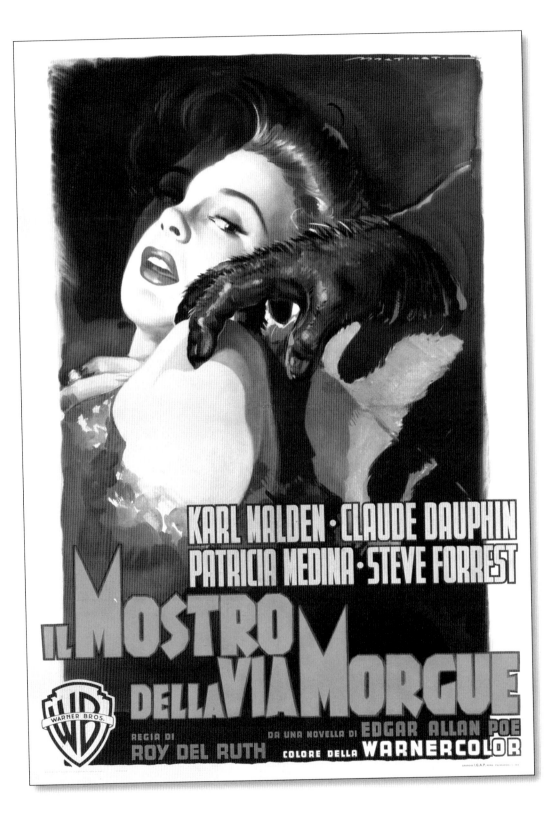

splayed; an attack on an artist's atelier becomes an action-painting shambles... This particular outrage is prefaced by a leisurely view of the beautiful and scantily-clad victim, Arlette (Veola Vonn) pulling on her stockings.'

The cracks in the Production Code had grown wider since 1952, and American filmmakers were becoming more and more daring. The most shocking scene in the film, and the best remembered, may be when the green-faced corpse of a woman (Dolores Dorn) slips down from its resting place in the chimney where it has been stuffed. It's a thrill that truly anticipates Hammer's shock approach to the horror film.

In 1957, when Hammer's *The Curse of Frankenstein* was released in the US through Warner Bros, it was advertised in some newspapers as 'From the people who brought you *House of Wax*,' thereby following a straight line from Warner's 3-D shockers to Hammer's 'girl and ghoul' movies, as *Time* Magazine christened them. Of course, this was the Grand Guignol approach made fresh and writ large; there are few quiet moments in *Phantom*, and, true to classic Grand Guignol themes, the villain lusts after the voluptuous Medina. In the film's climax, Marais is killed by his own ape, a scene which would be 'aped' in AIP's gory *Horrors of the Black Museum* (1959) when Michael Gough's assistant Rick (Graham Curnow) falls on him from atop a carnival ride.

*Phantom* received generally favourable reviews upon its release, with *Variety* noting, 'Murders and gory bodies abound in this Henry Blanke production, which gives fulsome attention to the bloody violence loosed by the title's *Phantom*... Not for the squeamish.'

*Phantom* grossed $1,450,000 in 1954, a tidy sum for those days, but by the time it was released, the 3-D craze was all but dead, and the film was released 'flat' in many venues. While *Phantom's* acting is adequate (there's even an appearance by future American talk-show host Merv Griffin in a featured role), it's the action the film is remembered for, providing the viewer a bloody good time. I'll let Rigby have the last word from his article on *Phantom:* 'It has three hair-raising, window-smashing, paint-spraying murder sequences – sequences that, for good or ill, were to have a decisive effect on future horror cinema.'

The mid-fifties found cinematic Poe adaptations very much in retreat, replaced by the rise of science fiction films. Every major studio invested in the relatively new genre, including Paramount (*War of the Worlds*, 1953), Universal-International (*This Island Earth*, 1955) and MGM (*Forbidden Planet*, 1956). During this period, only one Poe adaptation was filmed, and it was a real curiosity.

*Manfish* (1956) proclaims its origins in the opening credits as 'Based on The Gold-Bug and The Tell-Tale Heart by Edgar Allan Poe.' Although the celebrated author would probably be hard-pressed to find either of his stories in the film, at least the credits spelled his middle name correctly.

Directed by W Lee Wilder (the less talented brother of director Billy Wilder), *Manfish* tells the very modern-day story of three deep-sea divers who get mixed up in murder while searching for a buried treasure. Although more of a straight adventure than a horror film, second billing is given to none other than Lon Chaney Jr as Swede, the first mate to adventurer Brannigan (John Bromfield). Bromfield was an American film and television actor whose screen debut had arrived in *Harpoon* (1948) and who quickly segued into *Sorry, Wrong Number* (also 1948), Anatole Litvak's famous thriller starring Barbara Stanwyck and Burt Lancaster.

Also in the cast was Victor Jory, a busy Canadian-born actor who had co-starred in seven *Hopalong Cassidy* films in the early forties and ended up working mostly in television. He was cast in *Manfish* as the enigmatic criminal mastermind known as The Professor.

*Manfish* featured the screen debut of blonde bombshell Barbara Nichols (not counting her uncredited appearance as a dancer in *River of No Return*, 1954), as Mimi. Nichols was an established Broadway performer who had appeared in the 1952 revival of *Pal Joey*, and who would repeat her performance in the 1957 film version starring Frank Sinatra and Kim Novak.

The leading lady of *Manfish* was Jamaican actress Tess Prendergast, who had appeared in such films as *Song of Paris* (1952) and *His Majesty O'Keefe* (1954). Cast as Alita in *Manfish*, Prendergast ended up retiring from acting and is best-remembered today as the designer of Ursula Andress's iconic white bikini in the first James Bond movie, *Dr No* (1962).

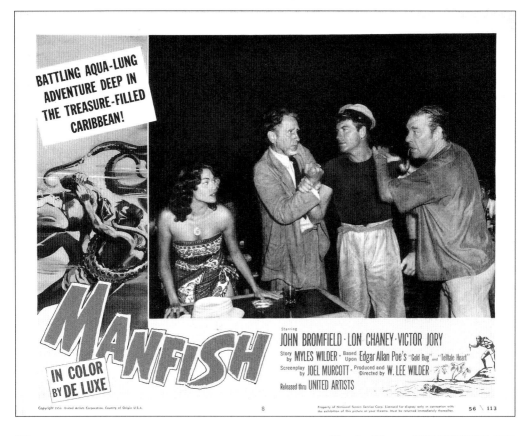

Released in February 1956 by United Artists, *Manfish* was the latest in a string of films Wilder had directed for the company, which included such Grade-B genre fare as *Phantom from Space* (1953) and *The Snow Creature* (1954). *Manfish* was originally filmed in Deluxe Color, but, for whatever reason, was released in black and white. United Artists played the same trick again in 1961 when it released the British film *Doctor Blood's Coffin*, starring Hazel Court,which had been shot in Cornwall in glorious Eastman Colour. However, stateside it was released in not so glorious black and white.

*Manfish* is a true oddity, not exactly a horror film but more of a slow-moving adventure story for the most part, with the fairly unlikable lead played by Bromfield being harpooned to death about seventy-five minutes in. The rest of the film becomes a variation on 'The Tell-Tale Heart', in which Bromfield's body, thrown overboard and weighted down, seems to cause bubbles to rise to the surface to torment the murderous character played by Jory.

There isn't a great deal of 'The Gold Bug' here, as Poe's original story had to do with breaking a cryptographic code. *Manfish*, on the other hand, is a mostly routine story of a search for lost treasure. The majority of the action concerns the various romantic problems of the lead characters, with Nichols (unusually for her, a brunette in her first film) smouldering in a variety of revealing costumes, while Prendergast is given little to do. The Jamaican locations absolutely cry out for colour, making the black and white release all the more unaccountable.

While neither fish nor fowl, so to speak, *Manfish* does come alive in the last fifteen minutes or so, when the story becomes a maritime version of 'The Tell-Tale Heart'. Jory is convincing in his madness, and the film even features a happy ending with Swede inheriting the Manfish, much to his childlike joy.

In 1957, Gothic horror made a shocking comeback on a number of fronts. In the Unites States, a film package called *Shock Theatre* was syndicated to television, consisting of horror classics from Universal and Columbia Pictures. The films became enormously popular again, with both older audiences and young viewers who had never seen them.

More to the point, perhaps, a British film called *The Curse of Frankenstein* was released in the summer of 1957 to fantastic business. Based on the original

Mary Shelley novel, it was produced by Hammer Film Productions in glorious Eastman Color, with large dollops of red blood, copious cleavage (courtesy of leading ladies Hazel Court and Valerie Gaunt) and excellent performances from its leads, Peter Cushing as Baron Frankenstein and Christopher Lee as the Creature. When Hammer followed this huge success with their now-classic version of *Dracula* (1958) starring the same two actors, a new horror cycle was solidified. Period Gothic horror films were suddenly back in style, and Poe was soon to follow with a cycle of his own for the first time in cinema history.

# CHAPTER FOUR
# THE AMERICAN
# INTERNATIONAL POE

*'The boundaries which divide Life from Death are at best shadowy and vague. Who shall say where the one ends, and where the other begins?'*

*– The Premature Burial*

In the early 1950s, the American film industry was in trouble. Its biggest competitor, television, had caused cinema attendance to fall from an all-time high of 90 million people in 1946 to 60 million in 1950. And that was just the beginning.

When Cinemascope appeared in 1953, it gave audiences something they couldn't get on television: colour and widescreen. The slow erosion of the Production Code after 1952 also helped to stop the bleeding caused by television's wounds to the industry. And a new company, American Releasing Corporation, came up with a revolutionary approach: why not make films geared to a specific audience, an audience that had spending money and liked to go out to, say, drive-in movie theatres? It was a market that was so far untapped: that of the American teenager.

Formed in April 1954, American Releasing Corporation, soon to be known as American International Pictures, was headed by James H Nicholson, a former sales manager for Realart Pictures, and Samuel Z Arkoff, an entertainment attorney. The company's specialty from the start was producing and distributing independent, low-budget films that could be packaged as double features. Their first release was the 1955 movie *The Fast and the Furious*, directed by young filmmaker Roger Corman.

In the early years of the company, Nicholson and Arkoff acted as executive producers, while Corman and producer/director Alex Gordon were the principal film producers. When several of their early films (mainly westerns) failed to earn a profit, Arkoff asked film exhibitors about their audiences: to whom should they gear their product? The answer was quick and, in hindsight, obvious: adults were staying home in droves to watch television, but the teenage market was just waiting to be exploited.

"Exploitation" was the operative word. AIP, as the company came to be affectionately called, was the first film studio to use focus groups, polling American teenagers about what types of movies they would like to see. This led to AIP producing such box-office hits as *I Was a Teenage Werewolf* and *I Was a Teenage Frankenstein* (both 1957), which encouraged the fledgling company to produce many more inexpensive black and white horror and sci-fi movies aimed at teenagers, such as Corman's *Teenage Caveman* (1958) and *Ghost of Dragstrip Hollow* (1959).

Corman was more than just AIP's cash cow; he was their *auteur.* He made films quickly and economically, but he also had an extraordinarily creative, restless mind. Born in Detroit, Michigan on 5 April 1926, Roger William Corman ended up attending Stanford University to study industrial engineering. Coming to the conclusion that he didn't want to be an engineer, as his father had been, Corman served in the Navy from 1944 to 1946, at which point he returned to Stanford to complete his degree in 1947. In 1948, he decided to join his brother Gene in the film business, where Gene was an agent. Roger was much more interested in the creative side of the business and worked at 20th Century Fox as a story reader, and, under the GI Bill, later studied English Literature at Oxford and lived in Paris for a short period.

After returning to Los Angeles, Corman did various jobs in the film business and wrote a script called *Highway Dragnet*, selling it to Allied Artists for $2,000. It was produced in 1953, starring Richard Conte and Joan Bennett. The fledgling filmmaker served as associate producer on the film for no salary, gaining valuable experience in the process.

Corman used his screenplay payment and his contacts in the industry to raise $12,000 to produce his first 'official' feature, *The Monster From the Ocean Floor* (1954), which was released by Lippert Pictures. The film turned enough of a profit for Corman to produce another film, *The Fast and the Furious* (1954), directed by John Ireland, who also starred along with Dorothy Malone.

Corman sold *The Fast and the Furious* to what was then called American Releasing Corporation, who gave him enough money to produce two more low-budget films, and the young producer/director was off and running. For Nicholson and Arkoff, he made westerns (*Five Guns West,* 1955), science fiction (*It Conquered the World,* 1956) and crime thrillers (*Machine Gun Kelly,* 1958).

By 1959, Corman was tired of the kind of budget AIP was giving him to make black and white genre films, which was under $100,000 each. He was not abandoning AIP, however; he was just trying to get them to think outside the box. The market for the black and white AIP genre films was declining. Their colour productions such as *Horrors of the Black Museum,* which they produced in Britain in 1959 with Herman Cohen producing and Arthur Crabtree directing, were making more money than the impoverished

*Chapter Four – THE AMERICAN INTERNATIONAL POE*

black and white movies that had been their bread and butter since the company's inception. Stories vary as to who actually initiated an upgrade in AIP's production quality. Corman always claimed that it was his idea, while Arkoff claimed it was his. The long and short of it is that AIP gave Corman $350,000 to bring Edgar Allan Poe's *The Fall of the House of Usher* to the screen in colour and Cinemascope.

There is no question that the success of Hammer's period Gothic horror films had played a role in this new approach at AIP. Hammer's films had been immediate hits with audiences and they had already spawned imitations (a sure sign of success) such as Tempean's *Blood of the Vampire* (1958) and *Jack the Ripper* (1959). Corman insisted that the idea to adapt Poe, a great *American* author of horror tales, was inspired by a bound volume of the author's short stories that his father had given to him when he was a child. He also said that he had become bored with the black and white format that had been imposed upon him. Corman's version of the tale was that Arkoff initially rejected the idea of adapting 'The Fall of the House of Usher' because there was no 'monster' in it. Corman told him that the house itself was the monster and that was that.

Arkoff, however, begged to differ with Corman's account over the years. He told Mark Thomas McGee for McGee's book *Fast and Furious: The Story of American International Pictures* (McFarland, 1984)*: '* There's a story out

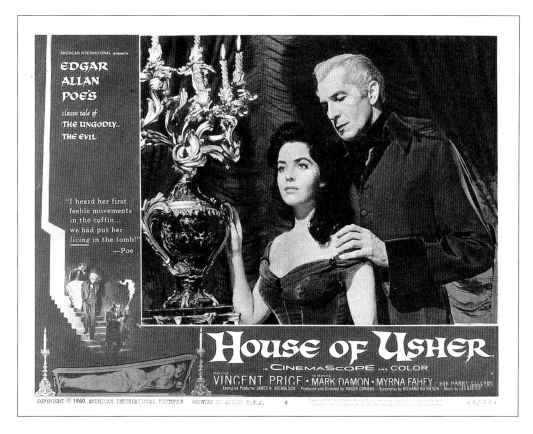

about me that I didn't want to do the Poe picture. That's all bullshit. That's something Roger made up... If people want to believe that old business that I didn't want to make *House of Usher* because it didn't have a monster... It's so ridiculous...'

In any case, Nicholson contacted prolific genre author Richard Matheson, who had written such classic genre novels as 'I Am Legend' and 'The Shrinking Man' (the latter having been made into a film called *The Incredible Shrinking Man* by Universal-International in 1957) to write the screenplay. Matheson was made aware of the limited budget on the film and its shooting schedule (fifteen days), but did not feel restricted by them. It was, essentially, a four-character screenplay that all took place in one house, so the budget restraints were no problem.

With an excellent crew that included art director Daniel Haller and cinematographer Floyd Crosby, *The Fall of the House of Usher* (in America the title was shortened to *House of Usher*) went into production in January 1960. Much of the film's budget went to the salary of its star, Hollywood veteran Vincent Price, who, during the fifties, had become America's most prolific horror film star, lending his arched eyebrows and velvet voice to such productions as the aforementioned *House of Wax* and *The Fly*, as well as the William Castle shockers *House on Haunted Hill* (1958), *The Tingler* (1959) and the inevitable *Return of the Fly* (1959). Cast as Roderick

Usher, Price leapt at the chance to play the role, shaving off his trademark moustache and dyeing his hair white to convey the character's fragility and allergy to sunlight.

The other cast members included Mark Damon, who played Philip Winthrop, the young male lead. Born in Chicago, Damon had worked in American television (including appearing on an episode of *Alfred Hitchcock Presents*) before entering the film industry with *Inside Detroit* (1956) starring Dennis O'Keefe and Pat O'Brien. Just previously to *Usher*, Damon had appeared in blackface as a bi-racial thug in a teenage gang movie called *This Rebel Breed*; a very different role!

Corman chose Myrna Fahey to play Madeline Usher, Roderick's doomed, tragic sister and the object of Philip's affections. Fahey had had an uncredited role in *I Died a Thousand Times* (1955), starring Jack Palance and Shelley Winters, and tiny roles in other high-profile Hollywood films, but most of her experience had been in television.

The only other major role in *Usher* was that of Bristol, the Usher family retainer. He was played by veteran actor Harry Ellerbe, who had been appearing in Hollywood films since the thirties and had more recently had been featured in numerous television series, including an episode of *Perry Mason*. Although he was in his fifties, Ellerbe was made up to look about fifteen years older in the film.

The behind-the-scenes personnel in *House of Usher* were just as important as the actors. Following Hammer's example, Corman decided that the look of the film was all-important. He had worked with cinematographer Floyd Crosby many times on his black and white 'monster' movies and knew that Crosby worked efficiently and creatively. With only a fifteen day shooting schedule, Crosby had his work cut out for him on *Usher*.

Just as Hammer had the services of a brilliant art director named Bernard Robinson (who worked wonders with little money), so Corman had the exceptionally talented Daniel Haller, who had cut his teeth on such Corman epics as *Machine-Gun Kelly* and, more recently, *The Little Shop of Horrors* (1960). Haller's job on *Usher* was to create the 'monster' – the House of Usher itself, and the 'deep, dark tarn' on which it sat.

The other key member behind the scenes was composer Les Baxter, who was hired to give a distinctive soundtrack to the film. Baxter had begun his career as a concert pianist but later scored a number of radio shows. He became a composer of popular tunes in the fifties (his recording of 'The Poor People of Paris' was a number one hit in 1956) and he composed the whistling theme for the television series *Lassie* in 1954. Baxter and Ronald Stein were staff composers at AIP for several years, and Corman employed both of them at different times. Baxter's previous genre credits for other studios included the scores for *The Black Sleep* (1956), *Voodoo Island* (1957), *The Invisible Boy* (1957) and William Castle's *Macabre* (1958), the latter of which earned him the tidy sum (for 1958) of $10,000. It is probably safe to safe that he did not make quite that much for his *Usher* score.

With all this talent in front of and behind the camera, AIP launched a more prestige advertising campaign than usual. Their radio spots for *Usher*, unlike those for their earlier films that had included hyperbolic ballyhoo, were more sophisticated: 'Only once did I risk the most distant glimpses of the grim and foreboding house of Usher. The mere sight of that awesome structure, huge and menacing, struck me chill with fear. It lay like a malignant sore that festered in the middle of the wasteland. Overhead the clouds hung low and a ghastly vapour rose from the ground. It seemed that the roots of the house touched the very coals of Hell.'

This voice-over was followed by Price quoting a line or two from the film, after which the announcer returned to proclaim: 'Edgar Allan Poe's demonic tale of the ungodly... The evil *House of Usher!*'

This was a new kind of advertising campaign for AIP, and it worked perfectly. Audiences flocked to see the new colour Gothic horror film, despite the fact that in many venues it was teamed with a more 'typical' AIP potboiler, the black and white *Attack of the Giant Leeches*, directed by Bernard L Kowalski. It was *Usher* that brought people into the cinemas however, and it was *Usher* that brought in the biggest percentage of the profits. In some venues, *Usher* was paired with Alfred Hitchcock's *Psycho*, and the queues stretched around the block.

Eugene Archer's review in *The New York Times* of 15 September 1960 was not charitable: 'American International, with good intentions of presenting a faithful adaptation of Edgar Allan Poe's classic tale of the macabre... blithely ignored the author's style... The film producers have made a horror film that provides a fair degree of literacy at the cost of a patron's patience.'

Other reviews were more favourable. *Variety* wrote: 'It is a film that should attract mature tastes as well as those who come to the cinema for sheer thrills... All things considered, pro and con, the fall of the *House of Usher* seems to herald the rise of AIP.'

In *The Los Angeles Times*, Betty Martin also liked the film for its 'fair amount of suspense throughout,' praising Haller's 'lavish' setting and Crosby's 'flamboyant' cinematography.' *House of Usher* received the best reviews of any movie from the company up to that time.

Over the years, the reputation of Corman's *House of Usher* has grown to such an extent that it is now considered *the* classic film adaptation of Poe's tale. Although Matheson's screenplay differs in a few particulars – Philip, the unnamed narrator of Poe's story, is Madeline's fiancée rather than Roderick's friend, and there is no mention by Poe of a servant in the house – Corman and Matheson remained faithful to the spirit of Poe in its grim, decadent atmosphere and in Price's tortured performance.

As was the case with the early Hammer Gothics photographed by Jack Asher, the colour in *Usher* is exquisite, and Crosby's camera is much more mobile than Asher's. He indulges in long tracking shots, crane shots (the opening, in which Philip rides his horse through a burned-out landscape, is especially fine) and whip pans. He accomplishes all of this despite having

less than half of the average schedule of a Hammer horror film of the time. His fluid cinematography is greatly enhanced by Haller's superb production design, as Gothic and doom-laden as one could imagine.

Baxter's score also adds much to the proceedings, with much less sensationalism and more romanticism than one is accustomed to hearing in horror films. He uses strings, voices and percussion sparingly but effectively,

It is Price, however, who dominates the film. His Roderick Usher is a masterclass in tragic, melancholy characterisation. It was his idea to dye his hair white, shave off his trademark moustache and leave his eyebrows black, all to suggest the fragility and sensitivity of the character. Early in the film, he has a long speech that explains nearly everything we need to know about him: 'Madeline and I are like figures of fine glass. The slightest touch and we may shatter. Both of us suffer from a morbid acuteness of the senses. Mine is the worst for having existed the longer... Any sort of food more exotic than the most pallid mash is unendurable to my taste buds. Any sort of

Vincent Price and Barbara Steele in *Pit and the Pendulum* (1961)

Vincent Price, John Kerr, Antony Carbone and Luana Anders in *Pit and the Pendulum* (1961)

*Chapter Four – THE AMERICAN INTERNATIONAL POE*

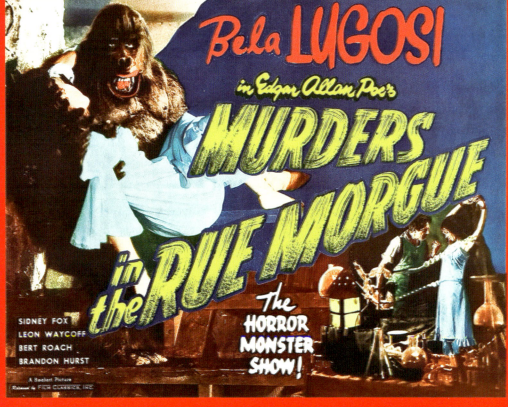

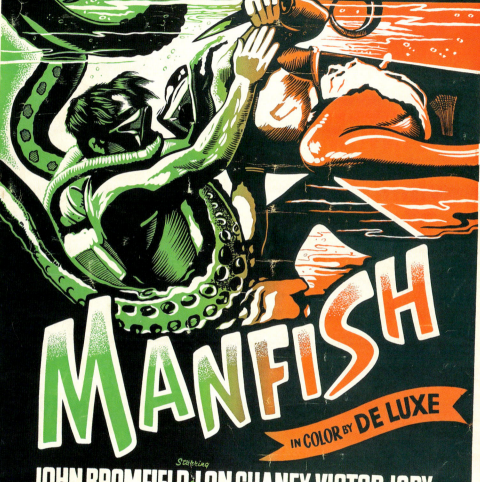

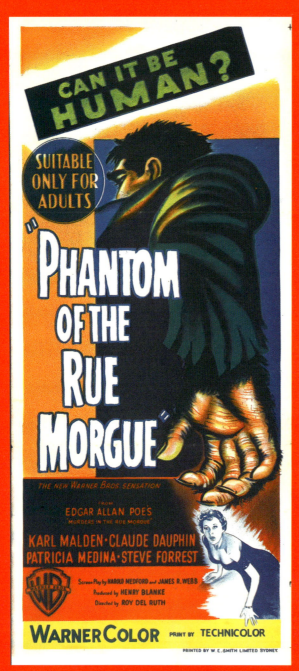

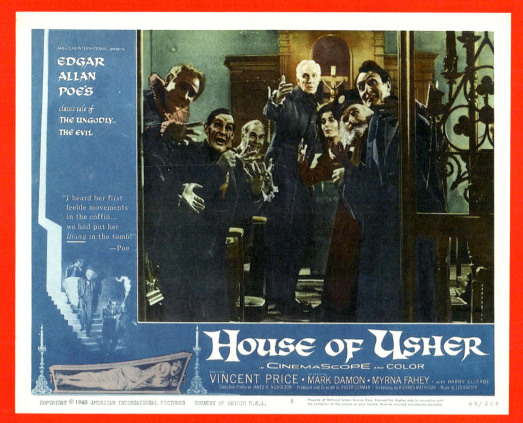

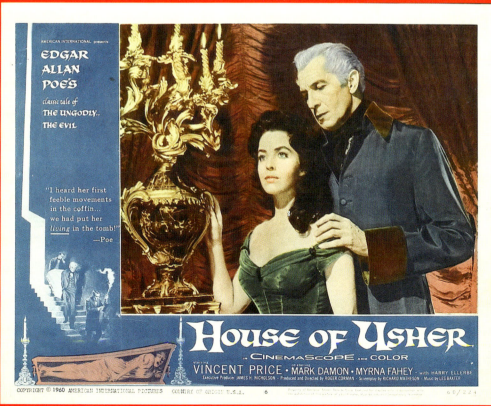

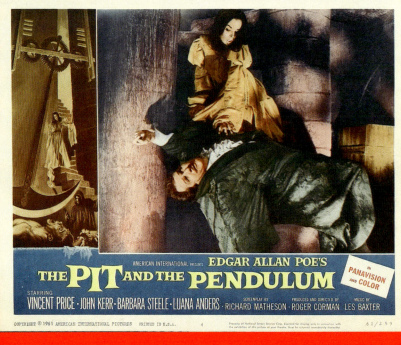

"WITHIN THE COFFIN I LIE... ALIVE!"

AMERICAN-INTERNATIONAL PRESENTS
RAY MILLAND
EDGAR ALLAN POE'S
HAZEL COURT · RICHARD NEY · HEATHER ANGEL
IN COLOR AND PANAVISION®
THE PREMATURE BURIAL

"WITHIN THE COFFIN I LIE... ALIVE!"

AMERICAN-INTERNATIONAL PRESENTS
RAY MILLAND
EDGAR ALLAN POE'S
HAZEL COURT · RICHARD NEY · HEATHER ANGEL
IN COLOR AND PANAVISION®
THE PREMATURE BURIAL

garment other than the softest is agony to my flesh. My eyes are tormented by all but the faintest illumination. Odours assail me constantly, and, as I've said, sounds of any degree whatsoever inspire me with terror.' Although not word for word from the story, this is the essence of Poe, and the lines are eloquently delivered by Price.

At the climax, after it has been revealed that Madeline has been buried alive, he conveys utter terror and guilt in a way few actors could. When he hisses, 'Did you know that I could hear the scratching of her fingernails on the casket lid?' he conveys the true *frisson* of mankind's fear of the grave.

Corman's direction is stylish, mature and assured. The influence of one of his favourite auteurs, Ingmar Bergman, can be seen in a haunting dream sequence, the first of many in his Poe films, involving surreal colour effects, sped-up and slowed-down action and weird Gothic imagery. His handling of the actors is also excellent; although Damon, Fahey and Ellerbe are no match for Price, they hold their own with Matheson's archaic dialogue, which would have been enough to challenge many an actor.

In 2005, *House of Usher* was chosen by the United States National Film Registry to be deemed 'culturally, historically, or aesthetically significant' to the history of American film, a rare honour for a horror film. Hitchcock's *Psycho* may have ultimately been more influential, bringing Gothic horror up to date in its chilling tale of the serial killer next door. At the time, however, *House of Usher* spawned dozens of imitations in Europe and around the world, and gave Poe a new lease on life in motion pictures. It also took Corman and AIP to a whole new level of quality filmmaking.

Corman was making more and more films for his own company, FilmGroup (including a script by Robert Towne called *The Last Woman on Earth*, which was filmed back to back with *Creature From the Haunted Sea* in Puerto Rico), but AIP would not let their cash cow get away from them that easily. After the runaway success of *House of Usher*, another Poe picture was the obvious way to go. Arkoff and Nicholson asked Corman to repeat the formula with *Pit and the Pendulum*, again from a screenplay by Matheson. As Poe's original story was only a few pages long, Matheson used it – an extended scene of a shackled man dreading the descent of a razor-sharp pendulum upon his body – as the climax of the film and came up with a Gothic tale leading up to it. The original story was a study in terror, of the anxiety of impending death: 'I was sick – sick unto death with that long agony,' writes the unnamed narrator. What goes through the man's mind is pretty uncinematic, but Matheson cooked up some interesting ways of visualising that agony.

Again, his story took place in a single setting – this time sixteenth century Spain, within an imposing castle by the sea. This gave Haller an opportunity to work his magic once again, this time removing the catwalks at Producer's Studio, thereby giving his sets more height and depth.

Price was, of course, invited back to play the lead role of Nicholas Medina, owner of the castle. Cast in the young male lead role this time (as an Englishman called Francis Barnard) was John Kerr, a stage actor who had received recognition for his sensitive portrayal of Tom Robinson Lee in the 1953 Broadway production of *Tea and Sympathy*, which he recreated for the 1956 film version directed by Vincente Minnelli. He had also received acclaim for playing the role of Lieutenant Joe Cable in Joshua Logan's film version of *South Pacific* (1958).

As Medina's 'deceased' wife Elizabeth, Corman cast British actress Barbara Steele, who had just become an overnight (no pun intended) horror star in Italian director Mario Bava's *Black Sunday* (UK: *Revenge of the Vampire*), which AIP had released only a few months earlier. *Pit and the Pendulum* further established Steele as one of the few female genre icons to specialise in sinister roles.

Luana Anders was cast by Corman as Catherine Medina, the sister of Price's patriarch. Anders had begun her film career as a messenger at MGM, along with fellow actor Jack Nicholson. She had gone on to appear in many television series, including the supernatural anthology *One Step Beyond*, before making her film debut in a lead role in Curtis Harrington's haunting fantasy *Night Tide* (1961), starring a very young Dennis Hopper.

Corman regular Antony Carbone, who had just appeared in *Creature from the Haunted Sea*, was recruited to play Doctor Charles Leon. Italian-born, Carbone was raised in Syracuse, New York and was a veteran of stage and television as well as film.

In the true Hammer tradition, in which personnel continued from film to film, the crew was virtually identical to that of *Usher's*, as was the fifteen-day shooting schedule. Although *Usher* had remained fairly close to Poe's original story, Matheson had to make up most of the script for *Pit and the Pendulum* out of whole cloth. His new story concerned Englishman Francis Barnard, who goes to Spain when he hears that his sister Elizabeth has died. Her husband Nicholas (whose father was one of the most sadistic torturers of the Inquisition) informs the young man that his sister has died of a blood disease, but Barnard feels that Medina is hiding something. After investigating, he discovers that Elizabeth may have gone into a cataleptic trance brought on by extreme terror and that she may have been buried alive. The last half-hour of the film takes some very unexpected twists and turns, culminating in Barnard being strapped down to a torture table in Medina's dungeon as a pendulum swings down slowly towards him.

The pendulum in question was designed and installed by Haller. The original version had a rubber blade, which, unfortunately, stuck to Kerr's stomach during rehearsals. Haller then created a metallic blade, which had to be set up in such a way that it could slash the actor's shirt without slashing the actor. A steel band was wrapped around his waist just to be on the safe side. Four men had to swing the pendulum manually, which allowed them to control it efficiently.

Kerr was understandably anxious about the pendulum, which undoubtedly worked for his portrayal. So in order to demonstrate that it was safe, Corman

himself stood in for him while the scene was being prepared. As Mark McGee wrote, 'The actor was a good sport about it all but Dan (Haller) noticed that he perspired a lot.'

To heighten the suspense of this climactic scene, Corman and editor Anthony Carras removed every other frame during the editing stage, which made the blade appear to move twice as fast. This, coupled with Les Baxter's pulsating music and Haller's stunning art direction, combined to make the sequence a masterpiece of terror.

Price gives one of his most over-ripe performances in *Pendulum*, slavering over such lines as, 'Do you know where you are, Bartolome? You are about to enter Hell. In hell, Bartolome, In Hell! The dead world, infernal zone, damned house, torture's place, pandemonium, purgatory, avernus, fire, Satan, *The Pit...* and the pendulum.' Indeed, Price's reputation as something of a 'ham' is predicated in part by his performance in *Pendulum*, but in the context of Corman's rich Gothic atmosphere, it works.

When the film was released in August 1961, it garnered some good reviews. *Variety* noted some pros and cons: '... An elaboration of the short Poe classic... The result is a physically stylish, imaginatively photographed horror film which, though needlessly corny in many spots, adds up to good exploitation.. (Matheson) has rendered it in some fruity dialogue. If audiences don't titter, it's only because veteran star Vincent Price can chew scenery while keeping his tongue in his cheek.'

In *Limelight*, Len Simpson wrote: 'Edgar Allan Poe would have been proud of the treatment American International has given his short story,' *The New York Times* raved about its 'rich colours, plushy decor and eerie music,' while *Time* Magazine referred to the film as 'a literary hair-raiser.'

*Pit and the Pendulum* was even more successful at the box office than *Usher* had been, proving to Arkoff and Nicholson that their first Poe film had been no fluke. From now on, the company's new cash cows would be Price, Poe and Corman.

Meanwhile, Corman felt that he was entitled to a more substantial percentage of the profits. Fortunately for him, he was in sync with Pathe Labs, who processed most of AIP's films. They were interested in starting their own distribution company and thought that a Corman/Poe film might be an excellent choice for a first feature. They offered Corman a better deal than AIP's.

Corman decided to adapt Poe's 'The Premature Burial' as his first production for Pathe. The film would be an exact duplicate of the AIP Poe pictures, with art design by Haller, photography by Crosby, costumes by Marjorie Corso, with music this time by Corman regular Ronald Stein. It would be set in the same 'country of the mind' as the other two Poe films, with swirling mists, eldritch graveyards and gnarled trees, all filmed on interior sets.

There was one major exception to the tradition, however: Vincent Price was under contract to AIP and Corman could not cast him in his 'renegade' Poe production. According to a contemporary article in the *Herald Tribune*,

Alan Napier and Ray Milland in *Premature Burial* (1962)

Price received $125,000 per picture in his AIP contract, plus a percentage of the profits, and they were not about to 'lend' him to Corman. Instead of Price, Corman hired Hollywood veteran (and Oscar-winner for *The Lost Weekend*, 1945) Ray Milland to play the lead role.

Milland had been born in Wales in 1907 and had a career in the British Army before playing his first major role in *The Flying Scotsman* (1929), which had led to a contract with MGM. Milland moved to the United States, where he appeared in supporting roles. It was at Paramount where he achieved international stardom opposite Dorothy Lamour in *The Jungle Princess* (1936).

By the mid-fifties, after leaving Paramount, he began directing and moved into the new medium, television. When Corman came calling in late 1961, Milland was a free agent and he liked the screenplay by seasoned horror authors Charles Beaumont and Ray Russell. Although he was as interested in directing as in acting by this time, he and Corman hit it off and Milland agreed to star in Corman's first film for Pathe.

Milland's leading lady in *Premature Burial* was a familiar face to fans of Hammer horror films, Hazel Court. She had co-starred with Peter Cushing and Christopher Lee in Terence Fisher's *The Curse of Frankenstein* (1957) and opposite Anton Diffring and Lee in Fisher's *The Man Who Could Cheat Death* (1959) for Hammer, and had moved to Hollywood in the early sixties, appearing in episodes of *Alfred Hitchcock Presents*, *Thriller* (hosted by Boris Karloff) and *Twilight Zone*. Corman cast her as Emily, the wife of Milland's character, Guy Carrell.

*Premature Burial* was the final film of veteran actress Heather Angel, a British-American thespian who had appeared in such films as Alfred Hitchcock's *Lifeboat* (1944) and John Brahm's atmospheric werewolf thriller *The Undying Monster* (1942), among many other films. Her role in *The Premature Burial* was that of Kate Carrell, Guy's sister.

The supporting role of Dr Gideon Gault was played by Alan Napier, a veteran of such genre films as *The Invisible Man Returns* (1940), *Cat People* (1942) and *Isle of the Dead* (1945). Napier would soon become best-known as Bruce Wayne's loyal butler Alfred in the 1966-1968 American TV series *Batman*, co-starring Adam West and Burt Ward.

Richard Ney, who had appeared in such films as *Mrs Miniver* (1942), *Joan of Arc* (1948) and, more recently, the thriller *Midnight Lace* (1960), stepped into the role of Miles Archer. The two actors who stole every one of their scenes in *Premature Burial* however, were John Dierkes as Sweeney and Dick Miller as Mole, two rather cheery grave robbers. Dierkes had had a long career as a character actor and had had a featured role in, among dozens of other films, Howard Hawks' and Christian Nyby's ground-breaking sci-

*Premature Burial* (1962)

*Chapter Four – THE AMERICAN INTERNATIONAL POE*

fi horror film, *The Thing From Another World* (1951). His six-foot, six-inch frame was in memorable contrast to that of the more diminutive Miller, a veteran of such Corman movies as *The Little Shop of Horrors* (1960.

Two days into production, Nicholson and Arkoff entered the Pathe sound stage. Corman was surprised to see them, to say the least. Arkoff informed Corman that he was, once again, working for AIP. It transpired that Arkoff had travelled to New York to speak with the owner of Pathe Labs when he had heard about Corman's upcoming Poe film and had 'politely' pointed out to the gentleman that Pathe was treading on AIP's territory by distributing *Premature Burial*. Arkoff went on to note that AIP was one of Pathe's biggest customers and, if they were going to compete with AIP in the distribution business, then AIP would find another lab to process their films. Unbeknownst to Corman, Pathe had already sold the production to AIP before principal photography had even begun.

After two months of negotiations, Corman received $500,000 plus an immediate $50,000 profit for his fifty-percent interest in the film. Not a bad deal for either AIP or Corman, and the film was brought in for $450,000.

Beaumont's and Russell's screenplay combines Poe's obsessions regarding burial alive with a sort of Jane Eyre plot. Emily Gault arrives at the Carrell mansion (amid the swirling mist), where she is determined to rekindle her old relationship with Guy Carrell, despite the fact that Guy's sister Kate disapproves. Guy overcomes his obsessive fear of being buried alive long enough to marry Emily, but soon his old obsessions return with a vengeance. He builds a crypt designed to prevent his premature internment that enables him to 'escape' should he fall prey to a cataleptic seizure. Ultimately, however, his worst fears become reality and he is lowered into his grave while yet alive. That is not the end of the tale, however, as the treachery of someone close to him is soon revealed.

The script is a good one and Milland acts out Poe's obsessions very well indeed. He quotes Poe nearly word for word in one memorable speech: 'Can you possibly conceive it? The unendurable oppression of the lungs, the stifling fumes of the earth, the rigid embrace of the coffin, the blackness of absolute night and the silence, like an overwhelming sea...'

In her autobiography 'Hazel Court: Horror Queen' (Tomahawk Press, 2008), Court wrote of the film: 'It is interesting to note that Francis Ford Coppola, not yet renowned, was Assistant Director on the picture... I was very excited about working with Ray Milland... Being Welsh, he wrote outstanding poetry, and being half Welsh myself, I loved talking to him.

'There is a scene in which I burst in upon my husband in his art studio, and I insist on seeing the canvas he is working on. He acquiesces but says something like, "You won't find it very pleasant." Then he whips off the fabric that is covering his painting and reveals a painting which was actually done by a very interesting artist, Burt Shonberg, who is also credited with having his paintings in another picture based upon a Poe story, *House of Usher*.

'At the end of the picture, I had to be buried alive. Roger asked me if I would do it or if I would rather have someone double for me. I said, "Heavens. no! I will do it." Well, I lay in the ground, with a straw in my mouth so that I would have air, as they shovelled the earth over me. The straw was removed when the director said, "Action!" I was to hold my breath for as long as possible. I made it for over one minute – long enough to get the shot. As I got to the end of the minute, the pressure on my body began, as the claustrophobia was setting in. It was one hell of an experience.'

*Premature Burial* is sometimes passed off as 'second-rate Poe' because of the absence of Price, but Milland truly carries the film and is highly effective in conveying both the pathos and the intensity of the long-suffering Guy. Although he is older than Price, his romance with the much younger Emily is convincingly portrayed and Court is equally effective as his duplicitous spouse. Court was always given more to sink her teeth into by Corman than she ever was by Hammer, and Emily is conniving, sensual and just plain evil, all traits superbly conveyed by the actress.

Stein's musical score is masterful, and the use of the old Irish tune, 'Molly Malone,' which features the phrase 'Alive, alive-o' is inspired. As whistled by Sweeney and Mole, the tune becomes a motif all its own amidst the moor, the mist and the graveyard. Crosby's use of the camera is just as inspired as in his first two Poe films, and Haller's art direction, which includes greyish clumps of Spanish moss draped over the dead trees like some macabre Christmas decoration, is a feast for the eyes. The characters seem to live in a blasted landscape; a God-forsaken heath where the sun never shines and the mist never lifts. Even the flowers which Emily plucks from a grave no less, seem dead and decayed.

Now that AIP officially owned the film, they let loose their publicity ballyhoo quite shamelessly. Their press book for the film included the following suggestion for cinema owners: 'Key exploitation stunt for *The Premature Burial*, which will result in top space in all newspapers and on television, is an actual burial alive demonstration by a man or pretty girl. Should you have difficulty in contacting a stunt-man or woman in your area for this purpose, get in touch with publicity department, American International Pictures, 7165 Sunset Blvd, Hollywood, Calif.'

Upon its American release in March 1962, *Premature Burial* received the usual mixed reviews. *Variety* quipped, 'By this time, many film fans (and at least one reviewer) are as familiar with Corman's downstairs dungeon as they are with their own basement hobby shops…'

*The New York Times* was more forgiving, noting that the film was 'no less attractively designed or tastefully coloured' than the two previous Poe pictures. Court's own thoughts on the film concluded with her writing, 'The *Premature Burial* was not as successful as the other horror films. Some critics felt it was because Vincent Price was not in it. I felt it might have been because a lot of people have fears of being buried alive – or of developing the condition of catalepsy in which one would be alive but accidentally presumed dead. The film was kind to me, and, as I've mentioned, a very good part.'

Milland's casting in Corman's film led to several more films for AIP. For Nicholson and Arkoff, Milland directed and starred in a dystopian survival story called *Panic in Year Zero!* (1962). Originally titled *Survival*, the project was first announced in The Hollywood Reporter on 4 January 1962: 'Survival will star Ray Milland, who also directs, with Frankie Avalon and Jean Hagen, rolling Feb 21.' He also starred in Corman's uniquely original sci-fi film *X: The Man with the X-Ray Eyes* (1963), written by Ray Russell and Robert Dillon.

Corman's next Poe picture, *Tales of Terror* (1962) more than made up for Price's absence in *The Premature Burial*, as it starred Vincent Price, times three. By the time he got around to this venture, Corman's restless mind was getting bored, so he and AIP asked screenwriter Matheson to turn Poe's *The Black Cat* (mixed with a dash of 'The Cask of Amontillado') into one-third of a trilogy of tales which would include *Morella* and *The Facts in the Case of M Valdemar*. The resulting film, *Tales of Terror*, featured the first teaming of Price and his old friend Peter Lorre for Corman, and it turned out to be a fruitful collaboration.

The casting of Lorre in *The Black Cat* segment was a terrific and fortuitous choice. Corman and Matheson tinkered with the by-now formulaic elements of the Poe series and couldn't resist the temptation to send it up a bit. *The Black Cat* became a horror comedy as Lorre ad-libbed his way through the role of the drunken lout Montressor, who walls up his voluptuous, adulterous wife (Joyce Jameson) and her lover (Price) in the cellar. Unfortunately for him, he

Peter Lorre in *Tales of Terror* (1962)

walls up his black cat as well, and it gives the game away to the police with its yowling, just as in Poe's original story.

Lorre's performance is comedic from the very start. His exchanges with his wife are consistently funny; when she reaches into her copious cleavage to give him money (much against her better judgment, as she knows that he'll waste it all on wine), he quips, 'Thank you for looking into your heart.' His wall-up of Price, who asks, 'What are you doing?' to which he replies, 'I'll give you three guesses,' is, well, priceless.

*The Black Cat* is the second story of the trilogy and a great improvement over the first, *Morella*. After the image of a beating heart fades from the screen, we fade in on a typical Corman/Poe opening of a young woman arriving by coach at an old, rundown mansion surrounded by the usual bent, moss-covered trees. The young woman's name is Lenora (Maggie Pierce) and she has come to reconcile with her long-estranged father (Price). It transpires that she is dying and that her father has resented her all these years, blaming her for her mother Morella's (Leona Gage) death; she had died shortly after giving birth.

We later discover, in true Poe fashion, that Lenora's father has kept Morella's body in the house since her death, on the bed where she died. The ending features a transmogrification of souls and the by-now expected conflagration, complete with stock shots from the ending of *House of Usher*.

*Morella* is the weakest of the three tales, although Price gives his usual sincere performance. The segment, however, is marred by rushed staging and a poor performance by Pierce, an ingénue at best.

Although *The Black Cat* is perhaps the best-remembered tale in the film because of its light approach to the grim material, the most frightening story is certainly saved for last. *The Case of M Valdemar* has the best cast of the three: Price, fellow horror icon (and world-famous Sherlock Holmes portrayer) Basil Rathbone, beautiful Hollywood actress Debra Paget (who had recently caused some controversy with her nearly-nude dance in Fritz Lang's *The Tomb of Love*, which was ultimately released by AIP after numerous cuts as *Journey to the Lost City*, 1961) and young British-American actor David Frankham.

The story of a mesmerist who attempts to keep communicating with a dying man, even past the point of death, is one of the most effective in the whole Poe oeuvre. Rathbone and Price excel in this segment, playing off each other brilliantly. Price, who also narrates all three tales, sets the tone with his mellifluous voice: 'What exactly is it that occurs within the moment of death, especially to a man within that moment who is not permitted to die, as in the case of Mr Valdemar?' And the final title card answers that question, per Poe: 'And there was an oozing liquid putrescence... all that remained of Mr Valdemar.'

When I interviewed him in 2015, Frankham explained how he ended up in *Tales of Terror*. It apparently happened as a result of his being hastily cast in a Jules Verne adaptation for AIP, *Master of the World:* (1961): 'Here's how I got the part in *Master of the World* (as I was told it): On a Friday, Vincent (Price) was at the studio getting wardrobe fittings for filming the following Monday, when he was told that a crisis had arisen: Mark Damon had apparently decided at the last minute to quit the picture and move to Rome. Panic ensued – until Vincent recommended a young actor he had worked with just the year before – *me*. Consequently, later that day I was sent out to the studio to meet William Witney (the director) and was told the part was mine.'

The film on which Frankham had worked previously with Price was *Return of the Fly* (1959), a sequel to Price's famous shocker *The Fly* (1958). Frankham, who had only arrived in the States from Britain a few years before to pursue acting, had played a dastardly villain in *Return of the Fly*, and he had impressed Price greatly.

Because of Frankham's stepping in at the last minute on *Master of the World*, he ended up receiving the important role of Dr James in *The Case of M Valdemar*. As Frankham told me: 'As the result of the casting crisis with *Master of the World*, my wonderful agent, Maurine Oliver, knew she had AIP over a barrel, and suggested, "Well, you know, David's helping you out so much, what about giving him a two-picture deal?" That's what they agreed to, with the second picture to be completed by the end of 1961. That's how I got *Tales of Terror*. They had to use me, or pay me anyway.'

Basil Rathbone and Debra Paget in *Tales of Terror* (1962)

Vincent Price scares Joyce Jameson with Peter Lorre's head in *Tales of Terror* (1962)

*Chapter Four – THE AMERICAN INTERNATIONAL POE*

Frankham said he was very impressed (and a little star-struck) with Rathbone: 'Like Henry Hull (in *Master of the World*), Basil Rathbone maintained the energy and enthusiasm of a 35-year-old every moment of that five-day shoot. He was actually seventy then. At first I was intimidated at the thought of meeting him – in part because when I was ten he terrified me as Mr Murdstone in *David Copperfield* – but at the first reading in Roger Corman's office, that evaporated. He had a wonderful sense of humour. He and Vincent were like teenagers between setups and of course they were old friends. On camera they were like two Rolls Royces.'

He was also impressed with Paget, who had made her film debut at the age of fifteen in Robert Siodmak's *Cry of the City* (1948) before appearing in such Hollywood productions as *Bird of Paradise* (1951) and *Prince Valiant* (1954). Frankham recalled, 'Debra was… a movie veteran since her teenage debut and a real pleasure to work with. We were so focused on the work, filming very fast, that we didn't have much chance to connect socially, but she was pleasant and professional. I remember her mother visited the set and kept saying, "Debra's going to marry a Chinese millionaire, you know!" And she did!

'During the parts where I had to pick her up off the floor, I could barely do it, even though she was so tiny. Vincent thought that was hilarious: "He can't get her off the floor!"'

For the American cable channel Turner Classic Movies, Corman recalled the making of *Tales of Terror*: 'With *Tales of Terror*, we tried to do something a little different, The screenplay was actually a series of very frightening dramatic sequences inspired by several of the Poe stories. To break things up, we tried introducing humour into one of them…'

Corman recalled how the final decomposition of Price's character was achieved in *Valdemar*: 'We settled for an old-fashioned mud pack – it dries and draws the skin up and then cracks open…' For the climactic scene of Price melting away, a mixture of glue, glycerine, corn-starch and make-up paint was heated and poured over the hapless actor's head. The resulting mess was so hot that Price could only stand it for a few seconds.

Each story in *Tales of Terror* was shot in five days, totalling Corman's usual fifteen-day shooting schedule. Upon release, the film was not well received by critics; with *The New York Times* review of 5 July 1962 a typical one: '… A dull, absurd and trashy adaptation of three Edgar Allan Poe stories, broadly draped around the shoulders of such people as Vincent Price, Peter Lorre and Basil Rathbone (who at least bothers to act).'

Nevertheless, the film made $1.3 million in domestic gross rentals, a tidy sum for those days; not as much as *Pit and the Pendulum*, but enough to ensure the continuation of the series. And there was no question by now: Corman and AIP had made a series out of the works of the celebrated Mr Poe, and fans eagerly awaited each new instalment.

*Tales of Terror* was the first in the series to be turned into an American comic book by Dell Comics. It was one of the early attempts by AIP to break into merchandising movie tie-ins, and it too was quite popular and helped to make audiences even more aware of the Poe films.

Arkoff and Nicholson determined that the most successful story in *Tales of Terror*, and the one most talked about by audiences and critics, was *The Black Cat*. It was decided that the next Poe film would be an unabashed horror comedy reuniting Price and Lorre.

Arkoff and Nicholson decided to make *The Raven*, probably Poe's most famous work and the one with the greatest name recognition. Interviewed for the book *The Making of the Raven*, Matheson told author Lawrence French, 'After I heard they wanted to make a movie out of a poem, I felt that was an utter joke, so comedy was really the only way to go with it.'

Starring alongside Price and Lorre in *The Raven* was the legendary Boris Karloff, who was having something of a career resurgence due to the current popularity of horror films. The novelty rock and roll song *Monster Mash*, by Bobby 'Boris' Pickett, had risen to number one in the American charts just before Halloween of 1962, and 'monsters' were 'in'. Karloff was in his seventies and afflicted with arthritis, but he was willing to do all that was asked of him.

Karloff had recently turned down an offer to be in the Hammer/William Castle remake of *The Old Dark House* because 'the new version..' he declared, 'was not to my liking.' He *did* like Matheson's screenplay for *The Raven*, however (and, ironically, he and Bela Lugosi had co-starred in *The Raven* for Universal in 1935, which had even less to do with Poe's poem than this version), and was pleased that Price and Lorre were also in the picture.

Vincent Price, Olivia
Sturgess and Peter Lorre in
*The Raven* (1963)

Corman asked Hazel Court to return for *The Raven*, and cast another actor he had worked with before, Jack Nicholson, who he had directed in *The Little Shop of Horrors* (1960). Rounding out the cast were Olive Sturgess, Connie Wallace, William Baskin and Aaron Saxon.

Matheson's screenplay recounts the misadventures of a medieval sorcerer named Bedlo (Lorre) who has been transformed into a raven by the evil wizard Dr Scarabus (Karloff). In raven form, Bedlo comes 'knocking at the chamber door' of Dr Erasmus Craven (Price) one evening, and asks him for help in transforming back to his former self. Craven discovers that his long lost wife Lenore (Court) is actually alive and well and living with Dr Scarabus, so he and Bedlo set off for the castle of the sinister sorcerer.

Although the film begins with Price reciting Poe's poem, we very quickly discover that this particular Poe picture is going to be a romp when the raven (with Lorre's voice) flies into his window and Price asks the bird, 'Will I ever see my lost Lenore again?' In one of his many ad-libs, Lorre replies with, 'How the hell should I know? What am I, a fortune teller?'

After Bedlo requests Craven to turn him back into a human again, the sorcerer takes him down into his cobwebbed, gothic basement. 'I don't get down here very often,' Craven says by way of apology for the state of the place. They find some interesting ingredients to be put into the transformation spell. Craven picks up a jar of eyeballs and quickly puts it back on the shelf. 'What was that?' Bedlo asks. 'I'd rather not discuss it, if you don't mind,' Craven replies. Another jar is labelled 'Entrails of Troubled Horse.'

Vincent Price and friend in *The Raven* (1963)

Boris Karloff in
*The Raven* (1963)

Vincent Price, Olivia Sturgess and Hazel
Court in *The Raven* (1963)

Much has been written of how Lorre improvised his lines. Years later, Corman pointed out, 'Peter kept everyone on their toes, myself included. He would just begin to improvise unexpectedly. Vincent was always willing to play along with it, but Boris, who was very methodical about his craft, was befuddled. Amused, but befuddled.'

A favourite line in the film occurs when Bedlo attempts to cast a spell on Scarabus with his magic wand. With one wave of his hand, Scarabus causes the wand to droop like a flaccid penis. 'Oh, you dirty old man!' Bedlo exclaims.

Apparently, Karloff was quite pleased that he got to dally with the luscious Court in the film. One of her best roles, the saucy Lenore allowed Court free rein to show off her comic delivery, as well as her considerable charms. The review of the film in *Time* magazine singled her out with the following unforgettable sentence: 'She is a lusty redhead with a cleavage that could comfortably accommodate the collected works of Edgar Allan Poe and a bottle of his favourite booze besides.'

When I interviewed Court in 1990, she told me what it was like to work with the horror veterans: 'Boris Karloff.... He was like a pussycat; a gentle, very sweet man. Peter Lorre wouldn't always know his lines. Boris would. ...The others would come on and kind of make it up a little. But it was always alright. Peter was very, very funny. He would be telling stories and intellectualising in between takes. It was fascinating. You'd just sit back and try to listen to them all. They'd all try and top each other with their stories.'

Court was somewhat less impressed with future superstar Nicholson. She told me, 'I always remember him saying, "I'm going home to write tonight." He was always talking about this great writing talent he thought he had... I never suspected he would become a great movie star. It was strange; he was this little person who popped around on the set. He popped around in a funny costume, with knee breeches and a funny hat! He looked rather like one of those little stone statues you can buy to put in your garden!'

In the book *Vincent Price: A Daughter's Biography*, Victoria Price quoted Corman as recalling, 'I said to Jack, who was a young actor, "You're good. I've seen you do improvisation in class. You are good with comedy. You can learn from Vincent and Peter and Boris because these are professional actors. They are good and they are funny and you can use your youthful vitality and your natural humour and combine it with them and learn to work with them."'

One of the ironic things about *The Raven* is that future Oscar-winner Nicholson is the weak link in the film. He is quite wooden, looks uncomfortable in his period costumes and is totally overshadowed by the other, more seasoned performers. The only moment he really comes to life is when he is suddenly possessed by an evil spirit and we see that killer smile. For that one brief, shining moment, he becomes the Jack Nicholson we know and love.

*The Raven* is comedy-horror triumphant, complete with the requisite beautiful gothic sets by Haller, lush cinematography by Crosby and Baxter's usual excellent musical score. There is an all-round sense of fun to the picture, as though the actors are enjoying making the film as much as we enjoy watching it. It remains one of Corman's own favourites, even though most critics dismissed it at the time. 'Strictly a picture for the kiddies and the bird-brained,' scoffed Bosley Crowther in The New York Times. The review in Variety, however, was favourable: 'The screenplay is a skilful, imaginative narrative and Corman takes the premise and develops it expertly as a horror-comedy, climaxing with Price and Karloff engaging in a duel to the death.'

*The Raven* turned out to be the most successful Poe picture at the box office up to that time. It was adapted into another successful Dell comic book. Corman was so enamoured with Haller's interior castle set that, when he finished shooting, he decided to take advantage of the leftover sets and paid actor/writer Leo Gordon $1,600 to write a script around them. He also made a deal with Karloff to be available for three days' filming for a small salary, plus a deferred payment of $15,000 that would be paid to him if the film earned more than $150,000. The so-called 'three-day wonder' that Corman ultimately produced and (partly) directed became the infamous *The Terror* (1963).

In the book *The Making of The Raven*, Karloff was quoted as saying, 'Corman had the sketchiest outline of a story. I read it and begged him not to do it. "That's alright, Boris, I know what I'm going to do. I want you for two days on this." I was in every shot, of course. Sometimes I was just walking through and then I would change my jacket and walk back. He nearly killed me on the last day. He had me in a tank of cold water for about two hours. After he got me in the can he suspended operations and went off and directed two or three operations to get the money, I suppose… (The sets) were so magnificent… As they were being pulled down around our ears, Roger was dashing around with me and the camera, two steps ahead of the wreckers. It was very funny.'

Some audiences found the resulting film to be very funny as well, although, this time, it was not intended to be. The credits for *The Terror*, however, read like a virtual *Who's Who* of future filmmakers. The film, contrary to

legend, was by no means shot in three days. Karloff's scenes were completed in three days by Corman, but then he sent his assistant Francis Ford Coppola to Big Sur for another three days to film additional scenes. Coppola ended up staying there for *eleven* days, attempting to shoot footage that made sense in the context of the story. Future directors Monte Hellman (*Two-Lane Blacktop*, 1971), Jack Hill (*Spider Baby*, 1967) and even Nicholson himself helmed some scenes. 'The Roger Corman Film School' was in full flower on this production.

*The Terror* is sometimes considered to be a part of the Poe cycle mainly because it *feels* like a Poe picture. The sets certainly go a long way in creating that mood, but so do the long, languorous shots along the beach at Big Sur, where the opening of *Pit and the Pendulum* was filmed. And, as in the Poe films, there is a doomed woman, a sort of 'lost Lenore,' played by Nicholson's then-wife Sandra Knight (who was in the scenes that Nicholson himself directed).

The story, some of it co-written on the set by Corman and Hill along with Gordon, is a confused mess that still befuddles audiences and critics to this day. In eighteenth-century France, Lieutenant Andre Duvalier (Nicholson) becomes separated from his regiment during the Napoleonic wars. He briefly encounters a beautiful young woman called Helene (Knight). Duvalier later meets an old witch (Dorothy Neumann, essentially reprising her role from Corman's *The Undead*, 1957) who lives alone in the forest and offers him

*Chapter Four – THE AMERICAN INTERNATIONAL POE*

shelter. She tells him that she has never seen the woman that Duvalier describes. The young woman fascinates him, however, and he ultimately follows her to the castle of Baron Victor Frederick Von Leppe (Karloff), where he discovers that the mysterious woman looks exactly like the Baron's late wife, who has been dead for twenty years. Eventually, the Baron admits to having murdered her when he returned unexpectedly to find her in the arms of another man. But there are even more plot twists to come, few of which make any sense.

The word 'dreamlike' comes to mind when describing *The Terror*, which no doubt has to do with the patchwork way in which the film was made. If the movie works at all, it is on a subconscious level, mainly because of the sheer beauty of its images and the power of the musical score by Ronald Stein.

The acting is spotty, at best. Karloff, ever the professional, does what he can with the material he is given, but even he seems to be somewhat at sea as to what the story is actually about. Nicholson is hopeless as the French soldier, his American drawl taking audiences completely out of the film. Yet, the movie has a genuine doom-laden atmosphere, complete with an attacking bird that gouges out the eyes of a character called Gustaf, played by Jonathan Haze.

Growing weary of the Poe adaptations, but with Nicholson and Arkoff expecting more, Corman decided instead to adapt a story by American fantasy/horror author H P Lovecraft. The Providence-born (in 1890) author was a cult figure, a master of tales of cosmic horror, mostly set in New England. He created the Cthulhu Mythos, a fictional universe dominated by the cosmic entity Cthulhu, and Lovecraft and his fellow authors such as Robert Bloch, August Derleth, Clark Ashton Smith and many others shared elements of this universe and expanded the mythos to meet the requirements of each tale. Lovecraft's most famous works include *The Dunwich Horror*, *At the Mountains of Madness* and *The Colour Out of Space*.

Most of Lovecraft's tales were short stories, but Corman was interested in adapting one of the late author's few novels, *The Case of Charles Dexter Ward*. The novel, written in 1927 but set in 1918, relates how a disturbed young man named Charles Dexter Ward becomes obsessed with his distant ancestor Joseph Curwen, an alleged sorcerer and necromancer. Ward has a strong physical resemblance to Curwen and he attempts to replicate his ancestor's magical formulae to bring Curwen himself back to life. Ward's family doctor, Marinus Bicknell Willett, investigates Ward's dark experiments and is horrified to find that Ward has summoned up an ancient entity.

The novel contains the first mention of the Cthulhu Mythos 'Old One' called Yog-Sothoth, who appears at several points in the narrative as an element in an incantation. Curwen owns a copy of the fabled and feared tome, the Necronomicon, and there are hints of occult activities in a fishing village that vaguely refer to lore referenced in another of Lovecraft's mythos stories, *The Festival*.

Scenes from *The Haunted Palace* (1963)

This was pretty heavy stuff for a horror film in 1963, the year that Corman decided to direct and produce *Charles Dexter Ward*. Arkoff and Nicholson, however, wanted him to make another Poe movie, so they insisted on downplaying the Lovecraft connection and wanted to call the film *The Haunted Village*. Ultimately, the final title became *The Haunted Palace*, derived, like *The Raven*, from a poem by Poe. At least, in this case, there was no reason to concoct an original story out of whole cloth; they had the entire mythos of Lovecraft at their disposal.

Most of the crew from the Poe pictures came back to work on *The Haunted Palace*, including cinematographer Crosby, but Corman entrusted him to use a darker colour palette this time to separate it from the 'true' Poe movies. While the finished film superficially resembles the Poe pictures, its mood is subtly different and the rather musty, pastel colours are a far cry from the bright shades with which Crosby had invested both *Tales of Terror* and *The Raven*. The atmosphere is sombre and grim, and, rather than 'doomed' women and black cats, one feels that perhaps demonic entities are lurking in the swirling fog in this unsettling landscape.

Price, of course, was signed to play the dual roles of Ward and Curwen, and Paget was brought back from *Tales of Terror* to portray his beautiful and long-suffering wife, Anne. In the absence of Karloff, another old Universal Pictures horror star boarded the Lovecraft train, Lon Chaney Jr in his only

appearance for Corman. He and Price had once been featured in the same film, *Abbott and Costello Meet Frankenstein* (1948), although Price did not actually 'appear' in the film at all, but merely provided he voice of the Invisible Man at the end of the picture. In that comedic romp, Chaney had played his most famous character, Lawrence Talbot, aka The Wolf Man.

The script for *The Haunted Palace* was by Charles Beaumont and, while certain portions of the adaptation are fairly faithful to Lovecraft, he took great liberties with the tale. Nevertheless, it stands as the first feature film ever based on a story by the famed 'Gentleman from Providence.'

In Beaumont's version, the narrative begins with the warlock Joseph Curwen placing a curse on a group of villagers who are about to burn him at the stake. Generations later, Curwen's descendant, Charles Dexter Ward, returns to the village of Arkham with his wife to claim his ancestral 'palace.' Ward, apparently possessed by the spirit of Curwen, eventually picks up where his necromantic ancestor left off by summoning up the cosmic entity Yog-Sothoth.

The score is by Ronald Stein, and what a powerhouse it is. Rich, magnificently orchestrated and beautifully played, it is one of the finest scores in Corman's 'Poe' cycle. Interestingly enough, Poe's middle name is misspelled twice in the opening credits as 'Allen' rather than 'Allan.' Could this be some sort of in-joke indicating this is not a 'true' Poe film? The name is spelled correctly in the end credits, which makes one wonder.

The justification for using the title *The Haunted Palace* is a bit of a stretch; the poem, which was originally published in 1839 and was incorporated into Poe's *The Fall of the House of Usher*, is heard, in part, when the opening scene fades into the main setting of the action (110 years later) and Price is heard reciting some lines from it. Another portion is seen, as per the tradition of the Poe pictures, in subtitles at the end: '…While, like a ghastly rapid river, through the pale door, a hideous throng rush out forever and laugh – But smile no more.'

Price is exceptionally fine in the roles of Ward and Curwen, an occasional arched eyebrow signalling when Curwen is taking over his soul. His performance is more subtle than usual, and can be quite unsettling when one is not quite sure whether Ward or Curwen is the dominant force. The scene in which he attempts to rape his beautiful wife is genuinely disturbing, and Paget – who would retire from acting after this film – is also memorable in the role of his doubting spouse.

Chaney is also very effective, although his screen time is limited, as Simon Orne, Ward's assistant in necromancy. His face made up to look pale and almost green, he lurks about in the shadows of Curwen's 'palace,' and there always seems to be the threat of violence beneath his apparently calm exterior.

The supporting cast is also up to the task. Frank Maxwell does a fine job as Dr Willett, who bears much of the exposition regarding the Lovecraftian pantheon of 'Old Ones.' Famed character actor Elisha Cook Jr, who had

Vincent Price trussed up in *The Haunted Palace* (1963)

appeared in everything from *The Maltese Falcon* (1941) to *House on Haunted Hill* (1959, with Price), is on hand as both Peter Smith and Mica Smith, the latter fated to bear the brunt of Curwen's curse upon the former. John Dierkes returns from *Premature Burial* and Leo Gordon (who co-wrote *The Terror*) appears as another villager, with Corman regular Barboura Morris portraying his wife. Statuesque Cathie Merchant plays Hester Tillinghast, Curwen's assistant in evil, with the kind of deep cleavage that Hammer horror was known for, but which Corman co-opted for many of his Poe films.

The Haunted Palace is one of the richest in Corman's 'Poe' cycle, either because of or in spite of the fact that it is not truly Poe. Beaumont gives Price some wonderful, wickedly humorous lines which the actor delivers with relish, such as when he says to Simon: 'I'll not have my fill of revenge until this village is a graveyard. Until they have felt, as I did, the kiss of fire on their soft bare flesh. All of them. Have patience, my friends. Surely, after all these years, I'm entitled to a few small amusements.'

Although Beaumont made many changes to Lovecraft's original story, *The Haunted Palace* captures the *atmosphere* of Lovecraft better than perhaps any other cinematic adaptation of the author's work. Reviews at the time were, of course, mixed. In *The New York Times* on 30 January 1964, Eugene Archer wrote: 'Roger Corman is an old hand at turning out lurid horror melodramas in low-budget colour such as *The Haunted Palace*... Nothing about it calls for comment, except perhaps the proficient colour photography by another old professional, Floyd Crosby.'

For those of us who are Lovecraft *aficionados*, however, the review by Andrew Migliore and John Strysik in their book *Lurker in the Lobby: A Guide to the Cinema of H P Lovecraft*, hits the coffin nail on the head: 'The Haunted *Palace* is a seminal film for Lovecraft lovers; it is the first major motion picture to introduce (Lovecraft's) creations – the Necronomicon, and those cosmic abominations Cthulhu and Yog-Sothoth – to a general audience. (Lovecraft's) obsession with the past is clearly presented, and in a heartfelt passage at the end of the film, so is his belief that mankind is a minor species adrift in a malevolent universe... Roger Corman did an admirable job as the first American feature-film director to stake out some cinematic high ground for the cosmos-crushing adaptations (of H P Lovecraft) to follow.'

One other point that Migliore and Strysik failed to mention: Poe was Lovecraft's favourite author, and the gentleman from Providence would have been thrilled and probably a bit bemused, that his work was conflated with Poe's for a motion picture, a medium about which he had decidedly mixed feelings.

AIP announced in 1963 that their next Poe picture would be *The Masque of the Red Death*, which Corman had wanted to film for some time but could never find a screenplay that he felt captured Poe's rather surreal moral fable. One draft of the script had been written by Robert Towne, who would later write the screenplays for such Hollywood blockbusters as Warren Beatty's *Shampoo* (1976) and Roman Polanski's *Chinatown* (1974). Corman was not happy with Towne's version, however, and the script was turned over to Charles Beaumont to rewrite. The eventual screenwriting credits went to Beaumont and R Wright Campbell, who also incorporated elements of Poe's *Hop-Frog* into the story.

At the same time that AIP were trying to get *Masque* off the ground, rival companies were attempting to make their own versions. All of Poe's stories were in the public domain, meaning that anyone could film them. Independent producer Alex Gordon said he wanted Price to star in his version, which made AIP quite unhappy, as Price was under contract to AIP. They put enough pressure on Gordon to make him withdraw his plans for the project, and *Masque* became AIP's most elaborate Poe picture to date.

One of the things that Corman liked about Beaumont's early draft of the script was that he made the protagonist, Prince Prospero, a Satanist. He felt that the screenplay still needed some work, however, but Beaumont was too ill by this time to complete it (he died of a mysterious brain disease in 1967 at the age of thirty-eight). Campbell was brought in to complete the screenplay and it was he who introduced the subplot concerning the dwarf from *Hop Frog*, which he renamed 'Hop-Toad' for the film.

*The Masque of the Red Death* (1964)

AIP's lucrative co-production deal with Anglo-Amalgamated gave Arkoff and Nicholson the idea to have Corman shoot *The Masque of the Red Death* in England. It was actually a practical decision; it meant that the film could qualify for the Eady levy and the budget could be larger than that for the previous Poe pictures. This financial choice led to a better quality of production as well; *Masque* was shot on a five-week schedule rather than Corman's usual three.

Price, of course, was cast as Prince Prospero, and Hazel Court received the role of Juliana, Prospero's consort in devil worship. Young British *ingénue* Jane Asher, who had appeared in Val Guest's *The Quatermass Xperiment* (1955) as a little girl (and who was currently the girlfriend of Paul McCartney as the Beatles conquered the music world), was cast in *Masque* as the innocent 'damsel in distress,' Francesca. Other cast members included David Weston as Gino, Nigel Green as Ludovico and Patrick Magee as Alfredo. Magee had already worked for Corman in *The Young Racers* (1963). He had also had a prominent role in *Dementia 13* (1963), a horror film directed by Francis Ford Coppola and produced by Corman in Ireland. In an introduction to the novelisation of the screenplay of *The Masque of the Red Death* in 2013, Corman recalled his fondness for Magee: 'He could find these strange little quirks which he would bring out during his performance, making it a richer and more fully rounded characterisation.'

Corman's usual art director Daniel Haller actually designed the film, but he went uncredited to allow *Masque* to qualify as a British production. Robert Jones is credited onscreen with the art direction.

The screenplay is very close to the spirit of Poe, while also featuring elements of Ingmar Bergman's *The Seventh Seal* (1957): Prospero, an evil prince in medieval Europe, rides through the village of Catania and sees that the peasants there are dying of the plague known as 'The Red Death.' Prospero burns the village to the ground, but saves three of its inhabitants: Gino, his father-in-law Ludovico and Gino's young and lovely wife Francesca. Prospero brings them back to his castle, where he intends to 'corrupt' Francesca into the ways of Satanism. Prospero also invites his noble friends to stay in the castle to protect them against the plague that ravages the countryside. When he invites all of his assembled guests to attend a masked ball, he notices a stranger dressed in red; he has specifically asked for no one to wear that colour. Soon, however, he learns who the guest really is, to his horror.

When *The Masque of the Red Death* was released in the US in June 1964 (just in time for the drive-in movie season), it garnered some of the best reviews that Corman and AIP had ever received. In *The New York Herald Tribune*, Eugene Archer positively gushed: ' On its level, it is astonishingly good… The film is beautifully costumed, the sets are lavish, the props exquisite.'

The 'lavish sets' in the film were actually leftovers from Peter Glenville's *Becket* (1964), which had just finished shooting at Elstree Studios only weeks before. And so the sets once occupied by the likes of Richard Burton, Peter O'Toole and John Gielgud were now romped upon by Price, Court and Magee. Not too shabby, as the saying goes.

Shortly after the film's release, a lawsuit against AIP was filed by Alex Gordon, who claimed that the screenplay was based on the script concocted by him, his wife and two other writers. The script, he said, had at one time been submitted to AIP. The judge, Macklin Fleming, dismissed the suit, claiming that the similarities between the two screenplays were 'coincidental,' a reasonable judgment considering the fact that they were based on the same public domain source material.

*The Masque of the Red Death* was not as financially successful as some of the other Poe pictures, which the ever business-minded Arkoff blamed on its being 'too arty farty'. In his introduction to the novelisation, Corman wrote, 'I think that is a legitimate statement… The fault may have been mine. I was becoming more interested in the Poe films as expressions of the unconscious mind, rather than as pure horror films.'

*Masque* found itself in censorship problems in the UK, mainly in the hallucinatory sequence in which Court is 'violated' by several demonic apparitions while she lies on a stone slab. In an interview for *Cinefantastique* Magazine by Steve Biodrowski in 1997, Corman recalled: 'From the standpoint of nudity, there was nothing. I think she was nude under a diaphanous gown. She played the consummation with the Devil, but it was essentially on her face; it was a pure acting exercise. Hazel fully clothed, all by herself, purely by acting, incurred the wrath of the censor. It was a different age…'

With all due respect to Corman, he may have forgotten just how 'diaphanous' that gown really was and how obvious it was when Court moved that she was naked underneath it. The combination of her near-nudity and the Satanic nature of the scene may have been what tipped the scales for the British censor.

*The Masque of the Red Death* was a clear example of how much Corman had matured as an artist, as this time, the critics were even more fond of a Corman Poe picture than the public, and *Masque* played at the prestigious Museum of Modern Art only a year or so after its release. 'Arty farty' it may be, but it is also the finest of all of Corman's Poe films. Its imagery captured by cinematographer Nicolas Roeg, who would later become a noted film director (*Don't Look Now*, 1973) remains unsurpassed for its dreamlike Gothic beauty and swirling colours. David Lee's musical score, Laura Nightingale's costumes, the sterling cast and Corman at the top of his game all combine to create an unforgettable cinematic experience.

Price's Prospero is one of his finest characterisations, pure evil yet somehow ultimately sad. Court also has one of her best hours here, all haughtiness and regal beauty until her violent death scene, which is straight out of Hitchcock's *The Birds* (1963). Asher is also surprisingly effective as the young, naive Francesca. When Prospero 'tutors' her in the ways of the world, he also reveals his beliefs to the audience: 'If a god of love and life ever did exist, He is long since dead. Someone, some *thing* rules in His place.'

His anti-Christian tirade continues when he shows Francesca his trained falcon: 'Do you know how a falcon is trained, my dear? Her eyes are sewn shut. Blinded temporarily, she suffers the whims of her God patiently, until her will is submerged and she learns to serve… as your God taught and blinded you with crosses.'

Prospero's dark vision of the world and the universe comes back to haunt him by the end of the film, however. When the 'Man in Red' (John Westbrook) arrives, he taunts the Satanic prince: 'Why should you be afraid to die? Your soul has been dead for a long, long time.' Yet the screenplay refuses to become preachy or overtly theological, as the Man in Red tells him, 'Each man creates his own God for himself, his own Heaven, his own Hell,' before Prospero rips the mask from the stranger's face, only to reveal his own.

The subplot regarding 'Hop-Toad' (Skip Martin) is seamlessly sewn into the story. The dwarf's tiny girlfriend Esmerelda (Verina Greenlaw) is cruelly mistreated by the sadistic Alfredo, and Hop-Toad enacts his revenge by convincing Alfredo to wear an ape costume during the Masque, whereupon he sets fire to him and burns him alive.

One of the strangest things about *Masque* is the casting of a little girl as Esmeralda, a dwarf. Her scenes with Martin are uncomfortable, and despite the fact that her voice is dubbed by an adult actress, it is still obvious that she is a little girl playing a fully grown dwarf. This could be considered a flaw in

Vincent Price in *The Masque of the Red Death* (1964)

Vincent Price in *The Masque of the Red Death* (1964)

David Weston and Jane Asher in *The Masque of the Red Death* (1964)

the film, yet in some respects it makes the subtext of certain scenes even more disturbing than they would have been otherwise. Alfredo lecherously lays eyes on Esmeralda and says to Prospero, 'You promised me entertainment, but I never expected this. Have such eyes seen sin?' Prospero answers, 'They will.' The discomfort of the audience becomes nearly palpable in such scenes, only adding to the unease of the film.

The final sequence is the one most obviously inspired by Bergman. The Red Death goes to join his fellows, all robed in different colours, upon a hillside. The Yellow Death says to him: 'This eternity of wandering! Ten thousand sleep where I walked. I am very tired.' The White Death sighs, 'The weariness of those to whom we bring rest burdens you.'

It is the Red Death, appropriately, who has the last word: 'I called many: Peasant and prince; the worthy and the dishonoured. Six only are left… a young man and woman; a dwarf and tiny dancer; this child, and an old man still in the village. Sic transit gloria mundi.'

*The Masque of the Red Death* is a stunning achievement, a horror film of intellectual depth and courage, one of the most elegant genre films ever made. It is not a perfect movie; the 'Dance of Death' does seem rushed and the 'tiny dancer' either works for or against the film, depending upon one's point of view. But it is Corman's masterpiece, beyond a shadow of a doubt.

Corman's final Poe film – as a director, at least – was *The Tomb of Ligeia* (1964), filmed this time in Norfolk, England, in a very different style. The ever-restless director wanted to get away from his usual technique of filming the Poe features entirely on sound stages. That approach had worked very well, of course, as Corman's *auteur* theory involved settings that existed mainly in the unconscious mind. With *Ligeia*, however, Corman decided to shoot many scenes on location, taking advantage of the beautiful English countryside. With a twenty-five day shooting schedule, there was plenty of time for this stylistic indulgence.

*Ligeia* was a fairly early story by Poe, first published in 1838. The tale involves an unnamed narrator and his beautiful wife Ligeia. In typical Poe fashion, she becomes ill and composes the poem 'The Conqueror Worm' shortly before she dies. After her death, the protagonist/narrator marries the Lady Rowena, but, again mirroring events in Poe's own life, she dies as well. The bereaved man stays with her body through the night and watches as Rowena returns from the dead; but she has morphed into Ligeia.

Corman hired Robert Towne to write the screenplay, which during production was variously referred to by such titles as *The House at the End of the World* and *The Tomb of the Cat*. And, because much of the film would be shot outdoors, Corman hired frequent Hammer cinematographer Arthur Grant to photograph it. Grant had become Hammer's most prolific lighting cameraman since the departure of Jack Asher in 1964 and he shot most of their Gothics of the 1960's, including such classics as *The Curse of the Werewolf* (1961), *The Phantom of the Opera* (1962) and *Captain Clegg* (US: *Night Creatures*, 1962).

The Tomb of Ligeia was a co-production between AIP and their usual British production partner Anglo-Amalgamated. In his desire to make this Poe film something 'different', Corman initially did not want to use Price in the lead role. He felt that Price was too old for the part, which in Corman's and Towne's minds was a character who was only twenty-five to thirty years old. Corman wanted Richard Chamberlain for the role; Chamberlain was a star of American television's *Dr Kildare* series and something of a heartthrob in the US. AIP insisted on casting Price, however; they felt that he was by now synonymous with the Poe series and was still under contract. Corman ultimately gave in. Towne had gone on the record as requesting that Price not be cast; when Corman told him that Price was in fact playing the lead, he reassured Towne by saying, 'Don't worry, Bob, I've got Marlene Dietrich's make-up man!'

When interviewed by Lawrence French for the magazine *Video Watchdog* (issue #138, Spring 2008), Corman recalled: 'Well, what we ended up doing was giving Vincent a wig and using a bit more make-up on him than usual. We were trying to make him look younger... When we decided to use Vincent again that did change the orientation of the film quite a bit.'

Price's leading lady, who had the challenging dual role of Ligeia/Lady Rowena, was Elizabeth Shepherd, an English Shakesperean actress whose career encompassed the stage, television and cinema. She had been the original choice

angielski film grozy

# GROBOWIEC LIGEI

wg. Edgara Allana Poe
Reżyseria: Roger Corman

w rolach
głównych:

Vincent Price

Elisabeth Shepherd

Derek Francis

Produkcja
Alta Vista
Roger Corman

to play Emma Peel in *The Avengers*, but after filming two episodes, she left the series, was replaced by Diana Rigg, and the rest is television history. The general consensus was that she could not handle the light comedy that was necessary for the role and her deep, throaty voice probably did not help matters.

For *The Tomb of Ligeia*, such concerns were irrelevant and she leapt into the role with relish. Supporting actors included John Westbrook as her would-be suitor Christopher Gough (an amalgam of Christopher Lee and Michael Gough, perhaps?). He was another Shakespearean who had previously appeared in such films as *Foxhole in Cairo* (1960), *A Prize of Arms* (1962) and, of course, was the Red Death himself in *The Masque of the Red Death*.

Familiar character actor Derek Francis, a regular in the *Carry On* films, was cast as Lord Trevanion. He had also appeared in Hammer's *Captain Clegg*. Richard Vernon (Dr Vivian) had just appeared in *Goldfinger* (1964) alongside Sean Connery as James Bond; he had also had featured roles in Wolf Rilla's *Village of the Damned* (1960) and Hammer's crime thriller *Cash on Demand* (1961) with Peter Cushing and Andre Morell.

*The Tomb of Ligeia* went into production on 29 June 1964 at Castle Acre Priory, Swaffham, Norfolk. Price 'had always wanted to do a picture in a ruin,' according to Mark Thomas McGee. In this case, however, the production team were not allowed to place furniture in the old priory because the place was 'a national monument.' Only the exteriors were filmed there, while the interiors were shot at Shepperton Studios. According to McGee, 'Good thing too since the climax of the film called for the whole place to go up in flames. The walls of the set were coated with liquid cement. Everyone was warned not to smoke. Vince and his co-star, Elizabeth Shepherd, were positioned under some debris, getting ready for the next shot, when somebody lit a match. All at once the place was an inferno. Vince dragged Liz to safety as fast as he could. Naturally, the shot and the set were ruined.'

Released in the UK on 8 December 1964 and in the US on 20 January 1965, *The Tomb of Ligeia* received some rather mixed notices. In *The New York Times*, Howard Thompson opined: 'Another film based on the writings of Edgar Allan Poe and directed by Roger Corman. The least effective of the… Poe films, it often drags and Price seems miscast…Mr Corman at least cares about putting Mr Poe – or at least some of the master's original ideas – on the screen. If they are frankly made to be screamed at, they are not to be sneezed at… These low-budget shockers generally evoke a compelling sense of heady atmosphere and coiled doom in their excellent Gothic settings, arresting colour schemes and camera mobility…Mr Corman has made stunning, ambient use of his authentic setting, an ancient abbey in Norfolk, England, and the lovely countryside..'

*Time* magazine wrote: '*Ligeia*, like its predecessors, offers meticulous decor, shrewd shock techniques, and an atmosphere of mounting terror that fails to deliver on its promise. Again, the cream-centred menace is Vincent Price, an actor who appears to be swooping around in a cape even when he stands perfectly still.'

In his interview for *Video Watchdog*, Corman noted: 'Actually, all of the Poe films made money, but *Tomb of Ligeia* made the least amount. I think it was because the series was just running out of steam and also because it was overly complicated.'

'Complicated' it may be, but *Ligeia* works on many levels. Although not as dreamlike as its predecessors because of the authentic locations, it is undoubtedly the most blatantly *romantic* of all the Poe pictures. Corman and Towne, both huge cinema fans themselves, included several nods to Hitchcock's *Vertigo* (1958) in the film. *Vertigo*, of course, has a similar plot: a man (James Stewart) is in love (or rather obsessed) with a woman (Kim Novak) who is dead. When he sees a woman who looks like her, he becomes obsessed with her and tries to make her into the exact duplicate of his beloved.

*Ligeia* inverts this idea by using the Poe concept of the transmigration of souls. During the course of the film, Rowena virtually *becomes* Ligeia, but this transformation is done with considerable subtlety. The scene in which a black cat (which may encase Ligeia's spirit) leads Rowena up some winding stairs into a bell tower is a virtual re-shoot of the climax of *Vertigo*.

Shepherd is first-rate in both roles, giving Lady Rowena just the right amount of spark to keep her from being the clichéd damsel in distress, while investing Ligeia with enough grim invincibility to convince the audience that 'Man doth not yield himself to the angels, nor unto death, save only through the weakness of his feeble will.'

Price is indeed miscast, physically at least. In his fifties by then, he is certainly too old for the role, yet he plays it with considerable vitality. The make-up helps, but he was an old hand at this sort of role by then. As Corman said, '… The character Vincent played in *Dragonwyck* was exactly what we were looking for in *Ligeia*, but as you know, *Dragonwyck* was made twenty years earlier… And as a matter of fact, I agreed with Vincent – *Ligeia* is one of the best Poe pictures and Vincent's performance in the film was very good. It was simply a matter of age.'

Grant's camerawork opens up Corman's metaphysical world of Poe into the purely physical; of all his Poe pictures, *Ligeia* looks the most like a Hammer film for obvious reasons. Corman's direction is often quite thrilling; there is a fox hunt that rivals the similar scene in *Tom Jones* (1963), the colour scheme is rich and varied and, despite the age difference, there is genuine chemistry between Price and Shepherd. *Ligeia* is indeed one of the best Poe pictures, and AIP wanted more.

While Corman had been filming *The Masque of the Red Death*, he had hired Charles B Griffith to adapt Poe's 'The Gold Bug' into a comedy. The script was to be written for Price, Lorre, Karloff and Rathbone. The latter was going to be a visiting English carpetbagger who comes to visit Price, who owns a burned-out mansion, shortly after the American Civil War. Price has a servant (Lorre) who carries a gold bug about in a matchbox. At night, Lorre lets the creature out of the box to play songs on the harpsichord. Anyone bitten by the bug turns to gold. Price discovers this and sells the gold bodies as statues to make ends meet, shades of Corman's *A Bucket of Blood* (1959).

Lorre's untimely death of a stroke in March 1964, before the screenplay of *The Gold Bug* was even finished, put an end to the project, and to any future comedy-horror films with him and Price. It was felt that Lorre had been the key to the funniest scenes in these films, and no one had the inclination to carry on without him.

As for Corman, he became utterly bored with the Poe series after *Ligeia* and he refused to do any more Poe pictures. His next film would be very different, a movie about motorcycles: *The Wild Angels* (1966) was a wildly successful 'counterculture' hit that kicked off a trend of so-called 'biker' films.

AIP was desperate for more Poe material, and, in 1965, they enlisted veteran director Jacques Tourneur (*Cat People*, 1942) to direct a project that was intended to continue the Poe series. Originally entitled *City in the Sea*, it was loosely based on the Poe poem entitled 'The City in the Sea' that had been published in 1845. Poe's earlier version of the poem, 'The Doomed City,' had originally been published in 1831.

The poem begins with the lines: 'Lo! Death has reared himself a throne/ In a strange city lying alone/Far down within the dim West/ Where the good and the bad and the dead and the rest/Have gone to their eternal rest.'

English screenwriter Charles Bennett, who had written some of Alfred Hitchcock's best-known British films such as *The Man Who Knew Too Much* (1934) and *The 39 Steps* (1935), was commissioned to write a screenplay adapted from the poem. Bennett had recently co-written the screenplay (with producer Irwin Allen) for the film *Voyage to the Bottom of the Sea* (1961), which later became a popular American television series, and he was instructed to turn Poe's poem into more of an underwater fantasy than a horror film, a la AIP's *Master of the World* (1961), which had starred Price as Jules Verne's Robur the Conqueror.

Price was still AIP's cash cow, and he was asked to play the Robur-like character in *City in the Sea*, The Captain. Set on the coast of Cornwall in 1903, the story concerned a group of people who discover an underwater city in which an organisation of smugglers dwell, never aging, living there unknown to the outside world alongside their amphibious slaves.

Tourneur was chosen to direct because he had recently completed *The Comedy of Terrors* for AIP, the final teaming of Price, Lorre and Karloff (along with Basil Rathbone). For the teenage set, American actor Tab Hunter was cast as the young male protagonist, Ben Harris. Hunter had made his debut in *The Lawless* (1950) and had become a teen heartthrob in such films as *The Burning Hills* and *The Girl He Left Behind* (both 1956), co-starring with Natalie Wood in each.

David Tomlinson, who had just appeared in *Mary Poppins* (1964), was cast in the role of Harold Tufnell-Jones, a sort of stereotyped eccentric Englishman, complete with a pet chicken called Herbert. AIP starlet Susan Hart, who ended up marrying James Nicholson, received the plum role of Jill

This page and opposite *War Gods of the Deep* (1965)

Tregillis, the heroine of the piece. In addition to appearing opposite Hunter in Columbia's *Ride the Wild Surf* (1964), she had just been featured in AIP's *Pajama Party* in 1964, prior to going to England to make *City in the Sea*.

Some veteran British character actors appeared in the film as well. John Le Mesurier, who had been featured in such genre films as *Jack the Ripper* and Hammer's *The Hound of the Baskervilles* (both 1959), was cast in the role of Reverend Jonathan Ives (a part originally intended for Boris Karloff), a citizen of the undersea city, while Henry Oscar (billed here as Harry Oscar) would play his final feature film role in the production as Mumford, after appearing in everything from Zoltan Korda's *The Four Feathers* (1939) to Terence Fisher's Hammer masterpiece *The Brides of Dracula* (1960).

The behind-the-scenes talent was equally impressive. Daniel Haller was promoted from art director to producer of the project, while the cinematographer was the distinguished Stephen Dade, who had photographed such epics as *Knights of the Round Table* (1954) and more recently had shot Sidney J Furie's *Doctor Blood's Coffin* (1961) on location in Cornwall.

One of the most important members of the production team was Louis M Heyward, a New Yorker who had begun his career as a scriptwriter for such television series as *The Ernie Kovacs Show* (1952) and had just written *Pajama Party* for AIP. He would soon be appointed the head of British production for the company after his 'baptism of fire' on *City in the Sea*, which came to be known as a 'troubled' production.

The problems arose when Heyward rewrote the screenplay, instructed by Arkoff and Nicholson to add humour; the character of Tufnell-Jones was an addition of his, as was the pet chicken, which was obviously inspired by a comic duck in the fantasy hit *Journey to the Center of the Earth* (1959), based on a Jules Verne novel. Although ostensibly a Poe picture, *City in the Sea* was produced very much in the style of the Walt Disney production of Verne's *20,000 Leagues Under the Sea* (1954), which also bears many similarities in plot.

In Tom Weaver's book *Double Feature Creature Attack: A Monster Merger of Two More Volumes of Classic Interviews*, Bennett was quoted as saying that AIP wanted him to go to England to work on the script but would not pay

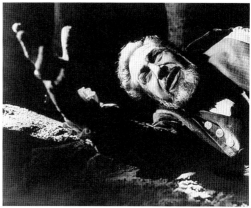

his way there or put him up at a hotel. Bennett refused to pay his own way, and, as a result, Heyward rewrote the script. Bennett detested the changes, calling the film as released, '...The worst thing I was ever involved in.' According to Hart, Bennett's original script was well done but was rewritten quickly, and she recalled tension between producers Haller and the British co-producer, George Willoughby, the latter of whom also disliked the humorous alterations to the screenplay. Willoughby hated both Herbert the chicken and the character played by Tomlinson, and he left the production after these changes were greenlit by AIP.

Released under its final US title as *War-Gods of the Deep* on a double bill with AIP's *Beach Blanket Bingo* on 26 May 1965 and in the UK later that year as *The City under the Sea*, the film did not, shall we say, make waves under either title. There is very little of Poe in it, although Price, as usual, gives his all as the doomed Captain (also known as Sir Hugh), but the film itself is neither fish nor fowl. Is it an undersea adventure a la *Mysterious Island*? There are gill-men and underwater shots reminiscent of Harryhausen's movie, minus the grand special effects. The gill-men in particular are disappointing, wearing sub-*Creature From the Black Lagoon* costumes and floundering about gracelessly under the waves.

Is it a Poe movie, with all the melancholy that implies? There is very little horror, although the scene at the climax in which The Captain ages as the sun's rays fall upon him, much like a vampire, is quite effective. Price does his usual voice-over Poe readings from Poe's poem, but that's about as Poesque as *War-Gods of the Deep* gets.

The music by Stanley Black (*Blood of the Vampire*, 1958) is unmemorable and not a patch on Baxter's or Stein's Poe scores. On the plus side, the visuals are striking, with magnificent undersea statues dominating the submerged city. Dade's cinematography and Frank White's art direction give the film a sumptuous, expensive look. Aside from Price, however, and a good supporting performance from Le Mesurier, the acting is lacklustre. Hunter and Tomlinson overact, while Hart is given little to do but to look decorative, which admittedly she does very well. Price, despite the uninspired script, is able to give The Captain a true sense of doom-laden melancholy. *War Gods of the Deep*, however, is a hopeless mishmash that never gels as a cohesive whole. The comic relief seems to have come from another film altogether and the film sinks under the waves, easily the weakest of AIP's Poe-related films. It would have been interesting to have seen what Corman would have made of it. It was Tourneur's swan song as director, and a sad one it was.

As censorship around the world gradually relaxed, cinema did a slow striptease throughout the sixties. In the 'continental version' of Michael Powell's controversial *Peeping Tom* (1960), model Pamela Green lies back on a bed waiting to be photographed. She undoes her top to expose one of her breasts. Many British films were 'double shot' with nudity included for 'Continental' versions. But that was just the beginning. In 1966, Michelangelo Antonioni's *Blow-Up* became the first English-language film to show a woman's pubic hair. There was also blatant drug use in the film.

By 1967, two ground-breaking Swedish films, *I Am Curious (Yellow)* and *Inga* broke new ground in showing not only full frontal nudity, but fairly explicit sex as well. British films continued to 'take it off,' with *This Sporting Life* (1963) showing flashes of male nudity, *Here We Go Round the Mulberry Bush* (1967) featuring Judy Geeson's uninhibited nude swimming romp and Ken Russell's film of D H Lawrence's *Women in Love* (1969) featuring frontal male nudity in the wrestling scene between Alan Bates and Oliver Reed, with just a hint of homosexuality into the bargain.

In the US, the by-now-obsolete Production Code was virtually extinct by 1966; *The Pawnbroker*, released in 1964, had defied the Code by fully exposing the breasts of actresses Linda Geiser and Thelma Oliver. After that, there was no turning back, and the Code was replaced in the US by a new rating system in 1968.

In 1966, Louis M Heyward had been appointed AIP's Director of Overseas Production and was set up in a London-based office to oversee AIP's British-based films in 1967, at which point he plunged into production almost immediately on Michael Reeves' *Witchfinder General*, a watershed film in British horror.

In the mid-sixties, British producer Tony Tenser had formed a company called Tigon Pictures. Tenser had previously run Compton-Cameo, a production company that had made a rather lurid Gothic horror film called *The Black Torment* in 1964, as well as an excellent Sherlock Holmes/Jack the Ripper thriller called *A Study in Terror* (1965). One of the first films he produced for Tigon was Michael Reeves' *The Sorcerers* (1967), a 'mod' horror thriller starring Boris Karloff, Catherine Lacey, Ian Ogilvy and a very young Susan George.

To Tenser's joy, and totally unexpectedly, *The Sorcerers* ran for three weeks in the West End, an extraordinary feat in those days for a low-budget horror film. It did equally well elsewhere, and in July 1968, the film won the 'Grand Prix' at the Sixth Film Festival of Trieste, with Catherine Lacey winning Best Actress and Karloff winning a special prize for his contributions to horror cinema.

The 21-year-old Reeves now found himself in the role of a cinematic 'Boy Wonder', and Tenser was now eager to find another vehicle for his young director's talents. Interestingly enough, Tenser received the galley proofs of a new horror novel called *Witchfinder General* during this period, written by British author Ronald Bassett. The book was based on the true story of Matthew Hopkins, a self-appointed witch hunter who had waged a reign of terror during the bleak days of the English Civil War. The novel was to be published in a few months, and everything fell into place because Tenser was acquainted with Bassett's agent.

Reeves had shown in his grim screenplay for *The Sorcerers* that he was fascinated with the dark heart of the human soul, and he jumped at the chance to write and direct *Witchfinder General* for the screen. He teamed up with a writer named Tom Baker to pen the script, which brought out the opportunism and misogyny of Hopkin's character and highlighted the brutality and violence of the era.

Originally, Tenser wanted Karloff to star as Matthew Hopkins, but his declining health made him physically unable to do the role, for which he would have been too old in any case. Reeves wanted Donald Pleasence for Hopkins; the busy character actor had excelled in such films as John Gilling's *The Flesh and the Fiends* (1959) and had just appeared in Roman Polanski's *Cul-de-sac*, which Tenser had produced.

When it came to funding, all of Tigon's fortunes were currently tied up in a production called *Death's Head Vampire*, later to be known as *The Blood Beast Terror*, a Gothic horror film starring Peter Cushing. Reeves wanted to start filming *Witchfinder* before the onset of winter 1967.

Stuck in the middle of a tricky situation, Tenser was forced to find a production partner. One arrived in the person of Louis M Heyward. Having been appointed AIP's Head of European Production by Nicholson and Arkoff in June 1967, Heyward was visited at his office in Grovesnor Square by Tenser. Heyward did not know much about Reeves but he loved the script for *Witchfinder* and felt this could be a great opportunity for him to flex his muscles for his bosses back home. Nicholson and Arkoff consented to put in £32,000 of the total £82,000 budget in return for distribution rights in the US – and on the condition that the film star Vincent Price.

Tenser had no problem with AIP's demands. For his part, Price – who was less than enthused about the script – would receive £12,000 for playing the role of Matthew Hopkins. All the contracts were signed by September 1967 and the project was set to commence filming.

Reeves made it clear from the start that he did not want Price for the role. Price's urbanity and sophistication were completely at odds with Reeves' concept of the character, and he was concerned about the horror film 'baggage' that Price carried with him. The agreement had been made with AIP, however, and Reeves had no choice but to go along with it. *Witchfinder General* went into production with Price in the lead on 17 September 1967.

Price and Reeves were at odds from the very first day. Their relationship never improved and, on his last day of shooting, Price showed up on the set obviously drunk. Reeves was outraged, but somehow they got through the scene, which concerned Hopkins' gory death by axe.

Principal photography was completed on 13 November 1967. In the end, Price's performance had been toned down by Reeves to a more 'serious' level than his rather more theatrical performances in the Poe films.

The director's cut was shipped to AIP's London office in spring 1968. When they saw the film in the States, Arkoff and Nicholson were as impressed as Heyward had been. Nevertheless, they had the right to 'final cut' and chose to exercise it. Arkoff felt that the title *Witchfinder General* was not commercial enough, but he believed that if the film could be somehow tied to Poe – especially with Price as its star – it could be an unqualified success. And so, in the US and Canada, *Witchfinder General* became *Edgar Allan Poe's The Conqueror Worm*, based on the title of a Poe poem about his favourite topic, death. Price was called back to the sound studio to read portions of the poem over the opening scene and the freeze frame just before the end credits, thereby linking the film – in a circuitous way – with the Corman/Price Poe series.

*Witchfinder General/Conqueror Worm* was released in both Britain and America in the autumn of 1968. It was met with great outrage from many British critics because of its violence. The controversy generated by the film's brutality only added to its box office success. In an interesting example of the difference in cultural attitudes between the two countries, *The Conqueror Worm* did not fall victim to any censorship problems, nor did it create a public or critical outcry against its violence. Few critics even bothered to see it, as it played the usual AIP drive-in circuit. 'Leave the children at home… and if you are squeamish, stay home with them!' screamed AIP's newspaper advertising. The movie earned nearly $2 million in its US release, bringing about a second wave of 'Poe' films from the studio, most of them starring Price.

Heyward wanted to get Reeves back for another Poe film, *The Oblong Box*, upon which the director began work on 18 November 1968. Sadly, Reeves died of a drug overdose during pre-production, so another director was found: Gordon Hessler, a British television veteran who had been story editor and associate producer on the American television series *Alfred Hitchcock Presents* and *The Alfred Hitchcock Hour* from 1960 to 1965.

Price, supporting actor Rupert Davies and leading lady Hillary Dwyer were all brought back from *Witchfinder General* to star in *The Oblong Box*. The writer of the screenplay, Lawrence Huntington, died as shooting began, and the script was quickly rewritten by Hessler and young screenwriter Christopher Wicking. Following in the footsteps of Reeves' film by adding

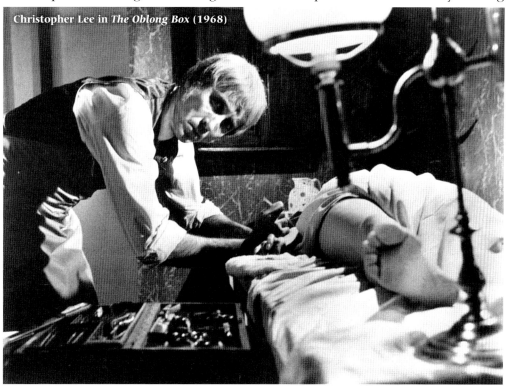

Christopher Lee in *The Oblong Box* (1968)

more gore and sex than Corman had put in his Poe pictures, *The Oblong Box* proved to be a very successful movie. Budgeted at £70,000, it made over $1 million in the US and Canada. Poe, Price and AIP were back together again, and Arkoff and Nicholson were going to make the most of it.

*The Oblong Box* plays more like a Hammer horror film than a Poe picture, in part because of the presence of Christopher Lee, who receives second billing after Price but whose role as a Victorian doctor who makes use of body snatchers is little more than a cameo. Davies, who receives third billing, had just co-starred with Lee in Hammer's *Dracula Has Risen from the Grave* (1968). For sex appeal, AIP cast Sally Geeson, sister of Judy Geeson, as Sally, a young woman who falls afoul of Edward (Alistair Williamson), the villain of the piece.

Once again, the story has little to do with Poe, although Williamson does recite a few lines from the short story 'The Oblong Box' late in the film. The plot is basic Victorian gothic: aristocrat Julian Markham imprisons his horribly disfigured brother Edward in a tower atop his mansion. Edward escapes with the help of Trench (Peter Arne) and N'galo (Harry Baird) who, with the aid of drugs and voodoo, simulate his death and remove him in a coffin. By a twist of fate, body snatchers bring his 'corpse' to Dr Neuhartt (Lee), Edward recovers and offers Neuhartt a large amount of money to stay in his house, where he wears a crimson hood to hide his disfigured face. Edward eventually goes on a rampage throughout the town and commits a series of murders.

As can be seen, the plot was nothing new, but the treatment of all these familiar elements was very much in the recently established, more realistic style initiated by Reeves. Few punches are pulled in the gore department, including a graphic throat-slitting, and, as the X Certificate in Britain was just about to be modified, raising the age for films under that classification from sixteen to eighteen, more could be made of sex as well. As a result, *The Oblong Box* was the most brutal and sexually charged 'official' Poe picture made up to that time.

Despite all the gore and excess (some of which was cut by AIP when the film was released in the States), *The Oblong Box* has little of the impact of *Witchfinder General*. Hessler's direction is adequate but doesn't have the headlong passion or inspiration of Reeves, and the script is perfunctory. Neither Price nor Lee is given much to do, Dwyer's considerable talents are wasted, and the film coasts mostly on the shoulders of its supporting cast, who just aren't all that interesting. Nevertheless, *The Oblong Box* made a ton of money for AIP and led to still more period horror films with Price.

Reviews, of course, were tepid or downright dismissive. In *The New York Times*, A H Weiler wrote, 'The British and American producers, who have been mining Edgar Allan Poe's seemingly inexhaustible literary lode like mad, now have created *The Oblong Box* to illustrate once again that horror can be made to be quaint, laughable and unconvincing at modest prices.' *Variety* was more charitable, noting, 'Price, as usual, overacts, but it is an art here to fit the mood and piece and as usual, Price is good in his part. Alastair Williamson as the brother is called upon for some strange goings-on but acquits himself well and Christopher Lee likewise scores as a doctor who becomes involved with Williamson.'

Prior to producing their next Poe picture, AIP hastily picked up a European film called *Histories Extraordinaires* in 1969, a French/Italian omnibus film containing three Poe stories, each helmed by a different 'A-list' director. Roger Vadim directed *Metzengerstein*, starring Jane Fonda and Peter Fonda; Louis Malle presided over *William Wilson*, starring Alain Delon and Brigitte Bardot; and Federico Fellini wrote and directed *Toby Dammit*, starring Terence Stamp.

For American distribution, AIP retitled the film *Spirits of the Dead*, and added a narration by Vincent Price, once again linking it, ostensibly at least, to their ongoing Poe series. Arkoff and Nicholson had offered the European producers $200,000 for the US and Canadian rights, but were turned down because Arkoff wanted to excise one scene from the Fellini sequence. A year later, however, the producers had not been able to find another buyer, so when Arkoff made them the same offer, they jumped at it. More about this film in the next chapter…

In 1970, AIP went the tried-and-true route once again, casting Vincent Price in a film supposedly based on the works of Poe, *Cry of the Banshee*. If that title is unfamiliar to Poe enthusiasts, it is because Poe never wrote such a story (or poem, for that matter). This did not prevent AIP from promoting the film with a verse supposedly written by Poe, which went:

'Who spurs the beast the corpse will ride?
 Who cries the cry that kills?
When Satan questioned, who replied?
Whenst blows this wind that chills?
Who walks amongst these empty graves
And seeks a place to lie?
T'is something God ne'er had planned,
A thing that ne'er had learned to die.'

This was the kind of spurious 'Poe' quotation that caused *Los Angeles Times* journalist John Mahoney to write: 'A phrase, a verse, is cribbed from Poe, tacked onto the main title and sprinkled into the ads. The tormented poet takes the rap again.'

*Cry of the Banshee* might be considered the third of a trilogy, featuring many of the cast and crew from *Witchfinder General* and *The Oblong Box*. Price starred again with Hillary Dwyer; Sally Geeson was back from *The Oblong Box*, as was Hessler; and John Coquillon, who had photographed the previous two films, returned to complete the trilogy.

The original screenplay was written by Tim Kelly, but Hessler was not keen on it and hired Christopher Wicking to do a rewrite. He wanted Wicking to change it even further, but AIP would not allow him to do so, probably for cost reasons. The story has echoes of *Witchfinder General*, but this time, the witches are real: In Elizabethan England, evil and powerful magistrate Lord Edward Whitman (Price) massacres nearly every member of a coven of witches, thereby becoming a target of their leader, Oona (Elisabeth Bergner). Oona calls up a supernatural entity, a 'banshee' (Patrick Mower) to kill off the lord's family one by one.

Somewhere during the course of the rewrites, any resemblance between this film's banshee and the actual being from Celtic folklore became very nearly coincidental. The Irish banshee is a sort of spirit whose haunting cry portends that someone will die. It has nothing to do with Satanism (and, in fact, neither does witchcraft), although in the film both the coven and the banshee are allied with Lucifer. As the banshee, Mower is more of a shape-shifter or 'werewolf' than he is any type of ghost or Celtic fairy.

And so, *Cry of the Banshee*, at its core, is a fraud. Although sold as a Poe movie, it has nothing to do with Poe; neither does it have anything to do with banshees. It is a fairly obvious attempt to cash in on the success of *Witchfinder General*, mixed in with a nod to the then-burgeoning neo-paganism of the 'youth culture.' What is interesting about the concept is that the witches are the 'good guys' and the so-called "Establishment' are the bad guys, a reversal of classic horror film tropes.

The three 'Poe' films produced in England – *Witchfinder General*, *The Oblong Box* and *Cry of the Banshee* – reflected the relaxed censorship of the

era. Spurred on to include more and more sex (the British cuts of all three films featured nudity) and gore (in keeping with the American market, which was still reeling from the gruesome impact of George A Romero's instant classic, *Night of the Living Dead*, 1968), they returned Grand Guignol to their Poe adaptations with a vengeance, so it was a natural progression that the company's next – and final – Poe picture would be placed against the backdrop of the Grand Guignol theatre itself.

Gordon Hessler was brought back one more time to direct a new adaptation of *Murders in the Rue Morgue* (1971), although it has very little to do with Poe's story. In fact, the film owes more to Gaston Leroux's *The Phantom of the Opera* and its various film versions than it does to Poe, even including the most recent Phantom, Herbert Lom, from Hammer's 1962 version of that tale. In an interview conducted for the American DVD release of the film, Hessler pointed out that he felt that most people knew the ending of Poe's story, so he thought that the story should be re-imagined and merely used as the jumping-off point for the narrative.

Written once again by Christopher Wicking, this time with the help of fantasy and sci-fi writer Henry Slesar, AIP's *Murders in the Rue Morgue* is set in Paris at the beginning of the 20th Century, where Cesar Charron (Jason Robards) runs the Rue Morgue Theatre, in which he directs and stars in the play *Murders in the Rue Morgue*, also starring his wife Madeleine (Christine

Kaufmann), who, offstage, is subject to terrible recurring nightmares. Inspector Vidocq (Adolfo Celi) is brought in to investigate a series of murders by acid at the theatre. The prime suspect would seem to be Cesar's former partner Rene Marot (Lom), but Marot had murdered Madeleine's mother (Lilli Palmer) and then killed himself. It couldn't possibly be Marot, then... could it?

Filmed this time in Toledo, Spain, *Murders in the Rue Morgue* features an exceptional cast, many of them new to the genre. Price had just segued from Poe into a new franchise, *The Abominable Dr Phibes* (1971) and *Dr Phibes Rises Again* (1972), so he was not available to appear in AIP's final Poe picture. Jason Robards was a highly distinguished American actor of stage and screen, best known on Broadway for his masterful portrayal of Jamie Tyrone in Eugene O'Neill's *Long Day's Journey Into Night* before making his film debut in *The Journey* (1959), gaining even more fame as a movie star. Eventually, he would win two consecutive Academy Awards for Best Supporting Actor for *All the President's Men* (1976) and *Julia* (1977).

Lom was another outstanding actor, born in Czechoslovakia, who had made his film debut in the Czech film *Woman Below the Cross* (1937) before moving to England where he spent most of the rest of his life making British films such as *The Ladykillers* (1955), *Mysterious Island* (1961) and becoming the long-suffering boss of Inspector Clouseau (Peter Sellers) in the *Pink Panther* comedies. Lom's role in *Murders in the Rue Morgue* was very much like his turn in Hammer's *Phantom*, and references to that film would seem to be intentional.

Christine Kaufmann was a young Austrian-born starlet who had already appeared in such international productions as *The Last Days of Pompeii* (1959), *Town without Pity* (1961) and *Taras Bulba* (1962). Despite those successes, her voice was dubbed in *Murders in the Rue Morgue* by another actress.

Adolfo Celi was best known for playing the villainous Emilio Largo in the James Bond film *Thunderball* (1965, in which his voice was dubbed by Robert Rietty), but was known in his native Italy as a versatile actor who had appeared in such films as *That Man from Rio* (1964), *Von Ryan's Express* and *The Agony and the Ecstasy* (both 1965). Maria Perschy (Genevre) was a ubiquitous Austrian-born actress who was popular in European genre films

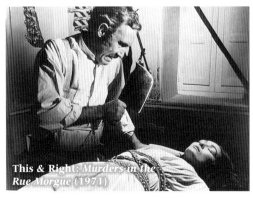

This & Right: *Murders in the Rue Morgue* (1971)

such as *Kiss, Kiss, Kill, Kill* (1966), *Five Golden Dragons* (1967) and *The Castle of Fu Manchu* (1969). Distinguished dwarf actor Michael Dunn had received an Oscar nomination for his role as narrator in *Ship of Fools* (1965) and was best known to American audiences for his continuing role as the villain Dr Loveless in the spy/western TV series *The Wild Wild West* (1965-1969).

Lilli Palmer was a veteran German-born actress who settled in Britain in the 1930s, making her film debut in *Crime Unlimited* (1935) before eventually moving on to such prestige productions as *Notorious Gentleman* (1945), *Body and Soul* (1947) and *But Not for Me* (1959). Unaccountably, most of her scenes in *Murders in the Rue Morgue* were left on the cutting-room floor.

British actor Peter Arne (Aubert) had been featured in such genre films as Val Guest's *The Men of Sherwood Forest* (1954) Ken Hughes' *Atomic Man* (1955) and Robert S Baker's and Monty Berman's *The Hellfire Club* (1961). He had also been featured in a supporting role in *The Oblong Box*. His next film after *Murders in the Rue Morgue* would be Sam Peckinpah's notorious *Straw Dogs* (1971).

Released almost exactly 130 years after Poe's story was first published, Hessler's *Murders in the Rue Morgue* is a fitting end to AIP's Poe series. Corman's Poe pictures always had stylish dream sequences, but *Murders* was the only one of AIP's series to be constructed entirely around dream sequences. Madeleine's nightmares are as creepy and perplexing to her as they are to the audience, and they're compellingly shot by cinematographer Manuel Berenguer (*Krakatoa: East of Java*, 1968) and elegantly staged by Hessler.

In keeping with the Grand Guignol theme, we're never quite sure if the gruesome events we are witnessing are part of the theatrical productions which are indeed, grandly grisly with decapitations, torture and acid thrown in faces; or are actual occurrences. It is, in a sense, the ultimate culmination of Corman's auteur theory concerning Poe Pictures: that they take place entirely in the country of the mind. It is no mistake that one of the key plot points in the film takes place on the stage, when Mrs Charron throws what she thinks is harmless liquid into Marot's face, but which is actually acid, to her absolute horror, Reality and fantasy merge, and we are left to wonder, which is which?

Robards felt that he was miscast in the film and told Hessler at one point that he would have liked to have played Lom's role, which was more interesting. Indeed, Robards flounders as Charron, and one wonders what Price would have made of such a character, who possesses light and darkness in nearly equal measures. The best performances by far come from Lom, basically playing the Phantom again (too bad *Phantom of the Rue Morgue* had already been used as a title), a character whose suffering has driven him to madness; and by Dunn, always a fascinating actor to watch, as a mysterious gentleman who has a connection to Marot that we don't understand until toward the end of the film.

It may be a Price-less Poe picture, but *Murders In the Rue Morgue* remains a compelling movie which could have been one of the very best in the series. Unfortunately, AIP tampered with it too much in post-production, removing nearly all of Lilli Palmer's scenes and making much of the film incomprehensible in the process. Although *Murders* has been partially reconstructed for DVD and Blu-ray, it is still somewhat incomplete. But what remains of screenwriter Christopher Wicking's and director Gordon Hessler's vision is one of the most dreamlike of all Poe Pictures. Sadly, it was not a box office success and the AIP Poe cycle came to an end not with a bang, but with a whimper.

After the failures of *Murders in the Rue Morgue* and *Dr Phibes Rises Again*, Heyward resigned from his post as head of AIP's London office and went back to Hollywood, where he ended up producing a TV game show called *Tic Tac Dough* and some cartoons for Hanna–Barbera Productions. The closest that he ever got to producing another horror film arrived when he became executive producer on the TV film *KISS Meets the Phantom of the Park* (1978).

AIP closed their London office and kept their future productions closer to home, for the most part. The mid to late seventies brought several major changes to the company and many difficult challenges in the brave new world of American film production, when big-budget blockbusters such as *The Exorcist* (1973), Steven Spielberg's *Jaws* (1975) and George Lucas' *Star Wars* (1977) all conspired to beat low-budget independent filmmakers at their own game.

# CHAPTER FIVE
# THE WORLDWIDE POE

*'A sombre yet beautiful and peaceful gloom here pervaded all things...'*

*The Island of the Fay*

**A**s we have seen, the works of Edgar Allan Poe had already been adapted many times in other lands besides his home country by 1960. Cinematic versions of *The Fall of the House of Usher* and *The Tell-Tale Heart* had been produced in France and Great Britain, respectively. World cinema truly came into its own however, during the postwar years of the late forties and early fifties, and international horror cinema later still.

Many of the greatest films of all time came from foreign lands. Japanese director Akira Kurosawa made two of them, *Rashomon* (1950) and *Seven Samurai* (1954), while Italian directors including Vittorio De Sica *(The Bicycle Thief*, 1948) and Federico Fellini *(La Strada*, 1954) and French directors such as François Truffaut *(The 400 Blows*, 1959) and Henri-Georges Clouzot *(Les Diaboliques*, 1955) became important players in world cinema. After the international success of *Les Diaboliques*, a Hitchcockian exercise in suspense, Georges Franju made one of the first out-and-out French horror films, the sublimely poetic *Les Yeux sans Visage (Eyes Without a Face*, 1959) while horror filmmakers in the United Kingdom found great worldwide success in the wake of Hammer's *The Curse of Frankenstein* and *Dracula* with imitations of Hammer's style in such films as *Blood of the Vampire* (1958) and *Jack the Ripper* (1959).

Perhaps because of the influence of Hammer, the cultural *zeitgeist* shifted around this time to conspire to bring about a worldwide renaissance of cinematic Poe adaptations. One year before Corman filmed *House of Usher*, Poe's stories were being filmed in an unlikely place: Argentina. A television series called *Obras Maestras del Terror (Masterworks of Terror)* debuted in that country in 1959, adapting stories not just by Poe, but by Gaston Leroux, Robert

Louis Stevenson, Guy de Maupassant, Eugene O'Neill and W W Jacobs, among others. It was the Poe adaptations that got all the attention, however: *The Facts in the Case of M Valdemar*, *The Cask of Amontillado* and *The Tell-Tale Heart* were all filmed, and Spanish actor Narciso Ibáñez Menta starred in all three.

Menta was, in some ways, the Spanish equivalent to Vincent Price. He specialised in films of the fantastic and had already explored Poe's macabre world in Argentinian television versions of *Berenice* and *Ligeia* (both 1959). A genuine student of Poe, he teamed up with director Enrique Carreras (no relation to the founder of Hammer films) to produce the Poe stories for *Obras Maestras del Terror*, and the result was so good that the Poe segments became the basis of an anthology film that was released in the US in 1965 as *Master of Horror*, excising, incredibly enough, the best sequence, *The Tell-Tale Heart*.

The film bears a marked resemblance to Corman's *Tales of Terror*, mainly because both *Valdemar* and *Amontillado* were adapted for both versions. Neither adaptation comes close to engaging the audience as much as Corman's, with the main attraction being the excellent performances of Menta in each. The black and white cinematography by Americo Hoss is also atmospheric and effective, but the direction is perfunctory, and in the English-language version, the dubbing is exceptionally poor. The stories also betray their television roots by relying far too much on close-ups and tight framing, although it does give the tales a certain claustrophobic flavour that may or may not have been intended.

The framing story is extremely weak: a maid (Mercedes Carreras, the director's wife), alone in an old house, is searching for a cat called Romeo. With no luck in finding him, and apparently with no work to do, she settles down to read a volume of Poe's short stories.

*Valdemar* is the first story presented, and it's reasonably faithful to its source, although the actor playing the title role (Osvaldo Pacheco) seems too young for the part and has none of the *gravitas* of Vincent Price in Corman's version. Menta acquits himself much more admirably as the mesmerist, Dr Eckstrom. The denouement seems rather rushed, and Valdemar rots to skeleton form with little dramatic effect.

*The Cask of Amontillado* is the second story, and it's somewhat more successful. Interestingly enough, it plays like the Corman version as written by Richard Matheson, with Menta (as the Montressor character, renamed John Samivet) again extremely effective, especially in the scene in which he walls up his duplicitous friend Maurice (Carlso Estrada). Again, as with Matheson's adaptation, the adulterous wife (Ines Moreno) is walled up as well, although she's already dead, drowned in a butt of wine a la the Duke of Clarence in Shakespeare's *Richard III*.

One wonders if Matheson saw this adaptation before he wrote his own; the resemblances seem far too blatant to be entirely coincidental. There is also, again as with Matheson's version, a fair amount of sexual suggestiveness, with Estrada's and Moreno's love scenes accompanied by a good deal of cleavage and heavy breathing.

Another Hammer imitation came about in 1960, courtesy of two brothers, Edward and Henry Lee Danziger. Native New Yorkers, they had operated a sound studio in Manhattan during the 1940s which had specialised in dubbing foreign films into English. Their first feature as producers was the American film *Jigsaw* (1949), starring Franchot Tone. In 1952, the brothers moved to the UK and began making television films at Shepperton Studios and Borehamwood, among other British facilities. They produced a TV series called *Adventure Theater*, which was broadcast on American television in 1956. That same year, they made a film called *Alias John Preston*, which starred a then-unknown actor named Christopher Lee.

The budgets for their films – designed as 'second features' – were extremely low, usually around £17,000. According to Brian Clemens, the screenwriter and producer who later became known for the hit series *The Avengers*, The Danzigers, as they came to be known, would shoot television episodes in no more than three days and feature films in eight to ten days. In 1956, the Danzigers founded the New Elstree Studios in Hertfordshire, where they converted a former World War II testing factory into a studio with six sound stages and a back lot.

It was at New Elstree that The Danzigers produced their Hammer-inspired version of Poe's *The Tell-Tale Heart* in 1960. As was the case with most of the

Laurence Payne in *TheTell-Tale Heart* (1963)

*Chapter Five – THE WORLDWIDE POE*

Hammer horrors, it was a period piece, but they couldn't afford Hammer's lavish Technicolor look, so the film was shot in black and white. Nevertheless, they obtained the services of some very high-quality technicians and actors.

Director Ernest Morris was a veteran of Danziger Productions Ltd; his first feature had been *The Betrayal* (1957), written by Brian Clemens and Eldon Howard. His most recent film for the Danzigers was *Three Crooked Men* (1959), also written by Clemens and Howard, and he was a successful television director as well, having helmed six episodes of the internationally successful series *William Tell* between 1958 and 1959.

The prolific writing team of Clemens and Howard also wrote *The Tell-Tale Heart*, adapting Poe's story into a tale of lust, betrayal and murder. Timid, meek Edgar Marsh flies into a jealous rage when he discovers that his lady friend (or at least he thinks she's his lady friend) is having an affair with his best friend, Carl. He murders Carl and conceals his corpse under the floorboards in his piano room. At nightfall, his conscience, and perhaps something else, induces him to hear strange sounds emanating from beneath the floor, and the rest of the script follows Poe's tale fairly closely.

Chosen to play Edgar Marsh was London-born actor/writer Laurence Payne, who had distinguished himself in television for such productions as *Ivor Novello* (1956) and *The Trollenberg Terror* (1956-1957), the latter of which was made into the Tempean Films feature *The Crawling Eye* (1958), in which he also appeared.

Adrienne Corri (Betty), born and raised in Scotland, was another television veteran who had appeared in *The Anatomist* (1956), an adaptation of the events surrounding the Burke and Hare case, starring Alastair Sim as Dr Knox, Diarmuid Kelly as Burke, and Hammer favourite Michael Ripper as Hare. Speaking of Hammer, Dermot Walsh (Carl) was married to actress Hazel Court, who had appeared in 1957 for Hammer in *The Curse of Frankenstein* and *The Man Who Could Cheat Death* (1959). He had previously worked for the Danzigers in *A Woman of Mystery* (1958), co-starring with his wife,

Cinematographer James Wilson's career stretched all the way back to the silent era; his first film was *The Constant Nymph* (1928), starring Ivor Novello and Mabel Poulton. Wilson had previously photographed *Satellite in the Sky* (1956), *Operation Murder* (1957) and several other B-films for the Danzigers.

According to Jonathan Rigby in his book *English Gothic*, the release of *The Tell-Tale Heart* was delayed until January 1963, when it was distributed on a double bill with the satirical film *Live Now, Pay Later*, starring Ian Hendry and June Ritchie. By that time, critics and audiences were used to Corman's Poe film, and, despite or because of its even lower budget, *The Tell-Tale Heart* received good notices from several critics. *The* Monthly Film Bulletin was especially kind: 'A modest but surprisingly effective little film, which contains much more genuine Poe atmosphere than many a more ambitious adaptation… The shoestring sets and lighting, in fact, contribute enormously towards achieving the correct oppressive aura of dank, seedy, gas lit Victoriana'.

When I interviewed Adrienne Corri for *Scarlet Street* Magazine #28, she remembered the film with fondness: 'Ernie Morris had been a cameraman, so that's why a lot of it is very interesting. It's shot very well… The film owed a lot to the way the actors interplayed and the way we discussed the scenes…'

Indeed, *The Tell-Tale Heart* is a little gem of both British and Poesque horror, with excellent performances by Payne, Corri and Walsh in what is essentially a three-hander. As is the usual case, the screenplay uses Poe's original tale as a springboard to the action: Edgar Marsh is a shy librarian who keeps a cache of erotica in his dingy little apartment on the Rue Morgue. He is also a voyeur, gazing longingly at Betty as she undresses in the flat across the street, never closing her drapes or turning out the lights first. His voyeuristic tendencies lead to his downfall when, on one particular night he is spying on Betty, Carl walks in and goes to bed with her. After Edgar beats Carl to death, he seems to go quite mad, hearing his heart beating no matter where he is, even when he has taken out the blood-dripping organ and buried it in the back garden.

*The Tell-Tale Heart* has some extremely gruesome moments for the time, and, had it been shot in colour, the censors may have trimmed several of the gorier scenes, especially the one in which Marsh removes his late friend's heart with his bare and bloodied hands. The sexual aspects are emphasised as well; the film was, after all, made in the same year as Michael Powell's *Peeping Tom* and Hitchcock's *Psycho*, both of which featured voyeurism as key plot points.

Payne is especially outstanding in the film, going from meek, mild librarian to brutal murderer to madman during the course of the story. Corri is also excellent as the rather cruel Betty, who uses Marsh to get to Carl. Walsh is also fine as the conflicted Carl, who doesn't want to betray his friend but is ultimately overcome by his desire for Betty.

The film has a circular ending, as does the Ealing classic *Dead of Night:* the proceedings we have just witnessed have been Edgar's dream, but now the 'dream' seems to be starting all over again and this is profoundly unsettling. In fact, the mood of a fever dream has been exquisitely maintained from start to finish, making *The Tell-Tale Heart* into a memorable, haunting experience.

Payne and Corri would be reunited years later in Hammer's *Vampire Circus* (1972), but their first onscreen appearance together remains their most unforgettable.

The first European film to be inspired by Corman's particular brand of Poe was *Horror* (1963), a neglected little Spanish-Italian item from director Alberto de Martino and producer Alberto Aguliera. Written by Gianni Gramaldi and Bruno Corbucci (with Spanish sources crediting Natividad Zaro as co-writer), Italian promotional material claimed it was based on a Poe story, but the finished film bears only a slight resemblance to three of Poe's tales, 'The Fall of the House of Usher,' 'A Tale of the Ragged Mountains' and 'Some Words with a Mummy'.

Drawing its real inspiration more from Corman than from Poe directly, or from other Italian gothic horrors such as *Black Sunday*, *Horror* (US: *The*

*Blancheville Monster*) is atmospherically shot by cinematographer Alejandro Ulloa at the Monastery of Santa Maria la Real de Valdeiglesias in Madrid and at Cinecitta Studios in Rome. The plot is routine gothic: The lovely young heiress (Ombretta Colli) of a somewhat depraved aristocratic family returns to her family home, where it becomes clear that she may fall victim to a family curse in which she will be sacrificed on her twenty-first birthday.

The leading man is Gerard Tichy, a German–born actor who mainly worked in Spanish films such as *Face of Terror* (1962). In the original version of *Horror*, Tichy portrayed Roderick Blackford, but in the English-language dub (which is quite poor), the location is transferred from Scotland to Brittany, and so the decadent aristocratic Blackford family became de Blancheville. One assumes that Roderick's given name came from Roderick Usher, and his sister Emily (Emillie in the English dub) is obviously based on Madeline Usher, meaning that, at some point in the narrative, she will be buried alive. Italian actress Colli was a veteran of such peplum films as *Gladiator of Rome* (1962).

One of the most interesting cast members in *Horror* is Helga Line as Miss Eleonore, the housekeeper. Line was a German–born actress who, like Tichy, specialised in Spanish films, and *Horror* was the first of many genre features for the beautiful and talented actress. Her next would be *Nightmare Castle* (1965), in which she co-starred opposite Barbara Steele.

Iran Eory (Alice) was born in Tehran and worked mainly in European films. She features in one of the most Poesque scenes in *Horror*, eloquently described by author Jonathan Rigby in his book *Euro Gothic: Classics of Continental Horror Cinema:* '… De Martino faithfully conforms to the Corman template with a masterfully confected scene in which Emily's college friend, Alice, is disturbed in her bed by distant bellows of agony. Taking up the regulation candelabrum, she ventures out and heads upstairs as midnight strikes. When she throws open a steel door in the tower room, De Martino's camera rattles in for a jarring reveal of the sinister housekeeper, hypodermic in hand, and a deformed nobleman who lurches into frog-faced close-up right on cue.'

De Martino was a journeyman director of such fare as *The Invincible Gladiator* (1961) and *Perseus against the Monsters* (1962), who rarely ventured into the realm of gothic horror. With *Horror*, however, he shows a genuine flair for the material, despite the rather perfunctory script by Grimaldi, Corbucci (who later became known for European westerns such as *The Great Silence* (1968) and Zaro (who may not have actually contributed to the script, but whose name is on the Spanish version because of its Spanish co-production status).

From the first scene, we see all the elements of a classic Poe picture, minus Corman's swirling colours: a monochrome forest lashed by rain, thunder and lightning, all accompanied by a pounding score by Carlo Franci. The atmosphere is maintained throughout, but aside from that and the score, *Horror/The Blancheville Monster* has little to offer. The pacing is lugubrious, the acting merely competent and, in the English language version, the dubbing is atrocious. As the film has been in public domain for some time, it is available in prints of widely varying quality. One notable aspect is the mask that features in the plot; it was sculpted by De Martino's father, Roberto Curti. Otherwise, De Martino himself, in an interview in later years, called *Horror* 'a little film of no importance.' It remains important in one way however: it was the first of many European films to have been inspired by the Corman Poe series.

The next one arrived the following year. Antonio Margheriti's *Castle of Blood* came with several pedigrees. In this case, the story, again written by Giannni Grimaldi and Bruno Corbucci, was not derived from anything written by Poe, instead featuring Poe as a character in an original story. The original title was *Danza Macabre*, which was highly appropriate. The plot involves a journalist who wagers that he can spend one night, which happens to be the eve of All Saint's Day, in a supposedly haunted castle. While he is there, he witnesses eerie and often gruesome events from the castle's grim past that seemingly come to life before him. And, not incidentally, he falls in love with a ghost/vampire of extraordinary beauty.

It is an intriguing and evocative tale, and it was originally slated to be directed by Bruno Corbucci's older brother Sergio, who was later to be known for helming the ground-breaking spaghetti western *Django* (1966). Due to a scheduling conflict, Sergio Corbucci could not direct the film, and brought in his friend Antonio Margheriti to helm it.

Margheriti often used the anglicized pseudonym 'Anthony Dawson' when directing genre films. As was the case with Corman, Margheriti had studied engineering before he entered the Centro Sperimentale di Cinematografia film school. He began working in Italian films at age 26 in various capacities such as editor, screenwriter and assistant director. His first film as director was *Assignment Outer Space* (1960), upon which he also did some of the special effects model work. He also directed *Battle of the Worlds* (1961), starring Claude Rains, and *Horror Castle* aka *The Virgin of Nuremberg* (1963), starring Rossanna Podestà, Georges Rivière and Christopher Lee.

Rivière, a French-born actor who appeared in all manner of international films, beginning with *El Vampiro Negro* (1953), an Argentinian reworking of Fritz Lang's *M* (1931), and even popping up in a featured role in *The Longest Day* (1962), returned for Margheriti from *Horror Castle* to co-star with Barbara Steele. Steele was by now the undisputed queen of European horror, having starred not only in Bava's *Black Sunday*, but in Riccardo Freda's *The Horrible Dr Hichcock* (1962) and *The Ghost* (1963).

In *Castle of Blood*, Riviere was cast as Alan Foster, the journalist, while Steele played the role of Elizabeth Blackwood, who dwells in the castle long after she has died. Also in the cast was Steele's co-star from *Black Sunday*, Arturu Dominici, as Dr Carmus. Other cast members included Norwegian actress Margrete Robsahm as Julia, who had appeared in Roger Corman's *The Young Racers* in 1963 and Silvano Tranquilli as Edgar Allan Poe, who appears at the beginning of the film relating the climax of his story 'Berenice,' and

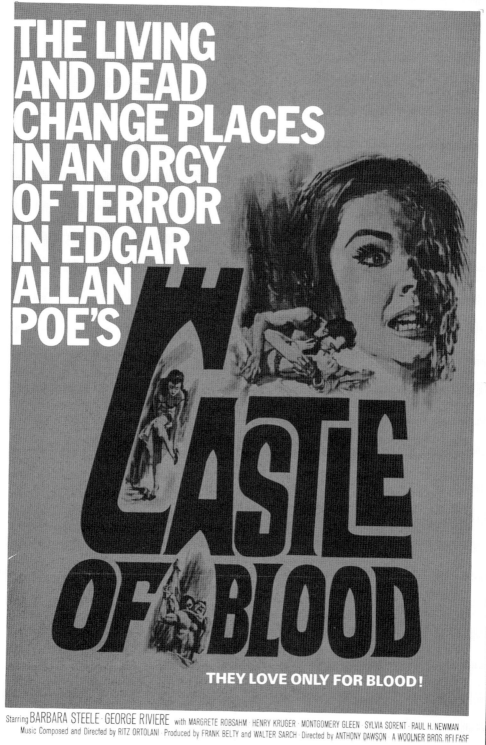

THE LIVING AND DEAD CHANGE PLACES IN AN ORGY OF TERROR IN EDGAR ALLAN POE'S

CASTLE OF BLOOD

THEY LOVE ONLY FOR BLOOD!

Starring BARBARA STEELE · GEORGE RIVIERE with MARGRETE ROBSAHM · HENRY KRUGER · MONTGOMERY GLEEN · SYLVIA SORENT · RAUL H. NEWMAN
Music Composed and Directed by RITZ ORTOLANI · Produced by FRANK BELTY and WALTER SARCH · Directed by ANTHONY DAWSON · A WOOLNER BROS. RELEASE

*Chapter Five – THE WORLDWIDE POE*

pops up again at the end when Lord Thomas Blackwood (Umberto Raho) travels to the castle to collect his wager.

The plot for *Castle of Blood* originated with Sergio Corbucci. He had just directed a comedy film called *The Monk of Monza* (1963) when the film's producer, Giovanni Addessi, asked him to make a film that would reuse *Monk's* medieval sets. Corbucci asked his brother Bruno to co-write the screenplay with Grimaldi. The film's credits indicate that it is based on a short story by Poe, but no such story exists.

According to assistant director Ruggero Deodato, it was difficult to persuade Steele to return to horror. She had just appeared in Federico Fellini's *8 ½* (1963) and had higher dramatic aspirations than continuing to do horror films. Having appealed to her better nature, and with the advantage of an excellent script, Deodato convinced Steele to star in the film.

When Corbucci found a conflict in his schedule, he asked Margheriti to direct *Danza Macabra*, which had a tight shooting schedule of only two weeks. Margheriti got around this problem by shooting the film using the techniques of television productions, setting up four cameras at once to capture the action. Nevertheless, he had to bring in Corbucci to finish the film on time, asking him to direct the scene in which Herbert (Giovanni Cinfriglia) murders Elisabeth. After a total shooting schedule of fifteen days, principal photography was completed on *Danza Macabra/Castle of Blood*.

Margheriti's film is a marked improvement over his own *The Virgin of Nuremberg*. Jonathan Rigby wrote, 'Though not stinting on the expected crepuscular atmosphere, the result pushed the fusion of horror and eroticism to new extremes.' Indeed, atmosphere, horror and eroticism pretty much sum up the whole of *Castle of Blood's* parts: the entire film takes place at night in a gloomy castle, there are several horrific sequences and there are subplots that hint at necrophilia and lesbianism; pretty heady stuff for a film released in 1964.

However, the English language version omits some scenes. The most complete version is the French, titled *Danse Macabre*, which was released in that country on 14 April 1965. The Gallic edition includes a longer coach ride on the way to the castle, during which Foster interviews Poe about his metaphysical theories of life and death. It is here that Poe gives us one of his more famous real-life quotes: 'The death of a beautiful woman is, unquestionably, the most poetical topic in the world.' There is also a longer murder sequence involving Julia, Elisabeth and Elisabeth's lover (Giovanni Cianfriglia), which is more explicit in its lesbian overtones than in the English-dubbed version. And finally, the scene in which Foster sees a ghostly re-enactment of newlyweds staying the night in the castle concludes with a sequence in which the bride (Sylvia Sorrente) is murdered in the nude.

Even with these cuts, however, *Castle of Blood* remains one of the most accomplished European gothic horror films of the sixties. Steele is darkly luminous, an otherworldly presence both of the flesh and of the spirit. After making love with her, Foster rests his head on her breast, yet fails to detect any heartbeat. She tells him, very matter-of-factly, 'My heart isn't beating, Alan. It hasn't beaten for ten years. I'm dead, Alan. Dead.' It is a chilling moment, almost immediately interrupted by the first of several murders.

As Rigby wrote, 'As the house's tenants replay their violent deaths, Margheriti ratchets up the already unhealthy erotic atmosphere considerably, moving from implied cunnilingus in the stables to three re-enacted sex murders in as many minutes – all of them focused on Elisabeth's four-poster bed, including a taboo-breaking lesbian interlude for Steele and the glacially blonde Margarete Robsahm.' Italian horror filmmakers, unconstrained by the censorship in English-speaking countries, broke taboos again and again in the sixties, and *Castle of Blood* was one of two Italian films in the same year (the other being Mario Bava's *Black Sabbath)* to include a lesbian subplot, something that would become common in horror films of the seventies after the collapse of censorship throughout most of the world.

At the film's climax, Poe travels with Lord Blackwood back to the castle to collect his wager. They discover that Foster is dead, impaled on the iron fence. Blackwood collects his wager anyway, callously reaching into Foster's pocket to relieve him of his cash. As Poe returns to the coach, he says to no one in particular, 'When I finally write this story, people will say… it's unbelievable.'

In the early to mid-sixties, Italy was the 'in' place to be, inspired to some extent by critically-acclaimed international hits such as Fellini's *La Dolce Vita* (1960) and *8 ½*, Vittorio De Sica's *Yesterday, Today and Tomorrow* (1963) and many more hedonistically-inclined films set in or near Rome, the Eternal City. So-called 'Swinging London' had not yet arrived, so Rome was the hot destination for the jet set. In part because of this Roman renaissance, Italian gothic horror flourished throughout the decade, with its combination of elegance, terror and sex, and *Castle of Blood* helped to pave the way.

The next European film to invoke Poe, at least in the credits, was another Barbara Steele vehicle called *Terror-Creatures from the Grave* (1965), a co-production between Italy and the United States. Directed by Domenico Massimo Pupillo, the film has little of the style or skill of Margheriti's work, but it does have its moments, even if it is another 'faux' Poe film, supposedly based on one of the author's works. A quick overview of the Master's oeuvre however, will reveal that no such story or poem exists.

The somewhat standard plot, cooked up by screenwriters Roberto Natale and Romano Migliorini, involves the arrival of attorney Albert Kovac (Walter Brandi) at a castle (of course) to settle the estate of the recently departed owner. Cleo Hauff (Steele), the owner's widow, and her stepdaughter Corinne (Mirella Maravidi), reveal that the late lord of the manor had the power to summon ancient 'plague spreaders' from the dead; evil victims of the black plague who deliberately spread the disease. The spirit of the castle's owner also supposedly haunts the place, and soon those staying in the ancient edifice begin to succumb to various types of gruesome deaths. The plague motif is somewhat unusual and includes an 'exhibit' of the mummified hands of the plague spreaders on display at the castle, apparently for the benefit of morbid curiosity-seekers.

Obviously, Poe never wrote anything resembling this plot, although there are elements of 'The Fall of the House of Usher,' but only in the generic strand of gothic horror with which the film concerns itself. The film came about because of American producer Ralph Zucker, a former child actor who had moved to Italy in 1958 to edit and produce films. It took him awhile to get anything produced; *Terror-Creatures from the Grave* was, in fact, his first feature film in any capacity, and for years fans thought he had directed it as well, as he receives credit for such on the film. An interview by Lucas Balbo in the book *Italian Gothic Horror Films, 1957-1969* by Robert Curti that was published years later set the record straight however: Massimo revealed that he had directed the film but was unhappy with it, and had let Zucker take the credit. In fact, Zucker did direct two scenes for the American version, which, unlike the case with most Italian horror films of the period, was actually more gruesome than the original cut. In the Italian and French editions, a man in a wheelchair (Ennio Balbo) hangs himself, but in the American version, he uses his wheelchair to run himself onto a sword, disembowelling himself in gruesome, graphic close-up. That scene was directed by Zucker, as was the pre-credit prologue in which a man is kicked to death by a horse.

An Italian-American co-production, *Terror-Creatures From the Grave* was not released in the US until 1967, on a double bill with another film directed by Pupillo, *Bloody Pit of Horror*, which had also been produced in 1965. *Terror-Creatures* was released in Italy on 23 June 1965 as *5 Tombe per un Medium* (*5 Graves for the Medium*), and the European cut included a nude scene involving Maravidi as well as several dialogue scenes that did not make the American cut.

In either version, the film is indifferent, although Steele, who apparently didn't get along well with Pupillo for the first few days (until he gave her a talking-to), gives her usual professional performance. She has one love scene which is a standout: in a perverse moment of passion, she bites her own arm rather than that of her partner's.

Brandi (billed here as Walter Brandt) was a veteran of such Italian horror films as *The Vampire and the Ballerina* and *The Playgirls and the Vampire* (both 1960) and was often a rather wooden actor. His performance in *Terror-Creatures* is no exception to that rule, and he brings little to the role of the 'hero,' who discovers that pure water will destroy the living dead.

Pupillo's film is beautifully shot in monochrome by Carlo Di Palma, who would later photograph Michelangelo Antonioni's *Blow-Up* (1966). The location shooting near Castel Fusano outside of Rome is especially evocative and impressive.

The film is sluggishly paced, and it isn't until the last twenty minutes or so that it picks up speed, as Rigby wrote in *Euro Gothic*: '…The severed hands start flexing, the bottled organs begin to pulse, and the victims acquire nasty plague sores prior to slumping dead beside globes, harps and grandfather clocks. It's a barnstorming climax, but perhaps not enough to justify the build-up.'

The film received few reviews in British or American trade papers at the time, although one in a 1968 edition of the prestigious *Monthly Film Bulletin* was decidedly mixed: '… Fortunately, in what is otherwise a rather routine and stilted exercise in horror, more grisly fare is provided in the form of a collection of mummified hands on permanent exhibition at the sinister villa, in which the ever-dependable Barbara Steele seems comfortably at home.'

While *Terror-Creatures from the Grave* is no great shakes as a motion picture, it does have moody and unsettling moments. The opening credits proclaim, 'Inspired by Edgar Allan Poe.' While Poe may have been surprised and a bit bemused to have seen his name in the credits, I don't think he would have been too ashamed.

The next Euro-Poe was from West Germany and went by many titles. Originally called *The Snakepit and the Pendulum* (1967), it was known in the UK as *The Blood Demon* and in the US as the lurid, unappetizing *The Torture Chamber of Dr Sadism*. A very, very loose adaptation of 'The Pit and the Pendulum,' the film was directed by Harald Reinl, known for Edgar Wallace mysteries such as *Face of the Frog* (1959) and *The Strangler of Blackmoor Castle* (1963), the latter starring Karin Dor, who would also co-star in *The Snakepit and the Pendulum*.

Dor was a beautiful red-haired actress who made a great impression on the Austrian-born Reinl: he had become her first husband in 1954. Prior to *Pendulum*, Dor had gone international with a role in Don Sharp's *The Face of Fu Manchu* (1965), starring Christopher Lee in the title role. Her big moment in the sun was as a Bond girl in the fifth 007 movie, *You Only Live Twice* (1967), opposite Sean Connery.

In *Pendulum*, Dor co-starred with former Tarzan Lex Barker, a stolid actor whose talent didn't quite match his aspirations. He first played Edgar Rice Burroughs' character in *Tarzan's Magic Fountain* (1949) after Johnny Weissmuller left the series. He played the role five times before moving onto other roles, ultimately travelling to Europe in 1957 to find more challenging work, with decidedly mixed results. He ended up slaving away in European potboilers such as *Kingdom of the Silver Lion* (1965) and *Die Slowly, You'll Enjoy It More* (1967) before being offered the leading role in *The Snakepit and the Pendulum* as heroic Roger Mont Elise opposite none other than Christopher Lee as villainous Count Regula.

The screenplay by Manfred R Kohler tells the tale of the evil Regula (the name sounds like the accent a New Yorker might use to order coffee). In the opening, we see him being drawn and quartered for his sorcerous crimes, although we're spared the gory details thanks to judicious editing. Thirty-five years later, he is brought back from the dead thanks to the blood of several virgins, assisted by his rather strange, green-blooded manservant Anatol (Carl Lange). Regula intends to exact revenge on Dor and Barker because their parents were involved in his execution. His vengeance includes

a lavish torture chamber that comes complete with the titular pendulum and snakepit.

In *Euro Gothic*, Rigby wrote of the film: '… A curiously charming film, owing more to Bava's *La Maschera del Demonio* and Fisher's *Dracula Prince of Darkness* than its supposed source in Edgar Allan Poe.' Indeed, there are visual references to both films, beginning with the opening scene in which a mask is nailed to Regula's face before he is drawn and quartered. His resurrection recalls that of Lee's own in *Dracula Prince of Darkness*, except for the fact that Anatol (a servant who recalls Philip Latham's Klove in Fisher's film) slashes his own wrist and drips his green blood not onto Regula's remains, but onto the lid of his glass coffin.

The plot of the film is more or less routine gothic; when it was released to American home video in the 1980s, it was retitled *Castle of the Living Dead*, a pretty generic title. Reinl's visuals, however, are outstanding, including an eerie coach ride to the castle through a forest full of hanging bodies, arms and legs protruding out of twisted, gnarled trees and other grandly gothic delights, all encased in swirling, bluish mist. When they arrive at the castle and are introduced to the torture chamber, art directors Gabriel Pellon and Rold Zehetbauer allow their imaginations to run riot, complete with human skulls encased in the walls, frescoes based on the 'Hell panel' by Hieronymus Bosch, and a pendulum that threatens to cut Barker's character in half *lengthwise*.

The scene with the pendulum is quite suspenseful and obviously inspired by Corman's version, even including cutting back and forth to the frescoes on the wall as Corman did. Most of the visuals, however, are quite original, with standout cinematography by Ernst W Kalinke and Dieter Liphardt. The dreamlike imagery includes lots of crawling things: spiders, snakes, scorpions and lizards, a virtual menagerie of unpleasant creatures in which Regula obviously delights.

Lee doesn't have a great deal to do in the film, although he looks great in it, with pasty, greenish-faced makeup and a dour, glaring expression throughout. Barker is a fairly wooden hero and Dor is the requisite beautiful heroine given little to do, but succeeding in looking wonderful doing it. The scene-stealer here is Lange, a German veteran of such films as *Mistress of the World* (1960) and *The Last Tomahawk* (1965), obviously relishing the daft villainy of the Renfield-like Anatol.

Under any title, *The Snakepit and the Pendulum* is a film that succeeds almost entirely on the strength of its imagery. The pendulum scene, while not as terrifying as Corman's, is more than sufficient to justify the original title and the nightmarish, colourful imagery will stay with the viewer long after the plot has been forgotten.

The next Poe-related film came from England, and from American-born producers Milton Subotsky and Max Rosenberg, whose Amicus Productions had recently scored a hit with the portmanteau movie *Dr Terror's House of Horrors* (1964), starring Peter Cushing and Christopher Lee. Helmed by cameraman turned director Freddie Francis, *Dr Terror* was the first of many anthology films that Amicus would produce.

The second was *Torture Garden* (1967), based on stories by American author Robert Bloch, who had started out as a contributing writer to H P Lovecraft's Cthulhu Mythos at *Weird Tales* magazine in the 1930s, later shooting to fame as the author of *Psycho* (1959), which was turned into one of the most famous films of all time by Alfred Hitchcock in the following year. *Torture Garden* had originally been planned to reunite Cushing and Lee, but as the film was being financed by Columbia, the Hollywood distributor asked for two American names to head the cast. The two actors chosen were Hollywood veteran Burgess Meredith, known at the time for playing The Penguin on TV's *Batman* and for gracing many an episode of *The Twilight Zone* with his presence. He was cast as Dr Diablo, a role originally intended for Cushing, who ended up being cast in one of the story segments instead.

The other American was none other than Jack Palance, Oscar-nominated for his roles in *Sudden Fear* (1952) and the classic western *Shane* (1953). The film was comprised of four Bloch tales, 'Enoch,' 'Terror Over Hollywood,' Mr Steinway,' and, the story relevant to this study, 'The Man Who Collected Poe,' which co-stars Palance as an obsessive collector of Poe memorabilia and Cushing as a fellow collector who has gone one step further and has collected Poe himself, who he keeps in his basement, where the author madly scribbles new tales for eternity.

'The Man Who Collected Poe' is typical Bloch, full of black humour and gleeful references to Poe tales, including an ending that is cribbed, more or less, from 'The Fall of the House of Usher.' The segment is generally considered to be the best tale in *Torture Garden*, which Francis, who again directed, acknowledged in his autobiography, *The Straight Story: From Moby Dick to Glory* (Scarecrow Press, 2013): 'The last story (was) about an obsessive Edgar Allan Poe collector who kills to acquire a collection of memorabilia. This last one was the best story, and because it was Poe and featured Peter and Palance, it allowed me a great deal of scope and flexibility. Peter and Jack delivered their characters as I knew they would, while I let my imagination run riot when it came to setups and camera angles.'

'The Man Who Collected Poe' is a fitting final story in *Torture Garden*, with Hammer horror veteran Cushing and Hollywood heavy Palance having a great deal of fun together, resisting the urge to go over the top into campiness. Cushing is the stronger actor here, especially in the scene in which Palance gets him drunk so that he will be more likely to show him the most priceless part of his Poe collection, Poe himself.

Palance, a 'Method' actor, treads dangerously close to caricature as the effete, highly mannered Poe collector. Nevertheless, he was chosen for the part because he was extremely good at playing characters that had psychotic tendencies, and he puts that across very well indeed when he relishes such lines as, 'Collecting can be a kind of mania.'

The story ends with an inferno, which finally releases Poe from his torment, letting the manic collector take his place in the dark basement. Poe, played by Geoffrey Wallace, is a haunting figure, draped in cobwebs, sitting at his desk, where he is forced to write new *Tales of Mystery and Imagination* forever and ever.

Although *Torture Garden* was released in the UK in November, 1967, it was held up until July 1968 for its US bow, the better to tie it in with the so-called 'drive-in season.' *Torture Garden*, however, was a bit too subtle and cerebral for the drive-in market, and it did not repeat the success of *Dr Terror's House of Horrors*. Reviews were mostly positive though, with The Times calling it 'A very superior horror film,' but it is likely that a film called *Torture Garden* didn't deliver the kind of sex and blood that its title would suggest at a time when censorship was crumbling all over the world, and was perhaps too 'timid' for 1968 audiences. Nevertheless, it remains a classic of the horror anthology format, and its superior performances and atmospheric visuals linger in the memory.

In 1968, American International Pictures acquired an Italian-French anthology film called *Histoires Extraordinaires*, which featured three Poe stories, each one helmed by a different, internationally-known European director. Roger Vadim (*And God Created Woman*, 1957) directed 'Metzengerstein,' starring siblings Jane and Peter Fonda; Louise Malle helmed 'William Wilson,' with Alain Delon and Brigitte Bardot; and Federico Fellini

(*La Dolce Vita, 1960*) took over the reins for 'Toby Dammit' based on Poe's 'Never Bet the Devil Your Head,' which starred Terence Stamp.

For American distribution, AIP retitled the film *Spirits of the Dead*, adding a voice-over (as they had done with *Witchfinder General/The Conqueror Worm*) by Vincent Price to ostensibly tie it into their Poe series. Originally, Sam Arkoff and James Nicholson had offered the producers $200,000 for the rights, but the producers had turned them down because Arkoff, not a fan of the 'artsy-fartsy,' as you may recall, had wanted to cut some footage from Fellini's sequence. With no other offers coming in after a year, the producers ultimately gave in and accepted AIP's offer.

*Spirits of the Dead* certainly arrived with a classy pedigree. Producer Raymond Eger had asked each director to choose and supervise a story based on a work by Poe. Each story, therefore, was a personal short film for the directors, who wrote their own segments as well. 'Metzengerstein' featured Vadim's then-wife Jane Fonda who falls in love with a cousin (Peter Fonda) who rejects her because of her profligate lifestyle. With Hell having no fury like a woman scorned, she sets his stables ablaze in revenge, and the young man is burned to death trying to save his favourite horse. The horse escapes the inferno and, in some unexplained supernatural fashion, carries the deceased man's soul within its body.

As was usually the case with Vadim, 'Metzengerstein' is saturated with sex. He adds a touch of incestuous perversity by casting real-life brother and sister as would-be lovers in the only instance of the siblings appearing on film together. The segment is given a lush look by cinematographer Claude Renoir, who had also photographed Vadim's adaptation of J Sheridan Le

Fanu's 'Carmilla,' which was titled *Blood and Roses* (1960) when it was picked up by Paramount Pictures. Jean Prodomides' musical score is also highly evocative and there is a considerable amount of atmosphere thanks to the fact that it was filmed in and around a genuine European castle, yet the tale never quite achieves what the French would call a frisson and it remains an intriguing exercise in unease, more style than substance.

Next up is Louis Malle's adaptation of 'William Wilson,' surprisingly dull considering it's by the director of *The Thief of Paris* (1967). Despite a large helping of nudity and a fine performance by Alain Delon *(Is Paris Burning*, 1966), Poe's story of a demonic *doppelganger* is poorly served by the director. Delon is excellent in both roles, as the tormented William Wilson and his evil double, but his performance is the only thing about the segment that is really worth watching. Brigitte Bardot is her usual sensuous self, but her screen time is limited, and the tale plods toward its inevitable and very telegraphed climax.

The most provocative of the three tales by far is Fellini's bizarre 'Toby Dammit' loosely based on Poe's 'Never Bet the Devil Your Head.' Terence Stamp dominates the proceedings as a down-on-his-luck Shakespearean actor who agrees to take a role in a film being produced in Rome. Flamboyantly alcoholic, he begins to have visions of a little girl (Marina Yaru) who may be the devil, and her ball (which may be Stamp's head).

Superbly photographed by Giuseppe Rotunno (Luchino Visconti's *The Leopard*, 1963) and scored by the masterful Nino Rota (Fellini's *La Dolce Vita*, and who later became known for his iconic themes for Francis Ford Coppola's *The Godfather*, 1972), Fellini's predictably surreal interpretation of Poe is the only one of the three tales that can still stand on its own today. In the 4 September 1969 edition of *The New York Times*, Vincent Canby panned the Vadim and Malle segments: 'The Vadim is over-decorated and shrill as a drag ball… and the Malle…is simply tedious.'; but praised Fellini's: 'Toby Dammit' is a short movie but a major one… I would never have thought that Fellini and Poe had much in common, but the Italian director has assimilated his source material in such a way that it has become a kind of postscript to *La Dolce Vita*, the picture of an exhausted, once beautiful person handing his soul over to the devil.'

As a foreign-made, *ersatz* addition to their Poe series, *Spirits of the Dead* was very successful for AIP. The nudity, something of a rarity for horror films of the period undoubtedly contributed heavily to the box office and it helped to keep both Poe and horror anthologies fresh in the collective mind of the audience, despite the fact that there is relatively little horror in it. Sex was all the rage at the time, and there was more – much more – to come.

A mere six years after his *Castle of Blood*, Antonio Margheriti directed his own remake of it, this time entitled *Nella Streta Morsa del Ragno* (US: *Web of the Spider*, 1971). Although advertised as being based on Poe's story 'Night of the Living Dead,' there was, of course no such story. In fact, Margheriti used the original screenplay by Bruno Corbucci and Giovanni Gramaldi and simply filmed it in colour. It is virtually a shot for shot remake of the original, and the addition of colour is not an improvement.

The remake came about because of the disappointing box office of *Castle of Blood*. *Web of the Spider's* producer Giovanni Addessi (who also co-produced the original film) felt that the addition of colour to an already intriguing story would guarantee commercial success. The cast this time around was headed by American actor Anthony Franciosa as Alan Foster. Known mainly for his television appearances on such American series as *The Name of the Game* (1968-1970), Franciosa was a handsome and charming actor, but of limited range. Replacing Barbara Steele was a tall order, but beautiful French actress Michele Mercier (Mario Bava's *Black Sabbath*, 1963) gave it the old school try. And cast as Edgar Allan Poe was none other than ubiquitous German actor Klaus Kinski, whose many appearances in 'spaghetti' westerns such as Sergio Leone's *For A Few Dollars More* (1964) were exceeded in quantity only by his numerous roles in horror films, such as Jess Franco's recent production of *Count Dracula* (1970), which starred Christopher Lee in the title role.

The only real difference between Margheriti's two versions (aside from the colour) arrives at the opening of *Web of the Spider*, which features Kinski's Poe carrying a torch through some catacombs to confirm the truth of a ghost story. Other than that, the remake comes across as a slavish attempt by Margheriti to imitate his own work. As Rigby put it in *Euro Gothic:* 'Foster has become an American, the wager has been reduced to a mere ten pounds (Foster can't afford anything more), the phantom bodybuilder is no longer shirtless, and Franciosa goes more extravagantly mad in the closing stages than Riviere did... The TV movie colour and Franciosa's TV movie face drain interest very rapidly, and all in all it's hard not to concur with Margheriti's contention that "it was stupid to remake it."'

*Web of the Spider* was released in Italy on 28 August 1971, distributed by Panta Cinematografica. The film didn't exactly set the world on fire, and, as Margheriti commented in an interview by Peter Blumenstock in *Video Watchdog #28*, Addessi 'spent a lot of money for nothing... because the colour photography destroyed everything: the atmosphere, the tension'.

The next European Poe film ratcheted up the sex angle to eleven. The giallo is a specifically Italian sub-genre of the horror film; the term arose from crime novels that were given lurid yellow covers. In film, a giallo is a horror movie that has elements of mystery, crime and slasher films. They frequently feature a fair amount of sex and nudity as well. The first giallo film is considered to be Luchino Visconti's *Obsessione* (1943), which was based on James M Cain's *The Postman Always Rings Twice*. As a genre, giallo didn't come into its own until the 1960s, when Mario Bava directed *The Girl Who Knew Too Much* (US: *The Evil Eye*, 1963), which, although filmed in black and white and lacking graphic violence and sex, established the template that nearly all giallo films would follow: someone witnesses a murder, reports it to disbelieving police and is left to his or her own devices to track down and

identify the killer. Bava's next giallo, *Blood and Black Lace* (1964), was shot in lurid colours and went much further in its violence and sexuality.

By 1972, the giallo had become such a well-established Italian cinematic tradition that screenwriters Adriano Boizoni, Ernest Gastaldi and Sauro Scavolini transformed Poe's 'The Black Cat' into one, with the exotic title of *Your Vice is a Locked Room and Only I Have the Key*. It was director Sergio Martino's fourth giallo, and the title was a reference to his first, *The Strange Vice of Mrs Wardh* (1971), in which the murderer writes the phrase as a note to his victim.

The plot of *Your Vice is a Locked Room and Only I Have the Key* is as over the top as its title: Oliviero (Luigi Pistillo) is a degenerate writer who owns an estate near Verona, where he throws orgies, much to the consternation of his wife Irina (Anita Strindberg), whom he humiliates in front of his guests. When a young woman is murdered, the authorities suspect Oliviero; when his beautiful niece Floriana (Edwige Fenech) stops in to visit, the action heats up in more ways than one. More women are killed and Oliviero fantasises about harming his wife. Meanwhile, there are two observers of the events; a mysterious white-haired stranger and Oliviero's black cat, Satan.

Fenech receives top billing in the film, although she doesn't appear until 32 minutes in. The French-born actress had won several beauty contests as a teenager before making her film debut in *All Mad about Him* (1967). Her obvious talent and smouldering looks led to her being cast in such films as *Sexy Susan Sins Again* (1968), and she soon became a favourite of director Martino, who cast her in *Blade of the Ripper* (1971) and *All the Colours of the Dark* (1972), as well as some sex comedies. Along the way, she was also cast by such directors as Mario Bava (*5 Dolls for an August Moon*, 1970), Andrea Bianchi (*Strip Nude for Your Killer*, 1975) and Umberto Lenzi (*The Biggest Battle*, 1978).

Once Fenech enters *Your Vice is a Locked Room*, she dominates the proceedings, coquettishly teasing everyone on the estate and seducing Irina in a languorous lesbian scene that was typical of the era. Lushly photographed by Giancarlo Ferrando with an elegant musical score by veteran composer Bruno Nicolai (*The Night Evelyn Came Out of the Grave*, 1971), *Your Vice is a Locked Room* is a stylish giallo, smoothly produced and tightly directed, but it gives short shrift to Poe's story, which only really enters into the plot toward the end, when investigating police officers discover that Oliviero's cat is mewing in agony from behind a recently-constructed wall, which they tear down, finding both the cat and Oliviero's body walled up within. Spoiler Alert: In an unexpected plot twist, Irina turns out to be the murderer (with some help from her friend Walter, whom she pushes off a cliff so she can have all the riches for herself).

One of the better examples of the giallo, *Your Vice is a Locked Room and Only I Have the Key* adds Poe's ending almost as an afterthought; one wonders why the screenwriters didn't just come up with an original denouement.

With solid acting from Fenech, Strindberg and spaghetti western veteran Pistilli (*For a Few Dollars More*, 1965) however, it is a memorable exercise in suspense, gore and sex.

Mexico is not a country usually associated with Poe, but Juan Lopez Moctezuma's *The Mansion of Madness* (aka *House of Madness* and *Dr Tarr's Torture Dungeon*, 1973) is an intriguing adaptation of 'The System of Dr Tarr and Professor Fether.' Filmed in English and dubbed into Spanish for its home audience, *The Mansion of Madness* is faithful to Poe's original intentions: The inmates of a remote insane asylum seize the place, imprisoning its staff, and then make their own decisions about how business in the asylum should be conducted.

Moctezuma was a Mexican actor/director who only helmed five films, but they were all horror and/or suspense: *The Mansion of Madness*, *Mary Mary Bloody Mary* (1974), *Alucarda* (1978), *To Kill a Stranger* (1983) and *El Alimento del Miedo* (1994). *Alucarda* is his most controversial work, a disturbingly over the top gothic horror set in a nunnery that is a sort of mash-up between J Sheridan Le Fanu's 'Carmilla' and Ken Russell's *The Devils* (1971).

Moctezuma co-wrote the script for *The Mansion of Madness* with Carlos Illescas and Gabriel Weiss. Poe's original story was a dark comedy, and the film uses that template and captures the basic plot quite well: Somewhere in France, Gaston LeBlanc (Arthur Hansel) travels deep into a mysterious forest to investigate the strange behaviour of the infamous Dr Tarr. Instead, he encounters Dr Maillard (Claude Brook), who performs bizarre experiments on the inmates, while at the same time allowing some of them free reign of the place. Others are tortured, placed in glass cages or forced to perform weird rituals and dances.

Moctezuma listed filmmaker Alejandro Jodorowsky (*El Topo*, 1970) as a friend and collaborator; among other things, Moctezuma was associate producer on *El Topo*. Jodorowsky's influence loomed larger over *The Mansion of Madness*, including Moctezuma's choice of cinematographer, Rafael Corkidi, who had just photographed Jodorowsky's *The Holy Mountain* (1973).

Claude Brook (sometimes known as Claudio Brook) was a distinguished Mexican actor who was best known at the time for Luis Bunuel's *The Exterminating Angel* (1962); he later played a featured role in the James Bond movie *Licence to Kill* (1989), which was filmed in Mexico and starred Timothy Dalton as 007.

Arthur Hansel was an American actor who had travelled to Mexico for a two week vacation and ended up staying there for four years, performing in such films as Sergio Vejar's *Trio y Cuarteto* (1972). He also appeared in Moctezuma's *Mary Mary Bloody Mary* in 1975.

Beautiful Ellen Sherman (Eugenie) made her film debut in *The Mansion of Madness* as the mysterious inmate whose seductive charms enthral LeBlanc, not to mention her uncle, Dr Maillard. Sherman's exotic good looks led to roles in sexploitation films such as *The Yum Yum Girls* (1976) and a guest appearance on the American TV series *Three's Company* in 1978.

The rest of the cast consisted of mostly Mexican actors, including Martin LaSalle (Julien Covier), David Silva (Cult Priest) and Susan Kamini (Cult Priestess). Co-writer Gabriel Weiss was also responsible for the production design, which gives the film a rich, Gothic appearance, with most of the interiors shot at Estudios America in Mexico City.

*The Mansion of Madness/Dr Tarr's Torture Dungeon* went virtually unnoticed when it was released to cinemas in the mid-seventies, but its cult reputation has grown over the years. It is a curious film, bizarre, nightmarish and just plain odd, but its images linger in the memory. The movie is encapsulated beautifully by Scout Tafoya, who wrote in RogerEbert.com on 4 November 2015: 'Pictures make the past impossible to deny, and they let us commune with what we've lost… (Moctezuma's) images may be upsetting, but they're clear, deliberate and stunning. The film's reputation suggests that atmosphere and winning visuals don't grant you a seat at the table critically. *The Mansion of Madness* was not well-liked at the time, nor is it well-regarded now. Its legacy is so negligible that it doesn't even have a Wikipedia page. But you cannot take its power away.'

*The Mansion of Madness* was Moctezuma's first film as director, yet its approach, no doubt influenced by Moctezuma's experiences working with Jodorowsky, is assured and powerful. The viewer is taken on a coach ride into the mysterious forest, then on a tour through the even more mysterious asylum, We know that something is 'off' about the place from the start, when we see men dressed as soldiers romping through the woods, ultimately attacking the passengers of the coach. And when we meet Dr Maillard, who later reveals himself as inmate Raoul Fragonard, we know he isn't quite right in the head either. Brook has a fine time chewing the scenery, giving a performance that is, well, daft. Hansel basically plays straight man to the bizarre events taking place in front of him, while Sherman remains a sylph-like presence throughout the proceedings.

As was the case with Jodorowsky's films, the visuals are most important. Even the intentional humour is visual, with Julien Couvier hopping away while bound and gagged to 'funny' music, and 'Mr Chicken,' a mental patient who thinks he's living in a barnyard.

There are also literary and cinematic allusions. These include quotes from black magician Aleister Crowley ('Do what thou wilt shall be the whole of the law'), from Mervyn LeRoy's classic 1931 gangster film *Little Caesar* as Fragonard is mortally wounded ('Can this be the end of Maillard?') and even a quote from John Donne's *Holy Sonnets* ('I run to Death, and Death meets me as fast/And all my pleasures are like yesterday'), the latter of which was also used in Mark Robson's *The Seventh Victim* (1943).

It's safe to assume that anyone going to see *The Mansion of Madness* under the title of *Dr Tarr's Torture Dungeon* would have been expecting a straight horror film and would have been somewhat bewildered by the strange goings-on. *The Mansion of Madness* remains an overlooked gem, undoubtedly the most imaginative cinematic treatment of 'The System of Dr Tarr and Professor Fether,' and one of the most intriguing of all Poe pictures.

The international cinematic Poe was quiescent for the rest of the seventies, a decade in which the horror genre itself was undergoing many changes. The British horror scene, which had dominated the market since Hammer's arrival in 1957 with *The Curse of Frankenstein*, ended with a whimper in the mid-seventies after William Friedkin's blockbuster adapted from William Peter Blatty's bestseller *The Exorcist* changed the face of horror films when it was released by Warner Bros in late 1973. After that watershed, (and ironically, Warners had also released *The Curse of Frankenstein* in the States in 1957) the smaller studios couldn't compete with the majors, and Hammer, AIP, Amicus, Tigon and Tyburn were all pretty much out of business by 1979. As a result, smaller independent producers carved out their own niche with such late-seventies horror hits as George A Romero's *Dawn of the Dead* (1978), which was followed by an unofficial 'sequel' directed by Italian goremeister Lucio Fulci called *Zombi 2* (US: *Zombie*, 1979).

The biggest horror trend, however, was toward so-called 'slashers,' low-budget films, mostly American, that usually involved teenage girls getting undressed before being horribly murdered. The film that started the trend was John Carpenter's *Halloween* (1978), which not only began a franchise of its own, but inspired a myriad of other producers to flood the market with imitations, such as *Friday the 13th* (1980), *My Bloody Valentine* (1981) and others too numerous to mention.

Needless to say, there wasn't much room for Poe, or any other classic authors in this new and rather mindless trend, so it wasn't until 1981 that Fulci, after directing a sort of follow-up to *Zombie* called *City of the Living Dead* (1980) took on a Poe adaptation by directing yet another version of *The Black Cat*. He supposedly did this project as a favour to its producer, Giullo Sbargia, who had produced Tinto Brass' infamous 'Nazi-sploitation' movie *Salon Kitty* (1976). The uncredited associate producer on Fulci's 1981 *The Black Cat* was veteran international exploitation specialist Harry Alan Towers, a British entrepreneur who went from one country to another in attempts to keep one step ahead of the law, which always seemed to be in hot pursuit of him. Nevertheless, he was a big fan of the classics (among other films, he had produced Franco's *Count Dracula*) and he probably had a hand in persuading Fulci to tackle Poe's oft-told tale.

Originally, Donald Pleasence, who had just reinvigorated his career by playing the 'hero' in *Halloween*, was to have played the leading role of Professor Robert Miles in *The Black Cat*, but he was forced to bow out because of his commitment to reprise his role of Dr Loomis in *Halloween II* (1981). Supposedly, the role was also offered to Peter Cushing, but he turned it down because of Fulci's reputation for gore movies. In any case, the part went to veteran Anglo-Irish actor Patrick Magee, who had appeared in Corman's *The Masque of the Red Death*.

As *The Black Cat* was going to be filmed mainly in English, as *Zombi 2* had been (resulting in great success in English-speaking territories), American actress Mimsy Farmer was hired to play Jill Travers, the female lead. Farmer had already appeared in such giallo films as Dario Argento's *Four Flies on Grey Velvet* (1971), Francesco Barilli's *The Perfume of the Lady in Black* (1974) and Armando Crispino's *Autopsy* (1975), so she was no stranger to Italian horror cinema.

Third-billed in *The Black Cat* was David Warbeck, who had starred opposite Peter Cushing in Hammer's *Twins of Evil* (1971) and who would segue from playing Inspector Gorley in *The Black Cat* into starring in Fulci's next gore-fest, *The Beyond* (1981). The rest of the cast was composed mostly of European performers, such as Dagmar Lassander, who had played Ligeia in the Italian TV series *I Racconti Fantastici di Edgar Allan Poe* (1979), Bruno Corazzari (Fulci's *The Psychic*, 1977) and Daniela Doria (Fulci's *City of the Living Dead*, 1980 ).

*The Black Cat* was filmed on location at West Wycombe Park in Buckinghamshire, with interiors shot at Elios Studios, Cine International and Incir De Paolis studios in Rome. The cinematography by Sergio Salvati (*City of the Living Dead*) is quite good, especially the exteriors, although there are too many tight close-ups of the eyes of Magee and Farmer included for no particular reason. During production, Lassander was nearly killed during filming of a fire scene when a breakaway wall fell on her. Most of the scene was ultimately accomplished with a stunt person.

The screenplay is strange and dreamlike: Robert Miles (Magee) is a psychic medium who can communicate with those from the Great Beyond.

He wanders about in cemeteries, recording voices of the dead onto tape. Miles also has the power to control the mind of his black cat, which he uses to take revenge upon those he believes have wronged him. Police photographer Jill Travers notices cat scratches on the bodies of some 'accident' victims and ends up visiting Miles to let him know of her suspicions regarding his cat. It's the cat's turn to seek revenge on its master after he murders Travers, and then walls her up along with the cat.

As was so often the case with adaptations of Poe, the only scenes from the original story arrive at the climax, although to little effect here. The biggest problems with Fulci's *The Black Cat* lie with the lacklustre script and Fulci's flat direction. For once, he doesn't include viscera flying all over the place, but the stilted dialogue and Fulci's seeming lack of interest in creating suspense mitigate against the film's success as a Poe adaptation.

In a review on allmovie.com, Simon Cavett wrote: 'Remarkably restrained horror from the man behind such flesh-rending epics as *Zombie* and *The Gates of Hell*, this is also nearly incomprehensible, possessing a nightmarish lack of cohesion that is more irritating than frightening. In fact, the most horrifying thing about this film is Fulci's aggressive tendency to shoot super-tight widescreen close-ups of Magee's eyes and nose.'

None of the characters really register as a three-dimensional human being, although Magee does his best with the dialogue he is given. There is only so much, however, that even a seasoned actor can give to such a poorly conceived script. Perhaps Fulci didn't really have enough of an understanding of Poe and his fiction to have been a good choice for director on this project. The best thing about the film, in fact, is the score by Pino Donaggio (*Carrie*, 1976), but aside from that, let's just say that Pleasence and Cushing were wise to turn this one down.

Speaking of filmmakers who were not sympatico with Poe, the ubiquitous Spanish director Jesus (Jess) Franco tackled his own adaptation of 'The Fall of the House of Usher' in 1983; at least that is allegedly what *Revenge in the House of Usher* was intended to be, but it's difficult to tell from the mess that resulted. The confused storyline (written by Franco) concerns one Alan Harker (Antonio Mayans), a doctor who visits the crumbling manse of Eric Usher (Howard Vernon), a man who is convinced that the house in which he lives has a life of its own and is attempting to drive him mad. He sees ghosts, among other things, and he informs Harker that when his daughter Melissa (Francoise Blanchard) passed away years ago, he had created a method by which he could bring her back to life by acquiring the blood of prostitutes. Usher and his assistant Morpho (Olivier Mathot) have kidnapped and murdered several women of the streets in an attempt to keep Melissa alive. Harker meets Dr Seward, Usher's physician, and tells him that Usher is quite mad. The truth is ultimately revealed to anyone who can stay awake.

As was the case with many of Franco's films, *Revenge in the House of Usher* was released in at least three different versions. The third cut, the French version, features flashbacks of the 'young Usher' from Franco's ground-breaking 1964 movie *The Awful Dr Orloff*, a pioneering Spanish horror film, as Howard Vernon, one of Franco's favourite actors, had starred in that film as well. As that movie was shot in black and white, however, the flashbacks stand out from the rest of *Revenge of the House of Usher*, which is in colour.

The original version, entitled *The Fall of the House of Usher*, featured no flashbacks from *Orloff*, and premiered (never to be seen in that form again) at a 1983 horror/fantasy film festival in Madrid. It was, to be put mildly, poorly received, and the film seemed to have no commercial future. Franco, however, was asked to film new scenes that ultimately went into the creation of two alternate versions of the film. The French version is the one most widely seen.

Bizarrely, the three versions of Franco's *Usher* have totally different storylines. In his original *The Fall of the House of Usher*, Usher is a mad killer who is haunted by the spectres of his victims; in the second cut, *Revenge in the House of Usher*, Usher is some sort of supernatural creature who, like a vampire, needs human blood to extend his existence; and in the final cut, also called *Revenge in the House of Usher*, Usher is a typical mad scientist who kidnaps prostitutes and uses their blood to keep his daughter alive.

Obviously, none of the three versions had much to do with Poe, and the names of two of the characters, Harker and Seward, are derived from Bram Stoker's *Dracula*, which only adds to the confusion. The original version that was shown in Madrid in 1983 is now considered to be lost, which is probably just as well.

It's best not to linger on *Revenge in the House of Usher*, so I shall attempt to be brief. Simply put, *Revenge in the House of Usher* is an abomination, an incomprehensible mess that has little to do with Poe or with real filmmaking, for that matter. The performers sleepwalk through their roles, with Vernon, a Swiss-born actor who was once quoted as saying, 'I act without distaste or conviction,' doing exactly that as Usher. Lina Romay, who was Franco's long-time lover and who starred in many of his films, is cast in her usual sexy type of role as a nymphomaniac maid, but curiously, Franco left out his usual extreme sex and graphic nudity in this production, rendering it even more boring than his usual schlock. The best part of the film consists of the clips from *The Awful Dr Orloff*, which at least looks like a real movie.

# CHAPTER SIX
# THE TELEVISED POE

*'I have reached these lands but newly*
*From an ultimate dim Thule –*
*From a wild weird clime that lieth, sublime,*
*Out of SPACE – out of TIME.'*

**Dreamland**

**A**daptations of Poe have been as ubiquitous in the medium of television as they have in the cinema, and it would be nearly impossible to list, let alone view, every television production that has alluded to Poe in some form or another. I shall, therefore, attempt to hit the high points of Edgar Allan Poe's televised exploits.

As most television transmissions were live in the early days of the medium, the majority of those productions have been lost over time. One of the earliest televised Poe adaptations to have survived (thanks to being preserved on kinescope) is the 1956 version of *The Fall of the House of Usher*, produced in the US for the National Broadcasting Corporation programme *Matinee Theater*, a live anthology series that featured original stories as well as adaptations of literary classics, including *Dracula* in 1956 and *Frankenstein* in 1957. Introduced by actor John Conte (*The Man with the Golden Arm*, 1955), the series debuted in 1955 and ran every weekday through 1958, with some episodes produced in New York and others in Los Angeles.

*Usher* was produced at California Studios in Hollywood, allowing for some top talent both behind and in front of the camera. The adaptation was by Robert Esson, who would later adapt Poe's 'The Cask of Amontillado' for the series the following year, and prolific television scribe and producer Albert McCleery, who would go on to produce the series' versions of *Dracula* and *Frankenstein*. The director was Boris Sagal, who would later helm such films as *The Omega Man* (1971) and the television miniseries *Rich Man, Poor Man* (1976).

The cast was even more impressive: Actor (later novelist) Tom Tryon was cast as Roderick Usher. Tryon had just made a name for himself in Michael

Curtiz's *The Scarlet Hour* (1956) and had previously played Heathcliff in the *Matinee Theater* production of *Wuthering Heights*. He would go on to star in the genre classic *I Married a Monster from Outer Space* (1958) and, as Thomas Tryon, would switch careers later in life to become an author of horror novels, with his best-known works being 'The Other' (1971) and 'Harvest Home ' (1973).

Cast as Usher's friend David was Marshall Thompson, a busy actor who would soon star in such horror and science fiction classics as *Fiend Without a Face, It! The Terror from Beyond Space* (both 1958) and *First Man into Space* (1959), before becoming a household name as the leading actor in the American television series *Daktari* (1966-1969). Veteran character actor Eduardo Ciannelli played the family doctor; Ciannelli's American film career stretched all the way back to 1917 with his role in Albert Parker's *The Food Gamblers*, followed by a stint on Broadway in the 1920s. The Italian-born actor later became known for playing a variety of gangsters and racketeers in such films as *Marked Woman* (1937) and *Law of the Underworld* (1938), while also portraying the evil titular mastermind in the Republic serial *Mysterious Doctor Satan* (1940).

Madeline Usher was portrayed by Joan Elan, a Ceylon-born actress who had previously appeared in *The Girls of Pleasure Island* (1953) with Leo Genn, Don Taylor and Gene Barry. She would later play the title role in the *Matinee Theater* production of *Jane Eyre* (1957).

With cast and crew assembled, *Matinee Theater*'s faithful adaptation of Poe's story was transmitted on 6 August 1956 in colour (the series was one of the early programmes to be broadcast in colour). While subject to the limitations of live, studio-bound television, *The Fall of the House of Usher* has much to recommend it.

The 50-minute television play begins with David (Thompson) arriving at the Usher abode, and the first glimpse we are given of Madeline comes shortly after, in a chilling scene in which we see her scratching madly at the walls of her room until she scrapes some of the wood from the wall – a rather eloquent foreshadowing of the grim scene late in the production when she is scratching at her coffin lid.

When we are introduced to Roderick Usher, at first Tryon seems too handsome and hearty looking. Ultimately, the sheer intensity of his performance transcends his seemingly healthy appearance, and by the time the climax rolls around, with all its blood and thunder, we have come to believe that, as Poe wrote, '…There was a species of mad hilarity in his eyes – an evidently restrained *hysteria* in his whole demeanour.'

*Chapter Six – THE TELEVISED POE*

Interestingly enough, David tries to calm Usher by reading to him, and he reads the final portion of Poe's poem, 'The Haunted Palace,' intoning:

'While, like a ghastly rapid river,
Through the pale door
A hideous thrown rush out forever
And laugh – but smile no more.'

Not exactly the sort of poem to calm one's nerves!

Thompson makes for a stalwart and compassionate hero, while Elan is a memorably tortured Madeline. In this version, the house of Usher is destroyed by the *deus ex machina* of a tornado; although the doctor points out that the storm seemed only to touch the Usher house and no other.

The production has a claustrophobic atmosphere, which is partly intentional and partly a limitation of the infant medium. The sets are sparse and somewhat unfinished, and Sagal includes a few too many clichéd wolf howls on the soundtrack, although the library music (supervised by Edward Truman) is effective enough – and some of the cues were later used in George A Romero's ground-breaking *Night of the Living Dead* (1968).

All in all, the *Matinee Theater* version of *The Fall of the House of Usher* is one of the more faithful adaptations of Poe in any dramatic medium, with powerful acting and a solid script. It makes one wish that Sagal's version of *The Tell-Tale Heart* for the series had also been preserved, but alas, t'was not to be.

We have seen that Argentinian television was among the earliest to adapt Poe with the series *Obras Maestras del Terror*, starting in 1959, which included *El aso de Mister Valdemar, Ligeia, Berenice, El Tonel del Amontillado* and *El Corazon Delator*, all starring Narciso Ibáñez Menta. Sadly, many of the early television adaptations of Poe have been lost, particularly those from South America and Europe. Once we entered the 1960s, however, more horror in general was being produced for American and British television, and Poe, naturally enough, was included in this boom.

In America, NBC's horror anthology series *Thriller* (1960-1962) was hosted by none other than Boris Karloff. The series adapted tales by such famed horror authors as Robert Bloch, August Derleth, and, of course, Poe. One of the advantages of episodic television was its brevity; the episodes ran for approximately 52 minutes, the television equivalent of Poe's dictum that short stories (especially horror stories) should be read in one sitting for maximum impact. The *Matinee Theater* version of *The Fall of the House of Usher* had run an economical 50 minutes, requiring very little padding, unlike most feature film adaptations.

The producers of *Thriller* chose to adapt *The Premature Burial*, one of the author's most unsettling works. It was broadcast in October 1961, just in time for Halloween.

Scenes from *Thriller: The Premature Burial* (1961)

Sadly, even episodic television's brevity required Poe's original story, which only ran a few pages, to fill fifty minutes' worth of running time. This required a bit of ingenuity on the part of the writers, and in the case of the *Thriller* version, there are many similarities to the screenplay of Corman's *Premature Burial*, which was released less than a year later.

The cast of *The Premature Burial* included Karloff himself, who occasionally stepped into roles in the episodes that he also introduced. Karloff plays Dr Thorne, family physician to Edward Stapleton (Sidney Blackmer), a wealthy old man who survives being buried alive early in the story. Unfortunately for him, his beautiful young fiancée (Patricia Medina) devises a plan to make use of his next cataleptic seizure by wedding him and then insuring that he stays dead this time, which will enable her to inherit his estate and be with her even younger lover (Scott Marlowe). Dr Thorne however, keeps a careful eye on her, suspecting that she is planning something duplicitous.

Blackmer was a veteran Hollywood actor who had previously appeared in a slew of classic (and not so classic) films, including *Little Caesar* (1931), *Charlie Chan at Monte Carlo* (1937) and *The Lady and the Monster* (1944). He achieved perhaps his greatest notoriety with his sinister portrayal of Roman Castevet in Roman Polanski's *Rosemary's Baby* (1968).

Medina, as previously noted, had appeared in *The Phantom of the Rue Morgue* (1954) and later in such films as *The Beast of Hollow Mountain* (1956). By the early 1960s, her had career shifted mainly to television, where she guest-starred on such series as *Zorro* (1959), *The Rebel* (1960) and *Rawhide* (1961). Marlowe was a young actor who had been featured in such American TV series as *One Step Beyond* and *Alfred Hitchcock Presents* in that same year.

Director Douglas Hayes had helmed several episodes of Rod Serling's *The Twilight Zone* (1959-1964), including two of its most memorable, *Eye of the Beholder* (1960) and *The Invaders* (1961). He had also directed two of the most influential and frightening episodes of *Thriller*, *The Purple Room* (1960) and *The Hungry Glass* (1961).

Hayes does his usual yeoman's job directing the episode, with good performances from all. Medina is especially effective as the duplicitous, voluptuous Victorine, ranging from lustful to greedy, with a final Ophelia-like 'mad scene' at the climax, when she believes her husband has returned from the grave for revenge. Karloff is also fine as Stapleton's old friend who is not about to let sleeping corpses lie, so to speak, and Blackmer is totally convincing as Stapleton, the embodiment of Poe's unnamed narrator whose obsessive fear of being buried alive haunts his every waking moment.

The resemblances in plot and story structure to Corman's version of the tale seem more than coincidental. Both versions feature a scheming bride and a scene in which the lead character demonstrates to her the gadgets in his newly-constructed vault, such as a coffin that pops open at the touch of a button and a bell that rings in the tomb to alert his friends and family that he has been buried alive. One wonders if Corman's writers, Charles Beaumont and Ray Russell, ever got together with episode scripter William D Gordon and Hayes to throw around ideas.

Whatever the case, the *Thriller* adaptation of *The Premature Burial* is both atmospheric and character-driven, with some plot twists that appear to have been borrowed from Henri-Georges Clouzot's *Diabolique* (1955), and all the better for it. Bud Thackery's monochrome cinematography captures the gothic mood very nicely indeed, and Morton Stevens' score is also evocative, hitting all the right notes, as it were. As Karloff, in host mode, intones at the outset, 'As sure as my name is Boris Karloff, this is a *Thriller.*'

The British equivalent to *Thriller* in the sixties (more or less) was ITV's anthology series *Mystery and Imagination*, which debuted on 29 January 1966 and aired its final episode on 23 February 1970. Produced by Jonathan Alwyn, Reginald Collin and Raymond Collier, *Mystery and Imagination* was a high-minded, literature-based series that adapted works by such famous authors as M R James, Sheridan Le Fanu, Algernon Blackwood, Bram Stoker, and, of course, Poe. The third episode of the first series was, in fact, yet another version of *The Fall of the House of Usher*, scripted by David Campton, who would later write for Hammer's *Journey to the Unknown* series (1968) and was directed by Kim Mills, who had directed episodes of the classic British series *The Avengers* in 1962, 1963 and 1964. *Mystery and Imagination* was hosted by actor David Buck, in character as Richard Beckett, one of the protagonists of Le Fanu's *The Flying Dragon*, which was adapted in the first series. Like Karloff in *Thriller*, Buck sometimes acted within the episodes rather than just hosting them. Buck segued from *Mystery and Imagination* into Hammer's *The Mummy's Shroud* (1967) and worked for Hammer again in the following year on *Journey to the Unknown*.

The ITV version of *The Fall of the House of Usher* is rather revisionist: Richard Beckett tracks down Madeline Usher (Susannah York), a young woman with whom he has fallen in love on first sight, to the isolated, crumbling mansion where she lives with her brother, Roderick (Denholm Elliott). There, he comes into conflict with Roderick, who is both highly protective of his sister and highly neurotic as well.

The addition of a romantic involvement to the story is reminiscent of Richard Matheson's adaptation for Corman's version, but, unlike any other adaptation, this one opens not at the house of Usher, but in the outside world, where Madeline is attempting to escape from her brother. It's an unusual and somewhat jarring opening, foreshadowing the rather unorthodox versions of *Dracula* and *Frankenstein* that the series would present in 1968.

Once we reach the Usher house (the estate is simply referred to as 'Usher' in this adaptation), we settle in to a slightly more faithful version of the oft-told tale. Elliott, who would later distinguish himself in such Amicus horror anthology films as *The House That Dripped Blood* (1970) and *The Vault of Horror* (1973) before achieving mainstream fame as Indiana Jones' sidekick in Steven Spielberg's *Raiders of the Lost Ark* (1981), is quite daft from the outset as Usher, chewing the scenery while wearing a shocking white wig. He's all broad strokes, whereas Vincent Price was all subtlety and meticulous detail in his portrayal.

Vincent Price in *An Evening of Edgar Allan Poe* (1970)

*Chapter Six – THE TELEVISED POE*

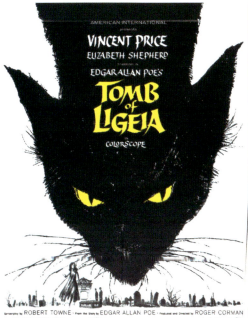

Even on her wedding night she must share the man she loved with the "Female Thing" that lived in the Tomb of the Cat!

AMERICAN INTERNATIONAL
presents
VINCENT PRICE
ELIZABETH SHEPHERD
in
EDGAR ALLAN POE'S
Tomb
of
LIGEIA
in COLORSCOPE

Screenplay by ROBERT TOWNE · From the Story by EDGAR ALLAN POE · Produced and Directed by ROGER CORMAN

They dared the most fantastic journey that has ever challenged imagination!

AMERICAN INTERNATIONAL STARS
VINCENT PRICE
TAB HUNTER
SUSAN HART
also starring
DAVID TOMLINSON
as HAROLD TUFNELL-JONES

WAR-GODS
OF
THE DEEP
COLORSCOPE

Directed by JACQUES TOURNEUR · Produced by DANIEL HALLER · Screenplay by CHARLES BENNETT and LOUIS M. HEYWARD · FROM EDGAR ALLAN POE'S "CITY IN THE SEA" · Executive Producer GEORGE WILLOUGHBY

DO YOU DARE SEE WHAT DR. DIABOLO SEES?

From the shock-author of "PSYCHO"

COLUMBIA PICTURES Presents

JACK PALANCE · BURGESS MEREDITH · BEVERLY ADAMS · PETER CUSHING

# TORTURE GARDEN

Guest Star Maurice Denham  Written by Robert Bloch  Produced by Max J. Rosenberg and Milton Subotsky  Directed by Freddie Francis  An Amicus Production

TECHNICOLOR®

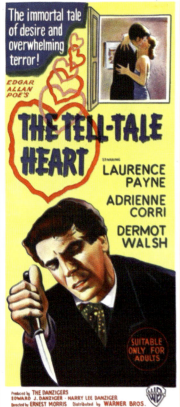

The immortal tale of desire and overwhelming terror!

EDGAR ALLAN POE'S

# THE TELL-TALE HEART

STARRING
LAURENCE PAYNE
ADRIENNE CORRI
DERMOT WALSH

SUITABLE ONLY FOR ADULTS

Produced by THE DANZIGERS
EDWARD J. DANZIGER · HARRY LEE DANZIGER
Directed by ERNEST MORRIS    Distributed by WARNER BROS.

THE LIVING AND DEAD CHANGE PLACES IN AN ORGY OF TERROR IN

EDGAR ALLAN POE'S

# CASTLE OF BLOOD

They love only for blood!

Starring
BARBARA STEELE · GEORGE RIVIERE  with MARGRETE ROBSAHM · HENRY KRUGER · MONTGOMERY GLEEN
SYLVIA SORENT · RAUL H. NEWMAN  Music Composed and Directed by RITZ ORTOLANI  Produced by FRANK BELTY
and WALTER SARCH  Directed by ANTHONY DAWSON  A WOOLNER BROS. RELEASE

# NON SCOMMETTERE LA TESTA CON IL DIAVOLO...

## 2 FELLINI 2

CON **TERENCE STAMP** E CON LA PARTECIPAZIONE STRAORDINARIA DI **SALVO RANDONE**

SCENEGGIATURA DI **FEDERICO FELLINI** E **BERNARDINO ZAPPONI** TECHNICOLOR

CINESTAMPA INTERNAZIONALE ROMA    ANNO DI EDIZIONE 1978

*The Haunting of Morella (1990)*

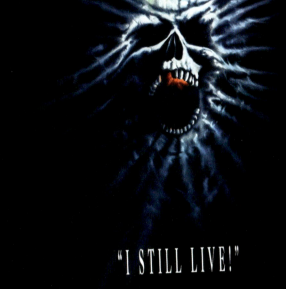

Edgar Allan Poe's
The
# HAUNTING of MORELLA

"I STILL LIVE!"

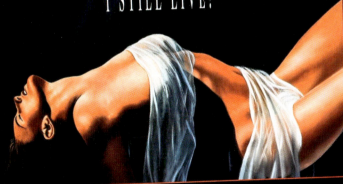

DAVID McCALLUM † NICOLE EGGERT

CHRISTOPHER HALSTED † LANA CLARKSON † MARIA FORD

PRODUCTION DESIGNER GARY RANDALL † DIRECTOR OF PHOTOGRAPHY ZORAN HOCHSTATTER † EDITED BY DIANE FINGADO

MUSIC BY FREDRIC TEETSEL AND CHUCK CIRINO † ASSOCIATE PRODUCERS ALIDA CAMP AND RODMAN FLENDER

WRITTEN BY R. J. ROBERTSON † PRODUCED BY ROGER CORMAN

DIRECTED BY JIM WYNORSKI

© 1990 CONCORDE

Concorde

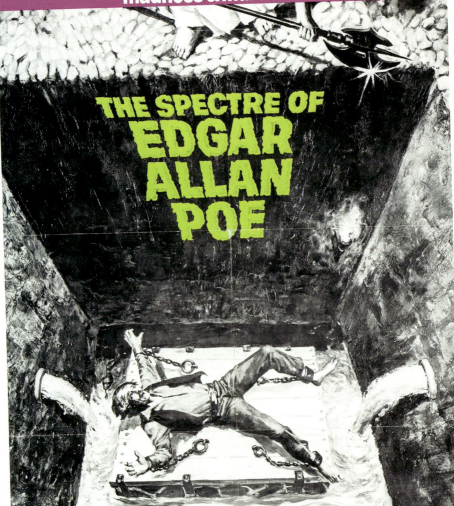

He wrote. MURDERS IN THE RUE MORGUE... THE FALL OF THE HOUSE OF USHER
THE RAVEN... THE PIT AND THE PENDULUM

What drove him
down into a bizarre world of
madness & murder?

THE SPECTRE OF EDGAR ALLAN POE

Cintel Productions presents
"The spectre of EDGAR ALLAN POE"
Starring
ROBERT WALKER JR. • CESAR ROMERO • TOM DRAKE • CAROL OHMART
Screenplay by Mohy Quandour  Based on original story and treatment by Kenneth Hartford and Denton Foxx
Produced and Directed by Mohy Quandour  In Color  PG  CINERAMA RELEASING

74/176

"The spectre of EDGAR ALLAN POE"

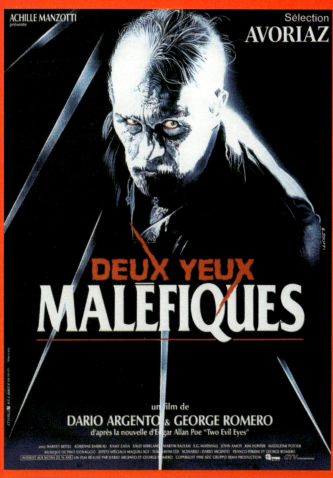

ACHILLE MANZOTTI
présente

Sélection
AVORIAZ

# DEUX YEUX
# MALÉFIQUES

un film de
**DARIO ARGENTO & GEORGE ROMERO**
d'après la nouvelle d'Edgar Allan Poe "Two Evil Eyes"

avec HARVEY KEITEL, ADRIENNE BARBEAU, RAMY ZADA, SALLY KIRKLAND, MARTIN BALSAM, E.G. MARSHALL, JOHN AMOS, KIM HUNTER, MADELEINE POTTER
MUSIQUE DE PINO DONAGGIO  EFFETS SPÉCIAUX MAQUILLAGE TOM SAVINI LTD  SCÉNARIO : DARIO ARGENTO  FRANCO FERRINI ET GEORGE ROMERO
INTERDIT AUX MOINS DE 16 ANS  UN FILM RÉALISÉ PAR DARIO ARGENTO ET GEORGE ROMERO  COPYRIGHT 1990 ADC GRUPPO RIMA PRODUCTION

John Cusack in *The Raven* (2012)

*The Raven* (2012)

Alice Eve and John Cusack in *The Raven* (2012)

Jim Sturgess and Kate Beckinsale in *Stoneheart Asylum* (2014)

Michael Caine in *Stoneheart Asylum* (2014)

York was best-known at the time for her highly visible role as Sophie Western in Tony Richardson's *Tom Jones* (1963) and would soon gain notoriety for co-starring opposite Beryl Reid in Robert Aldrich's *The Killing of Sister George* (1968), one of the first mainstream films to depict a lesbian relationship. She fares rather better than Elliott in *Usher* as the obviously deranged but beautiful Madeline, and the scene in which she returns from the grave is quite chillingly done.

ITV's *The Fall of the House of Usher* is an offbeat version of Poe's tale, but it is really no more successful than the 1949 British feature film edition. Shot on video in black and white, it features little atmosphere, but one wonders if the second Poe adaptation on *Mystery and Imagination* – another version of *The Tell Tale Heart*, this one starring Norman Eshley, Gillian French and Leslie French (and featuring Freddie Jones in a small role) – was more to the point. Sadly, that version, broadcast in 1968, has been lost, along with three-quarters of the other episodes.

In 1970, the same year that Corman's *Pit and the Pendulum* was released to American network television, American International Pictures produced one of their few forays into the medium with a one-man show starring Vincent Price called *An Evening of Edgar Allan Poe*. Directed by television producer/director/writer Kenneth Johnson, who would later be responsible for such science fiction series as *The Bionic Woman* (1976-1978) and *V* (1983), the one-shot was a 52-minute *tour-de-force* for Price, who obviously relished the opportunity to reach the vast television audience.

Scripter David Welch and Johnson adapted four Poe stories for the production, merely editing them for time rather than changing anything: 'The Tell Tale Heart,' 'The Sphinx,' 'The Cask of Amontillado' and 'The Pit and the Pendulum.' Price does far more than read the stories; he *performs* them, and superbly.

In fact, Price has never been better than he is in *An Evening of Edgar Allan Poe*. As each story has been carefully chosen to have a first-person narrator, he throws himself into the characters with all the energy of the Shakespearean that he was, running the gamut of emotion. In *The Tell Tale Heart*, he perfectly conveys the terror and guilt of the nameless narrator, ending the sequence by lifting up the bloody heart of his victim and presenting it to the camera.

*The Sphinx* is one of Poe's lighter tales, in which a man thinks that he has seen a hellish monster through his window, when in actual fact it turns out to have been a death's head moth that he was observing at close range. Price builds up the mystery of what the man might have seen, and then gently brings us back to the real world for the story's witty denouement. Johnson's direction is clever too, as we see just the slight representation of a skull superimposed over Price's face when he speaks of the 'death's head,' a nice touch reminiscent of the final shot of Anthony Perkins in Hitchcock's *Psycho*.

*The Cask of Amontillado* is a true *tour-de-force* for the actor, in which he plays both Fortunato and Montressor. He is filmed at different angles for

Vincent Price in *An Evening of Edgar Allan Poe* (1970)

A WORLD PREMIERE SPECIAL!

VINCENT PRICE
STARRING IN
FOUR POPULAR
POE CLASSICS

THE
TELLTALE HEART
THE SPHINX
THE CASK OF
AMONTILLADO
THE PIT
AND THE
PENDULUM

*VINCENT PRICE* presents
AN EVENING OF EDGAR ALLAN POE

each character, with Montressor the suave, icy yet charming murderer and Fortunato the drunken, clumsy victim. The conceit of this segment is that Montressor seems to be confessing his crime – which had occurred many years previously – to a friend while having dinner. Price's urbanity suits him well here, and this sequence may be his best-acted one of all.

The production ends with Price as the protagonist of *The Pit and the Pendulum*, and once again, he ratchets up the screws of terror and tension, aided by directorial touches that include a 'pendulum's eye view' of Price as he lies strapped to a table, the pendulum swinging down…and down. We also see the rats who chew through his bonds, freeing him.

*An Evening of Edgar Allan Poe* is a fitting swan song to the whole Corman/Price/Poe cycle, with the music of AIP house composer Les Baxter adding just the right amount of mood, and the simple but effective sets drenching the whole piece in atmosphere. We get a feeling for how Price must have come across onstage – the show was shot on videotape, giving it that 'live' look – and it's a joy to behold, an actor at the top of his game practising his craft by using every trick in the book to make us believe in him, and in Poe. *An Evening of Edgar Allan Poe* is, quite simply, one of the finest – and one of the purest – presentations of Poe in the history of television.

Edgar Allan Poe himself turned up, in the unlikely form of stand-up comic Marty Allen, in an episode of Rod Serling's *Night Gallery* in 1971. *Night Gallery* was the highly respected Serling's follow-up to his own *The Twilight Zone*, which had aired on the Columbia Broadcasting System from 1959 to 1964. Unlike *The Twilight Zone*, however, *Night Gallery* concentrated more on tales of horror than science fiction and fantasy in a format that recalled that of *Thriller*. As he had done on the previous series, Serling acted as the host of *Night Gallery*, which had begun life in 1969 as a made-for-TV movie on the National Broadcasting Network. It ultimately ran for three series, beginning in 1970.

The format featured Serling appearing in an art gallery, surrounded by paintings and sculptures, with each painting representing a story that he would introduce. Each episode of the show featured two or more stories, and, in the second season, comic vignettes were added into the mix. Poe turned up in a vignette entitled *Quoth the Raven*, sandwiched between an H P Lovecraft tale called *Cool Air* (*Night Gallery* was the first series to adapt Lovecraft's tale for television) and a story by Basil Copper called *Camera Obscura*, in an episode broadcast on 8 December 1971.

*Quoth the Raven* is a brief but amusing vignette written by producer Jack Laird and directed by Jeff Corey. Set in 1845, we see Poe sitting at his writing desk (he misspells his own middle name as Allen, possibly intentionally, as he's played by Marty Allen) attempting to compose what would become his most famous work, 'The Raven,' but he seems to be encountering a slight case of writer's block. The fact that he's throwing back several glasses of brandy may not be doing him any good.

'While I pondered weak and…while I pondered weak and…' he mumbles to himself, trying to get the line right. A live raven is in the room (voiced by

Mel Blanc, Warner Bros' go-to guy for cartoon voices such as Bugs Bunny and Daffy Duck), who exasperatedly fills in the blank for him: 'Weary, weary, dummy, weary!'

Poe throws his glass at the mocking raven and the vignette ends.

In 1979, a four-episode miniseries called *I Racconti Fantastici di Edgar Allan Poe* was broadcast on Italian television. Directed by Danielle D'Anza, the series was produced by Arturo La Pegna and starred numerous cult figures of European cinema, including Phillippe Leroya *(The Night Porter,* 1975) as Roderick Usher, Dagmar Lassander *(A Hatchet for the Honeymoon,* 1974) as Ligeia and cult Euro-horror star Erika Blanc (Mario Bava's *Kill Baby Kill,* 1966) in a featured role in one episode.

The individual episodes were all based on Poe themes without actually being based on any one story; the entire miniseries uses the template of 'The Fall of the House of Usher,' but reworks it in a modern setting, featuring elements of many other Poe stories. The first episode incorporates 'MS Found in a Bottle,' an idea taken from 'The Oval Portrait' and the ending of 'The Tell Tale Heart.' Episode two essentially recounts Poe's 'Ligeia,' but the character is changed to that of a silent movie actress whose career is destroyed by the transition to talking pictures. The third episode is essentially 'William Wilson', altering the title character (Nino Castelnuovo) from the military officer of Poe's story to a race car driver. The fourth and final episode is a more or less faithful adaptation of 'Usher,' but the ending is cribbed from 'The Masque of the Red Death.' In between, Usher entertains his guests with monologues based on 'The Pit and the Pendulum' and 'A Descent into the Maelstrom.'

*I Racconti Fantastic di Edgar Allan Poe* is still rarely seen outside of its native Italy, but for Poe completists, it's well worth tracking down.

Also in 1979, yet another version of Poe's most oft-told tale was remade for American television. Sunn Classic Pictures' production of *The Fall of the House of Usher* was the latest in the Utah-based company's line of 'Classics Illustrated,' loosely based on the comic book series derived from literary masterpieces. Sunn Classics Pictures (sometimes known as Schick Sunn Classic Pictures) had previously produced an adaptation of James Fenimore Cooper's *The Last of the Mohicans* for television in 1977, and later filmed Washington's Irving's *The Legend of Sleepy Hollow* (1980), starring a young Jeff Goldblum as Ichabod Crane.

Sunn's edition of *The Fall of the House of Usher* was helmed by James L Conway, who had directed some of their feature documentaries such as *In Search of Noah's Ark* (1976) and *The Lincoln Conspiracy* (1977), as well as *Last of the Mohicans.* Scripter Stephen Lord was a television veteran, having penned episodes of the classic science fiction series *The Outer Limits* in 1964, among others.

The cast of *The Fall of the House of Usher* was unusual, to say the least. Top-lining as Roderick Usher was the distinguished film and TV actor Martin Landau, who would later win a Best Actor Oscar for portraying Bela Lugosi in Tim Burton's biopic *Ed Wood* (1994). The leading lady was Charlene Tilton (Jennifer Cresswell), known at the time for lurid TV films such as *Diary of a Teenage Hitchhiker* (1979) and already famous for her role as Lucy Ewing in the night-time soap opera *Dallas* (1978-1990). Ray Walston (Thaddeus) had won a Tony Award on Broadway for his role as the Devil in *Damn Yankees* (1955) and was known to American television audiences as the star of the comedy-fantasy series *My Favorite Martian* (1963-1966).

Along with Tilton, cast member Robert Hays (Jonathan Creswell) gives *The Fall of the House of Usher* unintentional 'camp' appeal in the 21st Century: a year later, Hays starred in the uproarious movie parody *Airplane!* and repeated his role in the sequel, *Airplane II: The Sequel* (1982), and has forever been typecast for those two appearances. His *Usher* co-star, Dimitra Arliss (Madeline Usher) was a busy TV actress who later appeared as Mrs Stark in the short-lived series *Iron Man* (1994).

Sunn Classics' *The Fall of the House of Usher* is not a total disaster, but it is a bit of a mess, starting with the script: In 1839, architect Jonathan Criswell is summoned by old friend Roderick Usher to go to the Usher manse and attempt to save it from falling in upon itself. Criswell takes his new bride Jennifer with him (which seems rather unprofessional) and finds that Roderick and his sister Madeline are not, shall we say, in the best of health. Eventually, Jonathan learns that the Usher line has been involved in black magic and Satanism, bringing an unholy curse upon the House of Usher, condemning the Ushers to die before their 37th year. Jonathan attempts to save both the house and his friend, but the ending is, of course, not a happy one.

There are numerous problems with the teleplay. Jennifer is brought along for no apparent reason other than to provide the story with a damsel in distress. She spends most of the story ill and in bed, only arising in time for the climax when she helps to dispatch Madeline. Tilton is a mannequin throughout.

Walston is the loyal family retainer, roughly analogous to Harry Ellerbe's character in the Corman version, but he too comes to a bad end, killed by Madeline with a mace. Hays attempts to be a stalwart hero, but is ultimately rescued by his wife, rather than the other way around.

The worst conceit of this adaptation is the explanation that the Ushers were Satanists. While Corman's version noted the 'evil' that permeated the family, there was not even a hint of the supernatural. In this adaptation, Madeline is not buried alive by her brother – the ultimate horror of Poe and Corman – but is actually killed by a falling chandelier, then apparently resurrected by invisible supernatural forces that unscrew her coffin for her. This completely negates the crux of the story: Madeline's revenge upon her brother for his heinous act. Instead, it becomes a cheap paranormal gimmick, apparently inspired by the recent success of devil-themed movies such as *The Exorcist* (1973) and *The Omen* (1976), even to the point of 'borrowing' the apparition of a vicious black dog from the latter film.

On the plus side, Landau makes a good Roderick Usher, all self-torture and torment, although he is much less subtle than Price. He is not as over the top as Elliot, but he comes perilously close to it at times. Nevertheless, Landau grounds *The Fall of the House of Usher* in whatever it may possess in integrity.

Paul Staheli's art direction and Paul Hipp's cinematography provide the film with considerable atmosphere, and Dimitra Arliss, without a word of dialogue, makes a suitably creepy Madeline, crying tears of blood at the fiery climax. But let's face it: Corman's version is the gold standard of *Usher* adaptations, and very few others even come close. Sunn Classics' version is further away than most.

From one of Poe's most adapted stories to one of his least adapted, we find ourselves looking at *The Gold Bug* (1980), as, interestingly enough, an ABC Weekend Special that was originally broadcast on February 2 of that year. ABC Weekend Specials were aimed at children, and *The Gold Bug* was co-produced by Highgate Pictures and Learning Corporation of America, running 45 minutes (plus commercials).

Poe's original short story was published in 1843, and tells the tale of William Legrand, who is bitten by a golden bug. His manservant Jupiter fears that his master is going insane from the bite and gets Legrand's old friend (the story's anonymous narrator) to visit him at Legrand's home on Sullivan's Island, South Carolina, where they ultimately attempt to break an ancient code that leads to buried treasure.

The basic template of the story is retained in the ABC adaptation, but the time period is moved up to after the Civil War and the narrator is altered to a young boy who visits Sullivan's Island and encounters Legrand and Jupiter, who are obsessed with the idea that there is buried treasure there. He gets involved with their search after encountering a gold bug on the beach, which he finds so unusual that he wraps it up in what seems to be an ancient treasure map written in code.

*The Gold Bug* was directed by Robert Fuest, best known to genre fans as the director of the Vincent Price vehicles *The Abominable Dr Phibes* (1971) and its sequel, *Dr Phibes Rises Again* (1972). The television film starred character actor Roberts Blossom, who had appeared in everything from *Deranged* (1974) to Steven Spielberg's *Close Encounters of the Third Kind* (1977), as Legrand. Trinidad-born Geoffrey Holder, probably best known to international audiences as Baron Samedi in the James Bond film *Live and Let Die* (1973), played the role of Jupiter, while young Anthony Michael Hall, years away from becoming a member of Hollywood's so-called 'brat pack" in movies such as *The Breakfast Club* (1985), was cast as The Boy who discovers the gold bug on the beach and is the story's narrator.

Nicely photographed by Alex Thompson (*Jesus Christ Superstar*, 1973), *The Gold Bug* has little of Fuest's trademark flamboyant style aside from a few offbeat camera angles here and there. The performances are all solid, with Blossom a standout as the eccentric Legrand, who comes to a bad (and

Val Kilmer & George C Scott in *The Murders in the Rue Morgue* (1986)

somewhat mysterious) end. Holder is an evocative presence as the mute Jupiter, while Hall, who had only one previous acting credit in the 1979 TV series *Jennifer's Journey*, shows all of the promise that he would later solidify in such films as *Sixteen Candles* (1984) and *Weird Science* (1985).

Fuest's *The Gold Bug* is a modest, unassuming way to spend a Saturday afternoon, quite faithful to its source despite the change in the narrator's age. It would have been most interesting to have seen Fuest, who had a real flair for the genre, attempt more Poe adaptations, but, sadly, it was not to be.

Poe returned to American television in 1986 with a lavish new version of *The Murders in the Rue Morgue*, produced for the CBS Network by Robert A Halmi, a European-based producer who had already adapted classics for CBS such as *The Phantom of the Opera* (1983). Halmi's version of *Rue Morgue* was filmed in Paris, which gave it added authenticity, from a teleplay by David Epstein which, while closer to Poe's original story than some other versions, still found it necessary to 'improve' on the author by adding characters and situations not in Poe's story.

Epstein's script follows the basic blueprint of the tale: The grisly killings of a Parisian mother and daughter baffle the police and the only person who seems able to grasp the evidence is retired police inspector Auguste Dupin. As it happens, Dupin has a beautiful daughter whose fiancée is charged with the crime. It is up to Dupin to solve the murders in the Rue Morgue.

Veteran television director Jeannot Szwarc, who was born in Paris, was hired to direct the film. Szwarc had cut his television teeth on Rod Serling's *Night Gallery* series, of which he had directed several episodes. He had also directed several feature films, including *Jaws 2* (1978) and the cult classic *Somewhere in Time* (1980). Szwarc was well acquainted with horror, fantasy and suspense and seemed just the man for the job of directing *Rue Morgue*.

Starring as Dupin was no less a luminary than Oscar-winner George C Scott (*Patton*, 1970), who had already top-lined a number of TV movies including *Jane Eyre* (1970) and *A Christmas Carol* (1984), so he was no stranger to the medium. As his daughter, Claire (a character not in the original story), Szwarc and Halmi chose Rebecca De Mornay, fresh off the success of her feature film breakthrough *Risky Business* (1983, co-starring a young Tom Cruise), a highly talented 27-year-old actress who would go on to acclaim in such feature films as *The Trip to Bountiful* (1985) and *The Hand that Rocks the Cradle* (1992).

Another young actor who was 'hot' at the time was Val Kilmer, cast in *Rue Morgue* as Phillipe Huron. Kilmer had just starred in the 1984 movie parody *Top Secret!* and had segued from the box office hit *Top Gun* (1986), another Tom Cruise blockbuster, into *Rue Morgue*. Also in *Rue Morgue*'s cast was veteran British actor Ian McShane as the Prefect of Police. McShane's highest-profile role at the time was probably that of Judas Iscariot in the American miniseries *Jesus of Nazareth* (1977).

Changes notwithstanding, *The Murders in the Rue Morgue* is one of the more faithful adaptations of Poe. The murders themselves (and their aftermath) are indeed Poesque, complete with the body stuffed up the chimney and the various neighbours hearing what they think are foreign voices. Although the American television censorship of the time forbade anything too gruesome – the murders are shown in shadow and with quick cuts – we do see a plethora of blood splashed on walls, and, although it's too dark and partly out of frame, the point that one of the women has been beheaded is clearly made.

It is in the character of Dupin, however, that Poe is finally given his due. Whereas other filmed versions turned the master of ratiocination into a student or a bumbler, here at last we see Dupin the detective, with Scott giving a rip-roaring performance as the elegant Gallic precursor to Sherlock Holmes. The character has been altered somewhat from Poe's story: early in the film, he has become a self-pitying semi-hermit, interested only in chess. When the game's afoot, he springs into action and we see the wheels once again turning at immense speed within his brilliant mind.

Scott is given some good lines to utter, which he attacks with relish: 'I can no more consult with you than apologise to the dead,' he says to one policeman. In a lighter mood, he admonishes his daughter: 'Nothing comes before chess, my dear! Haven't I taught you anything?'

McShane's Prefect despises Dupin, of which Poe would have no doubt disapproved. There is a reconciliation of sorts at the climax, however, in which the ape attacks Claire. One might have wished for a more rousing denouement, although it's filmed well enough.

Claire is portrayed by De Mornay as a feisty, somewhat too-modern

Michael Anderson in
*Fool's Fire* (1992)

*Chapter Six – THE TELEVISED POE*

woman; as good an actress as De Mornay is, she was perhaps miscast in this role. Kilmer fares somewhat better as Dupin's godson, a faithful acolyte, while McShane is all bluster and self-importance as the Prefect.

The production is sumptuous, as is the cinematography by Bruno de Keyser, who also photographed Roman Polanski's *The Tenant* (1976) and Bertrand Tavernier's *A Sunday in the Country* (1984). Szwarc's direction is fluid, if uninspired; the location shooting in France adds immeasurably to the authenticity of the proceedings. *The Murders in the Rue Morgue* is one of the better adaptations of the Poe tale, and certainly one of the best-mounted versions of Poe to be presented on television.

Moving on several years, Julie Taymor's extraordinary *Fool's Fire* (1992) is an adaptation of Poe's 'Hop-Frog' that was produced for the Public Broadcasting System. Taymor is an American theatre, opera and film director who is known for, among other things, the stage musical version of *The Lion King* (1997), the film *Titus* (1999) and the opera *Oedipus Rex* (1992). She is an exceptionally gifted director with a unique vision, and many of her works include such elements as puppetry, dance and mime.

*Fool's Fire* is a heavily stylised yet faithful adaptation of Poe starring Michael Anderson, known for his role as the backwards-speaking dwarf in David Lynch's surreal TV series *Twin Peaks* (1990). His portrayal of the jester is heavily nuanced, elegant and unforgettable. As Trippetta, the object of his affections, Taymor and company cast diminutive actress Mireille Mosse, who would later become known for her role in Marc Caro's and Jean-Pierre Jeunet's *The City of Lost Children* (1995). Tom Hewitt, a television and theatre actor known for roles in such programmes as the soap opera *All My Children* (1970-2011), was cast as the vile, gluttonous King.

The storyline, adapted by Taymor, is even more faithful to its source than the 'Hop Toad' segment in Corman's *The Masque of the Red Death* had been: The protagonist (here called Hopfrog) is forced to be a jester for a despotic, overbearing king. A beautiful dwarf named Trippetta arrives, with whom Hopfrog falls in love. When the king mistreats her, Hopfrog plots his horrifying revenge.

The conceit of Taymor's vision is that the real 'grotesques' of the story are not the dwarves, but rather the gluttonous, debauched king and his ministers – hence the fact that they are portrayed by actors in puppet-like masks, and, in many cases, purely by puppets. They sit at the dinner table gorging, belching and farting, while forcing Hopfrog and Trippetta to dance and provide amusement. At one point, the king proclaims: 'Animals feed, men eat, but only a wise king knows the art of dining.' Hopfrog replies, 'Yes, and fat ones pay the fine of farting!'

Even more disgustingly, asides from the king describe his privy activities in more detail than we might like: 'I say there is no arse-wiper like a well-downed goose, if you hold her neck between your legs! Take my word for it, you get a miraculous sensation in your arse-hole both from the softness of the down and from the temperate heat of the goose herself, and this is easily communicated to the bum, gut and the rest of the intestines from which it reaches the heart and brain!'

As in Poe's story – and unlike the adaptation in Corman's *Masque* – Hopfrog takes revenge on the king and all of his ministers by dressing them as orangutans for a masquerade ball, and murdering them all in front of the assemblage by setting their costumes ablaze, after which he escapes with Trippetta. While preparing them for their impending doom, he recites, 'Hear your Hopfrog with his bells, silver bells/What a world of merriment their melody fortells!/How they tinkle, tinkle, tinkle in the icy air of night/ While the stars that over-sprinkle all the Heavens/Seem to twinkle with a crystalline delight!'

Poe's poem 'The Bells' makes up the final lines of the production, in Hopfrog's voiceover, and earlier, lines from Poe's 1849 poem 'A Dream Within a Dream' are heard. The Poesque nature of the production, shot on High Definition video, is second to none; *Fool's Fire* is one of the most faithful adaptations of Poe ever recorded in any medium.

As Hopfrog, Anderson is superb, from expressing his deep love for Trippetta to his deep hatred of the king. Mosse creates a strange, sweet presence and Hewitt's king is appropriately revolting and venal. Taymor's direction is confidently odd, with the final touch being a surreal shot of Hopfrog as a puppet master, holding the strings over the king and his cronies.

In the 25 March 1992 edition of the *Los Angeles Times*, television critic Ray Loynd wrote of *Fool's Fire*: 'What prepares you for this hour-long phantasmagoria are long-suppressed memories of childhood wonder, frightening fairy tales... and, on the deepest dream level, emanations of terror and madness...The lure here is that twilight between a state of amazement and dismay. Poe, whose poem "The Bells" concludes the piece, was always blending beauty and horror. And in this tale of sweet revenge, Taymor has dared to visualise Poe's dark, symbolist mind, leaving all prior Poe adapters in the dust.'

Poe himself was the subject of another PBS production called *Edgar Allan Poe: Terror of the Soul* (1995), an episode of the long-running series *American Masters*. Narrated by actress Ruby Dee, the one-hour documentary is constructed around interviews with such Poe aficionados as composer Philip Glass (who composed the opera *The Fall of the House of Usher* in 1988), literary critic Alfred Kazin and Poe biographer Kenneth Silverman. The documentary also covers the life of Poe (played by Anthony Maggio) and some segments dramatise scenes from his stories, including a partial adaptation of 'The Tell Tale Heart' starring Treat Williams. The dramatic highlight is a full adaptation of 'The Cask of Amontillado,' with John Heard as Montressor and Rene Auberjonois as Fortunato. Directed by Joyce Chopra and Karen Thomas, this segment benefits from elegant costumes by Hillary Wright and is word-for-word Poe, including the final devastating exchange when Fortunato pleads, 'For the love of God, Montressor!' as he is being walled up, with Montressor calmly responding, 'Yes, for the love of God,' as he lays the final brick.

Tales of Mystery and Imagination (1995)

Christopher Lee in Tales of Mystery and Imagination (1995)

*Terror of the Soul* is a splendid tribute to Poe, including the author in a series which has also covered such luminaries as Leonard Bernstein, Lon Chaney, Ernest Hemingway and Eugene O'Neill. The series would return to Poe over twenty years later, but more on that as we enter the 21st Century.

Meanwhile, also in 1995, there was an ambitious attempt to bring several of Poe's stories to the small screen in a series called *Tales of Mystery and Imagination*, with each of its twelve episodes hosted by none other than Christopher Lee. A co-production between the UK, South Africa and Croatia, the series, comprised of thirty-minute episodes, never aired that year, reportedly due to legal complications. It is now available on several streaming services and on some European DVDs.

*Tales of Mystery and Imagination* should have been a triumph, as it adapted several of Poe's best and most famous works. From the first episode, *The Fall of the House of Usher*, through the penultimate one, *The Masque of the Red Death* (in two parts) – and a final bonus program about Poe himself – the most memorable of Poe's tales are represented: *The Oval Portrait, Berenice, The Black Cat, Ligeia, The Cask of Amontillado, Mr Valdemar, The Tell-Tale Heart, Morella* and *The Pit and the Pendulum*, all hosted by one of the greatest horror stars of all time.

Sadly, the series' low budget mitigated against its success, and it was not broadcast until years later. The episodes themselves are perfunctorily produced and directed; although they are quite faithful to Poe's texts, their execution is often lifeless and lacklustre. In some respects, they almost seem as though they were made for the educational market, as Lee is popped in at a crucial moment in *Usher* to 'explain' some of its elements to us.

Each episode runs approximately thirty minutes in length. Consequently, in the case of the longer tales such as *Usher*, the story has to be somewhat truncated for a change, rather than expanded upon as in the feature versions. *Usher* stars Jeremy Crutchley as a very young-looking Roderick, with South African actor Graham Hopkins as Poe's narrator/protagonist, in this case called Paul.

There are a couple of points of interest in this version of *Usher*. For one, Crutchley, despite his youthful appearance, gives an intense and tortured performance. The character of Madeline, so pivotal to Poe's story, barely registers as a presence, to the extent that the actress who played the role isn't even credited. It is difficult to find much information on this series, but your humble author has a theory that perhaps Crutchley played Madeline in drag. There are a couple of hallucinatory sequences in which he does that very thing, and it may be that he played a dual role here, although he is not credited as doing so. Roderick does mention that he and Madeline are 'twins,' so, until I hear from Crutchley himself on the matter, and he has gone on to considerable success in such series as *Salem* (2015-2017), I'm sticking with my theory.

Under the somewhat torpid direction of James Ryan, however, the climax falls flat. There is really no 'fall' of the House of Usher, because the budget doesn't allow for it. We see a few scraps of material thrown at the camera, and a long shot of the Usher estate seemingly being engulfed by the surrounding forest, but that's about it.

The rarely-adapted *The Oval Portrait* stars British actor Patrick Ryecart as artist Bernard Bouvet, with Barbara Roko as the object of his obsession. Opening in the present day, the episode then flashes back to Bouvet's obsessional rendering of his beautiful wife on canvas. As this was one of Poe's shortest stories (running only two pages in its initial 1842 publication), there is a fair amount of material that is extrapolated upon, but the gist of the tale, the fact that the artist has quite literally put his wife's life and soul into the portrait, is still intact. The acting is mostly good, with Ryecart taking most of the honours under the direction of Bill Hays. Unlike the portrait, however, the episode itself is mostly devoid of life, and certainly of passion.

*Berenice*, adapted from one of Poe's most obsessive tales, completely lacks any sense of monomania, which is essential to the piece. Starring Croatian actor Bozidar Alic as Egaaeus, who is obsessed with the teeth of his new but ailing bride Berenice (Alma Prica), the episode ambles along when it should grip; someone like Alfred Hitchcock would have understood the obsessive nature of the character, but, alas, that is not the level of talent we are dealing with here. There is no heightened emotion, no operatic intensity, both of which are called for, and the climax contains no shock whatsoever. English dubbing of several of the Croatian actors doesn't help. Sluggishly directed by Dejan Sorak, *Berenice* is one of the weakest entries in the series.

*The Black Cat* is slightly better; although the teleplay is just as flat as the others, the acting is of a higher calibre, with Susan George, probably best known for her memorable performance in Sam Peckinpah's *Straw Dogs* (1971) receiving top billing as the long-suffering wife of a drunkard (Jon Laurimore) who ends up killing her cat (or so he thinks) and then killing her, walling them both up in his basement. Told in flashback, the story is set in Ireland for no apparent reason, and, despite the acting, this great tale still fails to thrill because of turgid direction. One of Poe's most gruesome stories is rendered nearly bloodless here, and with an almost total lack of suspense.

*Ligeia* is also quite perfunctory, noted mainly for a couple of tame sex scenes and some quotes from Poe's story, with the best performance given by Dorette Nel as Rowena/Ligeia. The poem within the story, 'The Conquerer Worm,' is quoted as well: 'While the angels, all pallid and wan/Uprising, unveiling, affirm/That the play is the tragedy, "Man,"/And its hero, the Conqueror Worm.' Directed by James Ryan, *Ligeia* has none of the style of Corman's film version and falls nearly as flat as *Berenice*.

The next adaptation is one of the finest in the series. *The Cask of Amontillado* shines because of the casting: With Freddie Jones as Fortunato, one could hardly go wrong. Jones, one of Great Britain's finest character actors, is probably best-known to American audiences for his role in David Lynch's *The Elephant Man* (1980), but he had already endeared himself to genre fans for his performances in Hammer's *Frankenstein Must Be Destroyed* (1969) and *The Satanic Rites of Dracula* (1973) as well as such television productions as *The Ghosts of Morley Hall* (1976) and *Children of the Stones* (1977).

Bill Simon plays Montressor, and he is nearly as effective as Jones. Also starring in the episode is Catherine Schell, a Bond girl from *On Her Majesty's Secret Service* (1969) and perhaps best known to international audiences for her continuing role on the television series *Space: 1999* (1975-1977), co-starring Martin Landau and Varb ara Bain. In *Amontillado*, she portrays Montressor's haughty and duplicitous wife. The episode is better directed (by Bill Hayes) than most, although the photography is so dark that, at times, it's difficult to tell whether the characters are in a wine cellar or somewhere in the lower circles of Hell. The costumes are colourful, however, and the acting superlative. *The Cask of Amontillado* is not only extremely faithful to Poe; it is a gripping exercise in poetic justice and suspense.

*Mr Valdemar* (note the shortened title) is one of the more gruesome efforts. It opens on a sexual note, with a mesmerist (Hugh Rouse) using his powers on a beautiful woman (Samantha Peo) to get her to strip for him. Somehow, I don't recall that scene from Poe's story!

Once the tale gets rolling, however, it's pretty faithful to its source, with Valdemar (Paul Slabolepszy) piercing the veil of death under the mesmerist's spell, and accenting the physical horror that is essential to Poe's vision. Valdemar's death rattles and his blackened tongue are difficult images to forget, and, for once, the series does not stint on the ghastly proceedings. James Ryan's direction is more assured this time, and *Mr Valdemar* has a visceral punch that many of the other episodes lack.

Incredibly, one of the most famous short stories ever written is mis-identified in the opening credits of the next episode: *The Tell Tail Heart* (sic), as it is misspelled, is an unmitigated disaster from start to finish. Whether or not something was lost in translation between Croatia and South Africa, spelling *Tale* as *Tail* is inexcusable, and sadly characteristic of the production's slipshod quality (or, rather, lack of quality) throughout, from the risibly artificial 'eye' worn by actor John Hussey, to the retrieval of said eye from beneath the floorboards by Michael McCabe at the not-so-thrilling climax.

Yes, you read that correctly: rather than removing his victim's 'hideous heart' from where he had placed it, he shows the police the 'hideous' eye, completely destroying one of the most famous endings in horror history. Hugh Whysall, who wrote every episode, also directed this one, so the entire mess can be laid at his feet. The less said about this entry, the better.

The next episode, *Morella*, also directed by Whysall, is another exercise in nothingness, or perhaps one should say being and nothingness, as Poe's story features elements of existentialism. Morella is a woman with a vast intellect who delves into the big questions: what is human identity and does it survive death?

Corman's version was essentially a rewrite of *Ligeia*, with the spirit of Morella literally possessing her daughter's body. Poe's original is more subtle; when Morella dies giving birth to her daughter, the unnamed narrator refuses to give the child a name. By her tenth birthday, her resemblance to Morella is downright disturbing and he decides to have her baptised, as he had believed that her mother was evil. At the ceremony, the priest asks the girl's name and the narrator bursts out with 'Morella!' at which point the girl dies.

While Whysall's teleplay is far more faithful to the original story than Corman's, once again the direction is lifeless and the dialogue stilted. While John Lesley and Camilla Waldman are both competent in their respective roles, the attempts to combine sex with the metaphysical just don't work, and Lesley's character comes across as a cruel, rather despicable husband rather than the frightened narrator of Poe's story. Matters are not helped by the fact that Waldman is required to play both Morella and her daughter, the latter of whom supposedly waits until she is seventeen to be given a name and a baptism. To say that having an actress obviously in her thirties attempt to play a seventeen-year-old is miscasting may be an understatement, and the episode falls apart at the end, where it should be at its most compelling, sharing a fate with so many others in the series.

*The Pit and the Pendulum* – set, unaccountably, in World War I – stars Alan Granville as a soldier who has visions of the Inquisition, and eventually finds himself strapped down to Poe's famous torture device. While there are attempts to create an atmosphere of dread, and some creative art direction, Whysall's flaccid direction is again in evidence, and there is no real suspense or horror. A coda, in which the soldier is rescued only to be thrown back into the horrors of war, is an obvious attempt at a social statement that just doesn't come off.

The piece de resistance of the series is a two-part dramatisation of *The Masque of the Red Death* that is a pale tallow candle next to Corman's full-blooded version. The good news is that Lee himself plays Prince Prospero, but Whysall's script gives him little to do, with none of the intelligent, witty dialogue that was given to Price in Corman's telling. Lee merely goes through the motions here, seeming hesitant and unsure of himself, a rare thing for the actor. One can only assume that Whysall gave him little to no direction and left it up to Lee to flounder in the role.

Again, the low budget dooms the adaptation, with no real atmosphere or sense of time and place achieved. If you're looking for Poe's purple, yellow and black chambers, you won't find them here. The supporting actors are given no direction either, and what could have been a real achievement – Lee as Prince Prospero sounds mighty indeed – fails to elicit any real sense of doom, despair or horror.

The final episode, titled simply *Biographical Portrait*, is credited to a director called N Hetherington – a pseudonym, most likely – and stars James Ryan as Poe. Ryan had directed some of the better episodes of the series, and he is actually quite good as Poe, giving a solid, tortured performance. The series ends, appropriately, with Poe's death.

Taken as a whole, *Tales of Mystery and Imagination* is a classic case of missed opportunities, a train wreck that should have been a high point of Poe on television. The most consistently good elements of the series are, predictably, Lee's intros and outros. Every episode ends with him intoning, in that deep, basso voice, 'Goodnight and…sleep well.'

Poe was absent from the tube for a while after that, with the exception of a reading by Sean Pertwee on 6 March 2001 of 'The Black Cat' on a British series called *The Fear* and readings by Giancarlo Giannini of 'The Masque of the Red Death,' 'Morella' and 'The Tell-Tale Heart' on a similar Italian series called *Racconti Neri* in 2006. A much more full-blooded adaptation of Poe arrived in 2007 as an episode of the series *Masters of Horror* on the American cable channel Showtime.

*Masters of Horror* showcased one-hour terror tales directed by 'masters' of the genre, such as George A Romero, John Carpenter and Stuart Gordon, the latter of whom directed the H P Lovecraft adaptation *Re-Animator* (1985), starring American actor Jeffrey Combs in the title role of Dr Herbert West. For *Masters of Horror*, Gordon wrote and directed another Lovecraft tale, *Dreams in the Witch-House* (2005) and co-wrote and directed Poe's *The Black Cat* (2007), the latter co-written by his *Re-Animator* collaborator, Dennis Paoli. Their version of Poe's tale starred Combs as Poe himself in 1840 Philadelphia, dealing with his alcoholism, near-poverty, his wife's illness and her pet black cat, Pluto.

Combs is a highly talented theatrically-trained actor who has specialised in genre roles since his breakthrough success in *Re-Animator*, following up with *From Beyond* (1986), *The Pit and the Pendulum* (1991) and *Castle Freak* (1995). He also starred in *Bride of Re-Animator* (1989) and in the final film of the series (so far), *Beyond Re-Animator* (2003), both directed by Brian Yuzna.

When I interviewed Combs in 1991, I told him that I thought he was one of the few actors working at that time who recalled the glory days of such genre specialists as Vincent Price, Peter Cushing and Christopher Lee. He responded that he wanted to 'bring back some of that style. All of those guys in the earlier horror films were stage-based. That's where that kind of grand attitude comes from – a little larger than life. A lot of actors don't have that sort of base. They just come in and don't kick it in the rear. It's very flattering to be compared to people like Vincent Price, Peter Cushing and all those great actors.'

Combs and Gordon turned out to be a match made in Horror Heaven, as he said of Gordon: 'He understands the process. A lot of film directors don't really know how to talk to actors other than to say, "Stand there," or, "Can you say it louder and faster?" Stuart really knows how to get the detail. He can really base it in honest-to-goodness motivation and reality. Although it's fantastical, he likes to base it in fact. He's a great guy. We have a lot of good laughs.' Also starring in *The Black Cat* was Elyse Levesque as Virginia Poe (*nee* Virginia Clemm). Levesque is a Canadian actress who has gone on to be quite ubiquitous in television, later playing a continuing character in the series *Orphan Black* (2013-2017). *Masters of Horror* was a Canadian-American co-production based in Vancouver, so a great deal of Canadian talent was involved.

When *Re-Animator* was released in 1985, its distributor, Empire Pictures, had decided to distribute it without an MPAA rating, meaning that the extreme gore contained in Gordon's vision could remain intact. George A Romero had started the trend of unrated horror with his sequel to *Night of the Living Dead* in 1978 called *Dawn of the Dead*. It was a risky decision that paid off, but by 1985, unrated theatrical horror had become even more of a gamble. *Re-Animator* didn't really find its audience until it was released on home video, and that changed the whole ball game.

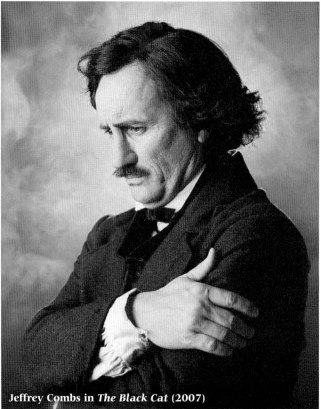

Jeffrey Combs in *The Black Cat* (2007)

Movies released on video didn't have to adhere to a ratings system, nor did premium cable television, so Gordon's extremely gruesome take on *The Black Cat* didn't have to concern itself with the formerly strict American broadcasting code. In the case of Showtime, viewers were paying to have the service beamed into their homes, and they weren't paying for censorship.

*The Black Cat*, therefore, has Gordon's trademarked gore, including the graphic gouging out of the cat's eye in close-up (with the added gross-out factor of Poe's stepping on the eye and squashing it after it falls to the floor) and an equally detailed axe to the cranium. The only items missing from Gordon's theatrical features are sex and nudity.

The conceit of Paoli's and Gordon's adaptation is that Poe himself is the unnamed narrator of the tale; we don't discover until the end that (Spoiler Alert!) Poe is actually fantasising his story in a drunken, hallucinatory nightmare. In his fantasy, the black cat is trying to destroy his life, but in reality, as we learn in the denouement, the cat has inspired him to write one of his greatest stories, which he can sell to his publisher, George Graham (Aron Tager).

*The Black Cat* is a tour-de-force for Combs, who gives one of the greatest portrayals of Poe ever committed to celluloid. During the fever dream, he goes completely mad, killing the cat in a horrible, sadistic way that ends in the poor creature's hanging. Yet before this ghastly act of brutality, he has shown total devotion to his wife, whom he refers to as 'Sissy,' especially when she becomes ill with what was then referred to as 'consumption.' Yet Poe's 'imp of the perverse,' which is referred to in the opening titles, causes him to do exactly the wrong things at the wrong times, which culminates in him accidentally cleaving an axe through Virginia's skull.

Although Poe's original tale only unfolds during the final act, when it arrives, it is quite faithful to its source. Gordon and Combs capture the essence of Poe, not just in the telling of the tale, but in the depiction of the man himself. Combs is pitch-perfect, both as the physical incarnation of the man and in the interpretation of his psyche. The episode is at times difficult to watch, not only because of its animal cruelty (no animals were actually harmed, thankfully), but in Combs' masterful portrayal of Poe in a state of madness. Life imitates art, and, at the conclusion, art imitates life.

Levesque is also fine as Virginia, and the scene in which she plays the piano and attempts to sing before vomiting blood all over the piano keys is genuinely disturbing. But it's Combs' show all the way, and he runs with it, giving perhaps the best performance of his career. *The Black Cat* has none of the jokiness that pervaded *Re-Animator*: the subject matter is treated entirely seriously and respectfully. Gordon, like Corman before him, can take pride in the fact that he has honoured both Poe and Lovecraft with superior adaptations of their work.

In an age when most films are now shot on digital formats, traditional television is also undergoing a tremendous upheaval. Gone are the days when the networks and, in the US, the Nielsen ratings held sway. It is now

*Theatre Fantastique* (2014–2017)

the age of Netflix, Amazon and many other 'streaming' services, and the medium has become more experimental than it ever was. Both quantity and quality are in abundance. It is something of a golden age for television, with new methods of distribution that would have been unheard of even thirty years ago.

One such innovation is the rise of the 'web series,' episodic videos that are released on the Internet and are part of the web television medium that debuted in the late 1990s and rose to prominence in the early 21st Century. These so-called 'webisodes' are often independently financed, and, now that high-definition television is the norm, can be viewed both on computers and TV sets.

One of the pioneers of independently produced web series is a young man named Ansel Faraj, a writer/director/producer who seeks his inspiration from such filmmakers as Fritz Lang, from whom he derived his 2014 feature *Doctor Mabuse: Etiopomar*; and, of course, from Poe, upon whose stories he based four episodes of his web series *Theatre Fantastique*, a horror anthology that debuted in 2014 and had a belated second series in 2017.

a THEATRE FANTASTIQUE Halloween 2015 Special — a short film by ANSEL FARAJ "A POEM OF POE" online October 16 2015 www.hollinsworthproductions.com

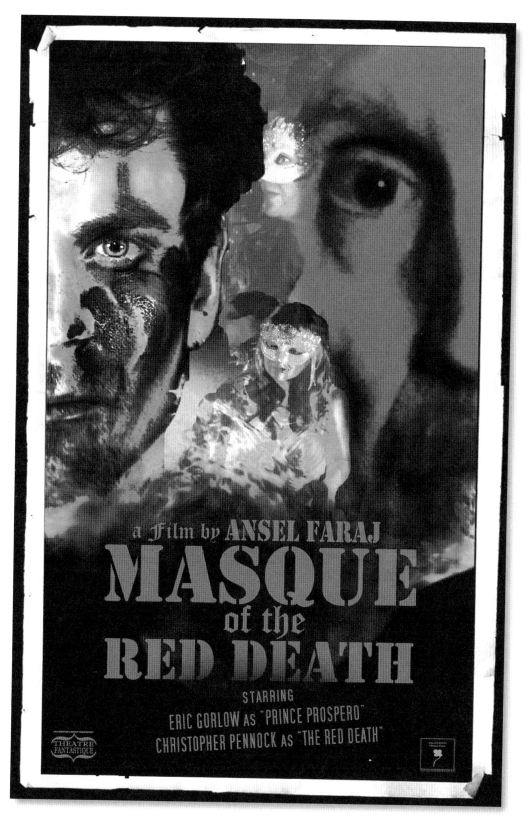

a
THEATRE FANTASTIQUE
Halloween 2015 Special

a short film by ANSEL FARAJ

" A POEM OF POE "

starring
CHRISTOPHER PENNOCK  KELSEY HEWLETT  ERIC GORLOW  ELYSE ASHTON

online October 16 2015  www.hollinsworthproductions.com

Born in Los Angeles in 1991, Faraj casts veteran actors from TV's *Dark Shadows* in many of his projects, including Jerry Lacy, Kathryn Leigh Scott, Lara Parker and Christopher Pennock. All of his productions are made on shoestring budgets, but they are made with a love of the genre that fairly bursts from the filmmaker's (tell tale) heart.

Interviewed for this book, Faraj related to me how such a young man could have been inspired by such old films: 'When I was six years old, I decided I would be a film director, though none of my family was in the industry or had industry friends. I used to make movies on VHS tape with friends from school, and with Lego toys and action figures, and I just never stopped. I did not attend film school, I just kept at it, teaching myself everything I could on movies, both history and technique. And part of that self-schooling was watching every movie I could. I would sit in front of TCM (Turner Classic Movies) all day long as a kid, and the Universal monsters were my pathway into the world of film.'

Aside from Fritz Lang, Faraj lists Roger Corman, Robert Altman, Christopher Nolan, Federico Fellini and Ken Russell as his favourite directors. Too young to have seen the original run of *Dark Shadows* in the late sixties and early seventies, Faraj fell in love with its first film incarnation: 'I saw *House of Dark Shadows* (1970), the first *DS* feature film, on VHS when I was far too young to be watching it, and it scared the hell out of me. But I could not get enough. It and *Night of Dark Shadows* (1971), the second feature film, kind of became obsessions of mine, and obviously extended out into the original series. When I was writing *Doctor Mabuse*, I wrote it for Jerry Lacy, his voice, his... intensity – but I was seventeen and I never thought I would ever get him, or any of the cast, in a movie... But when I was twenty, I took a leap of faith, and reached out to the actors with the script; they liked the story and my vision for the project, and came along for the ride. I'm eternally grateful. They have all become family to me, and they are phenomenal actors to work with.'

One of the things that makes Faraj's Poe pictures special is the fact that they seem to be set in some nebulous, Poesque underworld. Faraj told me they were shot in his garage! He continued: '... My makeshift studio, a cramped 8 by 8 foot space where I've shot nearly everything... And they were all made with the lowest resources. It's all cardboard and chewing gum tied with a shoestring. I studied a lot of Mario Bava and tried to channel him and his magic tricks for how to create worlds and atmosphere with an empty stage, and to create this strange netherworld landscape, where it could be alternately creepy and unsettling, but also fun, like a carnival haunted house... We had a great time making the two seasons of *Theatre Fantastique*.'

I pointed out to Faraj that he seemed to have established a kind of repertory company for his films. He responded, 'Yes, this is the *Dark Shadows* influence on me – a strong, reliable and talented acting troupe – and my group of actors are some of the best people I know... Nathan Wilson... when he's not acting, he writes and produces, and was a producer on *A Poem of Poe* and played the

Phantom of the Opera in *Masque of the Red Death*. From the four Poe films (*The Madness of Roderick Usher*, *A Descent Into a Maelstrom*, *Masque of the Red Death* and *A Poem of Poe*), Eric Gorlow, who plays Poe and Prince Prospero is a good friend... Elyse Ashton, who is Madeline Usher, is awesome; Kelsey Hewlett is Annabel Lee; this is not her genre – she always bugs me to write a "normal" movie – but I really appreciate that she enthusiastically returns time and time again... And then there is Chris Pennock, who I cannot say enough about. He is amazing. He gives so much.'

Each of Faraj's short Poe pictures – the average running time is around 15 minutes – is positively brimming with Poesque mood. *The Madness of Roderick Usher* manages to tell Poe's tale in a brisk but surreal fourteen minutes: Told entirely from the viewpoint of Roderick Usher (as played by Pennock), it takes the viewer to the brink of insanity and beyond. *A Descent into a Maelstrom* is equally effective, mixing in elements of both 'Annabel Lee' and the legend of the Flying Dutchman, again with Pennock in the lead role. Pennock both narrates and stars (as the Red Death) in *Masque of the Red Death*, part of the 2017 series, which includes a 'guest appearance' by Wilson as the Phantom of the Opera. Finally, *A Poem of Poe* is a 2015 Halloween tribute to Poe, with Pennock presiding over all as Death, Hewlett as Annabel Lee, Gorlow as Poe and Elyse Ashton as Madeline Usher. This may be the director's most authentic Poe picture of all, a phantasmagoria of the author's fears and loves set to the strains of Camilla Saint-Saens' *Danse Macabre*. Faraj's short film is

like one of Poe's alcohol-induced fever dreams come to life, a delirious delight of decadence and doom.

As for his future projects, the talented young Faraj told me, 'I had to take a break from the genre for a moment and challenge myself; as a result I directed a love story entitled *Will & Liz*, which is now streaming on Amazon Prime, and it's a film I'm very proud of. And we're working on a new horror project – I've always wanted to make a kind of "folk horror" film, along the lines of *Blood on Satan's Claw* (1971) or *Cry of the Banshee* (1970), and this new project is in that vein, which is exciting, hopefully in release for Halloween 2019.'

PBS returned to Poe in October 2017, just in time for Halloween, for another *American Masters* documentary, this time running to feature length and more in depth. *Edgar Allan Poe: Buried Alive* is perhaps the finest television biography of Poe to date, setting the record straight on many of the apocryphal stories about his life and death in the process. Written and directed by Eric Strange, the one hour, 24-minute production is chock full of conversations with Poe scholars, many of whom point out that the initial obituary for the author was written by none other than editor/poet/critic Rufus Wilmot Griswold, one of Poe's more vindictive enemies, who acidly penned that 'few will be grieved' by Poe's death, that the author had few friends and that he suffered from 'madness or melancholy', all of which gave rise to Poe's reputation as somewhat akin to the characters in his horror stories. In actual fact, Poe had many friends and was by all accounts a kind and loving husband; Griswold was, in many respects, jealous of Poe's talents and success with 'The Raven,' among other works. He tarnished Poe's reputation for many years, yet Griswold is forgotten while Poe is as popular now as he has ever been.

*Edgar Allan Poe: Buried Alive* is narrated by actress Kathleen Turner, whose deep, throaty delivery suits the subject well. Appearing as Poe himself, and reciting some of his poetry, is actor Denis O'Hare, previously seen on the FX Network series *American Horror Story*. He is a very convincing Poe, both in appearance and manner, and his recitations of some of the author's more poignant poems such as "A Dream within a Dream," are superbly performed.

There have been countless adaptations of Poe on television, and to cover all of them in depth would require a book of its own, but that is another story for another day.

# CHAPTER SEVEN
# THE EXPLOITABLE POE

*'Convinced myself, I seek not to convince.'*

***Berenice***

Regional horror exploitation films began to rear their frequently ugly heads in the United States in the late 1950s and early 1960s. Although the trend started out rather innocuously with fare made for the drive-ins such as the double bill of *The Killer Shrews* and *The Giant Gila Monster* (both filmed in Texas in 1959), independent filmmakers far outside the studio system quickly decided that they could give the public what Hollywood still did not dare to do: as much sex, gore and violence as the waning production code would allow.

Florida-based filmmaker Herschell Gordon Lewis began the so-called 'splatter movie' trend with *Blood Feast* (1963), in which young women in various stages of undress are horribly mutilated and murdered. Filmed in less than glorious Eastman Color, the film cleaned up at the box office, despite outrage from critics and other arbiters of good taste.

In Connecticut, producer Alan Iselin came up with another double bill aimed at the drive-in market, *The Horror of Party Beach* and *The Curse of the Living Corpse* (1964). The former featured as many bikini-clad girls as the screen could hold and monsters that tore them to shreds, with gore filmed in black and white (in which the blood was actually chocolate syrup). The latter film is distinguished by the casting of a young Roy Scheider (*Jaws*, 1975) in a supporting role, along with brief female nudity and a scene in which a human head is served up on a dinner plate. Incredibly, the double bill was released by 20th Century-Fox.

Most regional horror films didn't get that sort of treatment and had to settle for distribution from smaller, lesser-known companies. One such outfit was Hemisphere Pictures, who, in 1966, put together a double bill of a Filipino

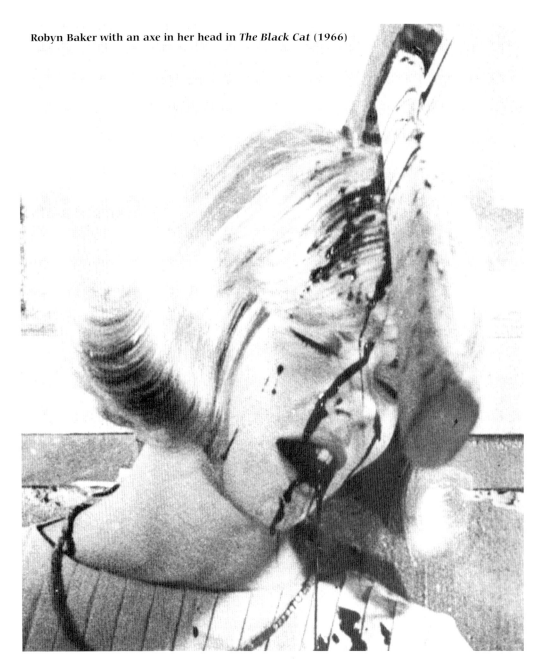

Robyn Baker with an axe in her head in *The Black Cat* (1966)

picture called *The Blood Drinkers* paired with yet another version of Poe's 'The Black Cat', filmed in Texas. Billed onscreen as Edgar Allen Poe's (sic) *The Black Cat*, the low-budget black and white film is actually fairly faithful to Poe's original, although the setting is updated to contemporary Dallas.

Written and directed by Harold Hoffman (*The Trial of Lee Harvey Oswald*, 1964), *The Black Cat*, as was the case with many regional features, starred local, unknown actors. Robert Frost (not the poet, obviously!) portrays Lou, a mentally disturbed alcoholic who is obsessed with the idea that his black cat, Pluto, is somehow possessed by the spirit of his late, apparently abusive father, or perhaps sent by him to Lou as a demon from Hell with the object of tormenting him. His long-suffering wife Diana (Robyn Baker) puts up with his alcoholism, but, after he tortures and kills the cat, she has him committed to an asylum.

Seemingly cured, Lou returns home to find another black cat, or perhaps the same one risen from the dead, hanging about the house. Lou's mental illness returns and he is now convinced that the cat has returned from the dead to seek revenge.

The final reel of *The Black Cat* is pure Grand Guignol, with Lou bashing his wife's head in with an axe, then walling her up in the basement. As in the original story, the police show up and question Lou about his wife's whereabouts, and the cat, also walled up behind the wall, gives him away. Unlike Poe's story, however, Lou runs out of the house, gets into his car and speeds off, with the police giving chase. In a nice touch of poetic justice, Lou sees the cat sitting in the middle of the road, swerves to avoid it, and ends up in a fatal car crash. Another interesting dramatic choice is that, as we see in the final shot of the film, his eye has been gouged out, just as he had gouged out the cat's eye.

Filmed in crisp, moody black and white by Walter Schenk *(Faster, Pussycat! Kill! Kill!, 1965) The Black Cat* establishes what might be called 'Poesploitation.' Although there is relatively little sex in the film (a prostitute coming onto Lou in a bar is about the extent of it), the blood flows like, well, chocolate syrup in the gore scenes. The sequences involving the torture, hanging and electrocution of the cat are grimly disturbing, and rumours have circulated on the Internet that a cat was actually killed for the film. That seems doubtful, however, as the sequence in question is achieved with a series of cuts, and there is an animal trainer named Scott Shawmake listed in the credits, so one fervently hopes that no cats (or anything else) were harmed in the making of the film.

The acting is quite amateurish, as might be expected, yet the film has some highly effective moments, although Hoffman's direction is merely perfunctory. Technically, it's a vast improvement over the 1934 *Maniac*, the first exploitation version of Poe's story. The rock-bottom budget is a virtue in some respects: the film has a gritty, immediate quality that makes it all seem quite believable. And as if to wallow in the film's exploitation roots, several rock and roll songs are played (poorly) in a bar, including the old classic 'Bo Diddley.' I wonder if Poe would have been amused or horrified.

By 1972, the nature of the film industry had completely changed. The introduction of the rating system in the US led to a spate of 'X-rated' cinema the likes of which the entertainment world had never seen. A mere four years after the rating system was instituted, hard-core porn movies such as *Deep Throat* were playing at public cinemas for the first time in history. Mainstream filmmakers started putting a great deal of sex, nudity, violence and strong language into their films, and the results were blockbusters like

John Boorman's *Deliverance* (1972), as dark and nasty a film as Hollywood had ever made up to that point – and released to great acclaim.

In this highly permissive climate, the stories of Edgar Allan Poe seemed positively quaint. Nevertheless, enterprising filmmakers still explored his works because of their exploitation possibilities. After all, Poe's tales were rife with implied incest, necrophilia, psychosis and all manner of dark, grim suggestion. Implicit elements could easily be made explicit in the audio-visual medium of film.

The same year that *Deep Throat* and *Deliverance* ignited the box office queues, Poe returned in a small independent film called *The Oval Portrait*, aka *Edgar Allen Poe's* (sic) *The Oval Portrait*, aka *One Minute before Death*. Directed by Mexican filmmaker Rogelio A Gonzalez, but filmed in the United States in English, *The Oval Portrait* keeps the bare bones of Poe's story intact, but updates the setting to the Civil War and its immediate aftermath.

In the screenplay by Enrique Torres Tudela, a woman who has arrived with her mother at her uncle's mansion for the reading of his will becomes apparently possessed by the soul of a dead woman whose spirit is trapped inside a painting. American actors were cast, headed by Wanda Hendrix (*Ride the Pink Horse*, 1947) as the possessed woman in question, with Barry Coe (*Peyton Place*, 1957) as a doomed lover and Maray Ayres (*The Cycle Savages*, 1969) as the woman in the portrait. Also in the cast was Gisele MacKenzie, an actress who had distinguished herself in the early days of television on such programmes as Lux Playhouse and The United States Steel Hour, as the possessed woman's mother.

Scenes from *The Oval Portrait* (1972)

*Chapter Seven – THE EXPLOITABLE POE*

For most of its 86-minute running time, *The Oval Portrait* plays like a star-crossed romance, a la Wuthering Heights. While staying at the old mansion to hear the reading of the will, Lisa Bickingham (Hendrix) seemingly becomes possessed by the spirit of the late Rebecca (Moray Ayres), whose portrait hangs on the wall downstairs and whose room she is occupying. The story quickly becomes a soap opera when we learn that the will being read is that of Lisa's uncle, a colonel in the Union Army who left his daughter Rebecca alone when he went off to war. During that time, a renegade Confederate soldier named Joseph Hudson (Coe) hid in the house and Rebecca fell in love with him. Hudson is captured as he and Rebecca are about to be married, and Rebecca – who is now pregnant – is thrown out of the house by the colonel. She loses her baby, the colonel dies of grief and Rebecca dies just before Hudson escapes and attempts to return to her. In very Poesque fashion, he goes mad with grief himself. By the end of the film, we learn that he has unearthed Rebecca's mummified corpse and keeps it with him, dragging it out of storage occasionally to dance with it.

Somehow, the filmmakers obtained the rights to some of Les Baxter's music, mostly from the American version of *Black Sunday*, which adds a certain richness to the soundtrack, although the rather over-ripe main theme, 'Haunted Love' by Tudela, is played over the opening credits and throughout much of the film. Obviously, the use of Baxter's music is an attempt to give the film the flavour of a Roger Corman Poe picture, but it isn't enough to elevate the rock-bottom budget and grainy, murky 16mm cinematography.

The acting is spotty at best. This was the final film for Hendrix, and for whatever reason, her voice is dubbed – atrociously. As such, Lisa becomes a non-character. McKenzie as the housekeeper fares better, although her histrionics seem outdated for the seventies, and the slightly out-of-period wigs and costumes don't help. Coe probably comes across best, as his grief slowly turns into madness; the final scene in which he dances with the corpse is actually effective and disturbing.

On the whole, though *The Oval Portrait* is dismal; a film that doesn't quite know what it wants to be. As such it is neither fish nor fowl, neither a Gothic romance nor an out and out horror film. Since1972, the film has fallen into – perhaps deserved – obscurity.

One of the most bizarre films to feature Poe as a character, *The Spectre of Edgar Allan Poe* (1974) is another independently produced movie, in this case directed by one Mohy Quandour, who didn't make another feature film until 2010. As was the case with *The Oval Portrait*, *The Spectre of Edgar Allan Poe* mostly starred actors who were a bit past their prime, although Poe is played by Robert Walker Jr, the son of Robert Walker and Jennifer Jones, a young actor who would ultimately make his mark in television. During the early seventies, however, he was trying his hand at feature films and was relegated to roles in such low-budget jobs as *The Man from O.R.G.Y.* (1970) and *Beware! The Blob* (1972).

**LO SPETTRO DI EDGAR ALLAN POE**

ROBERT WALKER Jr. TOM DRAKE CESAR ROMERO CAROL OHMART

Regia di MOHY QUANDOUR distribuzione ARDEN CINEMATOGRAFICA produzione CINTEL PRODUCTIONS EASTMANCOLOR

Hollywood veteran Cesar Romero, cast here as Dr Richard Grimaldi, had certainly seen better times. Praised for his roles in such features as *Captain from Castile* (1947), his most recent pop culture fame had arisen from his numerous appearances on the *Batman* television series (1966-1968) as The Joker, arch-enemy of Batman (Adam West) and Robin (Burt Ward). Romero would continue to work in television for some time to come.

Tom Drake (*Meet Me in St Louis*,1944) was cast as Dr Adam Forrest, while Carol Ohmart (*The House on Haunted Hill*, 1958) assumed the role of Lisa Grimaldi. The whole project was pulled together by Quandour, who, in addition to his directing duties, produced and wrote it as well,

The screenplay, from a story and treatment by Kenneth Hartford and Denton Foxx, is a weird one: Poe's beloved Lenore falls into a coma and is believed to be dead. Her burial starts to take place, but she awakens from her cataleptic trance and is ultimately rescued from being buried alive. Sadly, the traumatic experience has left her quite mad. Her friend Dr Forrest advises Poe to take her to Dr Grimaldi's asylum. Gradually, Poe and Forrest discover that there are disturbing goings-on at the asylum, and they make a plan to break into the place at night and find out for themselves.

It transpires that Dr Grimaldi is performing experiments on his patients that have to do with injecting them with snake venom. All hell breaks loose in the final act, complete with a PG-rated axe murder, and it is postulated that Poe's macabre imagination was inspired by the 'true' events of this film.

Needless to say, the story itself is a total invention and not a very clever one. Much of the film takes place in the dank, murky asylum, complemented, if that is the word, by dank, murky photography. Walker looks the part as Poe and gives a competent performance, but the script gives him little to do. All of the other performers walk through their roles. The film was sold as a gore picture, yet there is relatively little carnage in it; it may have been cut for the PG rating. Ultimately, then, *The Spectre of Edgar Allan Poe* is neither a Poe biopic nor a gore movie. In fact, the ghastliest thing in *The Spectre of Edgar Allan Poe* is the folk-rock song 'Lenore,' played under the opening credits.

Once *The Spectre of Edgar Allan Poe* had vanished into the ectoplasmic mists of obscurity – which was almost instantaneous – Poe was absent from cinema screens for fifteen years, making way for killers with chainsaws, killers wearing ski masks, and killers entering the nightmares of teenagers. The horror film had devolved into the slasher film, where cardboard characters, R-rated nudity and extreme gore held sway. When Poe finally did return in 1989, it was with a vengeance, and with a kind of Grand Guignol fervour that had only been hinted at previously.

A whole new market had opened up for what used to be called B-movies: Home video. The 1980s had seen the home video market explode, much as television had in the 1950s, and it was a new world for exploitation, horror and sex film producers. Home video all but killed the drive-ins, and movies that once would have been made for outdoor cinemas were now made for home consumption, bypassing theatrical release altogether. Porn movies were hugely popular on video as well: no longer did men and couples have to join the 'raincoat crowd' in dingy cinemas to watch coupling on the screen. Now they could do so in the privacy of their own homes.

Similarly, the drive-in crowd no longer had to endure rain, noisy patrons or poor lighting at outdoor venues; now they could view such exploitation fare as *Sorority Babes in the Slimeball Bowl-O-Rama* (1988) with as few – or as many – distractions as they chose, thanks to their VCRs. It was in this atmosphere that such disparate producers as Harry Alan Towers, who had made films such as *The Face of Fu Manchu* (1965) and *The Bloody Judge* (1970) – and none other than Roger Corman himself – decided that the time was ripe for a Poe revival, albeit with an exploitation angle.

Towers was first past the post with a very modern update of *The House of Usher* in 1989. Towers was a colourful figure, a London-born producer who made over 80 feature films, mostly of the exploitation variety. Always a somewhat shady character (in 1961, he was charged with operating a vice ring in New York, but he jumped bail and went to Europe), he often operated one step ahead of the law, producing films in first one country, then the other. By 1989, he was based in South Africa, where most of *The House of Usher* was filmed.

Towers always had a knack for casting excellent actors in his rather lurid productions. He had somehow coaxed Herbert Lom to star in the 'women in prison' film (complete with X-rated lesbian scenes) *99 Women*, directed by Jesus Franco in 1968, for example. The brilliant but alcoholic actor Oliver Reed, who had made his mark in Hammer's *The Curse of the Werewolf* (1961) and had gone on to be Oscar-nominated for Ken Russell's *Tommy* (1975), had previously appeared for Towers in his 1974 version of *Ten Little Indians*, and he was cast in *The House of Usher* in the starring role of Roderick.

As his brother Walter Usher (a character not in Poe's story), the distinguished actor Donald Pleasence appeared. With a long career in films (including a key role in Roman Polanski's *Cul-de-Sac* (1966), Pleasence had often found himself in horror films such as *The Flesh and the Fiends* (1959), *Circus of Horrors* (1960) and *From Beyond the Grave* (1974); he had also played Blofeld in the James Bond epic *You Only Live Twice* (1967). Pleasence had recently enjoyed a career resurgence by playing the role of Dr Sam Loomis in John Carpenter's watershed slasher *Halloween* (1978), a part that he reprised in several of the film's sequels.

American actress Romy Windsor played Molly McNulty, the female lead, while South African actor Rufus Swart essayed the role of her fiancé, Ryan Usher. The remainder of the cast was filled by South African actors.

The screenplay by Michael J Murray is an obvious attempt to transform Poe's classic tale of brooding horror into a 1980s slasher film: Ryan and Molly travel to the Usher house to visit Ryan's uncle Roderick. They discover that Roderick's brother Walter has gone insane, however, and that Roderick isn't exactly in his right mind either. On the way to the predictable conflagration at the film's climax, we encounter ghost children, a premature burial and a few gore scenes.

Directed by Australian-born Alan Birkinshaw (*Killer's Moon*, 1978), *The House of Usher* is something of a mess. For one thing, there are far too many occupants in this house, including the butler, Clive (Norman Coombes), his wife (Anne Stradi), a mute servant girl (Carole Farquhar), and a devious doctor (Philip Godawa). Plot points include Roderick attempting to 'mate' with Molly, thus ensuring the future of the Usher line; Ryan lying in a coffin through most of the film in a cataleptic trance; the doctor also having designs on Molly; and the aforementioned ghost children (Lenorah Ince and Jonathan Fairbirn) wandering through the proceedings with no explanation at all. To make matters even more confusing, the coda, a la *Dead of Night* (1945) seems to indicate that everything we have witnessed has been a dream, and that it is now starting again on a continuous loop, which also echoes the ending of the 1960 version of *The Tell-Tale Heart*.

Reed gives his usual intense performance, although his lines are mostly delivered in a whisper, as Roderick can't stand loud noises, smells, etc., which is just about the only Poesque touch in the movie. The other actors flounder through the rather stylised sets by Leonardo Coen Cagli, while one hopes they won't bump into the furniture. Pleasence doesn't show up until an hour into the film, and then proves to be the story's counterpart to the looney in the attic of James Whale's *The Old Dark House* (1932).

Reed is physically miscast as Roderick, his big, burly frame utterly at odds with such a sensitive, effete character. The other performers, with the exception of Pleasence, who seems to be having a wonderful time chasing the other characters around with a drill strapped to his wrist, are pretty much hopeless. The insipid Molly takes the honours for the most annoying character in the film, which is unfortunate, as she is the female lead.

In place of mood, Birkinshaw inserts gore sequences that include Clive forcing his wife's fingers into a meat grinder, with her head later turning up on a dinner plate, a la the similar scene in *The Curse of the Living Corpse*; the doctor stripped naked and tied to a table while Roderick releases a starving rat onto the poor man's genitals; and the mute girl sliced and diced by Walter's drill. Poor Poe...

The best thing that can be said about Birkinshaw's *House of Usher* is that it isn't as unwatchable as Jess Franco's version. It didn't bode well for the new wave of Poe films to come as the 1980s drew to a close.

Next up was Corman's second version of *Masque of the Red Death*. After leaving AIP and directing behind in 1970, Corman had founded his own company, New World Pictures, to produce exploitation films. Corman also distributed foreign films through New World, including Ingmar Bergman's *Cries and Whispers* (1971) and Federico Fellini's *Amarcord* (1973). Corman sold New World in 1983 and formed New Horizons to produce basically the same types of genre films. In 1985, he created Concorde Pictures, which, among other titles, produced a remake of Corman's own 1956 *Not of this Earth* in 1988. Apparently in a mood to remake his own movies, he financed *Masque of the Red Death* in 1989, which Concorde released straight to home video through MGM-UA in October of that year.

Unlike Corman's masterful 1964 version, his 1989 take on the story was filmed in California. As a result, the great British acting talent that graced the earlier version was not available to this production, which was directed by Larry Brand *(The Drifter*, 1988). The screenplay by Brand and Daryl Haney is philosophical in tone – unusual for this period in exploitation movies – and the exploitable elements are kept to a minimum.

The bare bones of the story are the same: The plague of the Red Death ravages the kingdom of Prince Prospero, who invites his friends to his castle, where they will be protected from the disease; meanwhile, the peasants are left to die while Prospero and his debauched followers have nightly revels in the castle – that is, until the Red Death itself gains entrance...

Patrick Macnee, late of TV's *The Avengers*, receives top billing as the Red Death, here referred to as Machiavel; the role had originally been offered to Michael York *(The Three Musketeers*, 1973), who turned it down. No Vincent Price here; Prospero is played by young London-born actor Adrian Paul, who later gained fame as the star of the television series *Highlander* (1992-1998). At the time of filming *Masque of the Red Death*, Paul was probably best known for his recurring role on the American TV drama *The Colbys* (1986-1987).

Julietta, the damsel in distress – roughly equivalent to Jane Asher's role in the 1964 film, was portrayed by Clare Hoak, a young American actress who had only one other credit at the time, a role in the horror TV series *Freddy's Nightmares* (1988). Tracy Reiner, another American actress, took on the role of Lucrecia, analogous to Hazel Court's role in the original version.

Not even a patch on the original Corman version, the 1989 *Masque* is distinguished (if that is the word) by its obvious cheapness, with cardboard sets and dull performances the order of the day. Unlike the lavish-looking 1964 version, this one also lacks the gravitas that its fine British actors had in spades, replacing it with insipid American-accented juvenile leads and a Prince Prospero who looks barely out of high school. One wonders why Corman decided to remake what many critics consider to be his directorial masterpiece; if ever there was a movie that didn't need to be made again, it was his 1964 classic.

Having said that, all was not lost; the camerawork of Edward J Pei, who later went on to photograph many television productions, including the miniseries based on Stephen King's *The Stand* (1994), includes some arresting Gothic images, despite the rather tatty-looking sets. Macnee does well enough as Machiavel, Prospero's boyhood tutor who becomes the first victim of the Red Death, and, ultimately, the Red Death himself. As Prospero, however, Paul gives a charisma-free performance, bland, melancholy and without any of the black humour that Price injected into the role. Reiner, the stepdaughter of director/actor Rob Reiner *(This is Spinal Tap*, 1984), gives an okay performance as Prospero's sister-wife, but with none of the sensuality or elegance of Court's role in the '64 version.

The music by Mark Governor is bland 80s synthesizer stuff, and the masque itself, the supposed climax of the film, is a rather tepid affair in which the actors attempt to perform medieval dances with some authenticity, but just miss the mark. Although the script is literate, it is also dour, and the performers act as though they're literally sleepwalking through their roles.

Reviews of the time included one from American uber-critic Leonard Maltin, in which he noted, '…Despite an interesting approach to the figure of the Red Death and a literate (if talky) script, overall cheapness and very slow pace cripple this medieval melodrama.' Pop culture writer Joe Bob Briggs was much more sarcastic: 'The original Edgar Allan Poe movies starring Vincent Price are great, but when they made this one, they did something a little different. They not only wanted to portray the Red Death, they wanted to use dead actors for enhanced reality. It's a pretty amazing feat, all of them talking like they're dead, moving like they're dead, even dancing like they're dead…'

The first two Poe movies in the new cycle couldn't compete with their thirty-year-old ancestors, even when they were produced by Corman himself. Suddenly, in one of those moments of synchronicity (or, more likely, Hollywood's plagiaristic plundering of ideas), exploitation producers had discovered Poe for a new generation. But the original cycle of Corman/ AIP/Price films were in no danger of being eclipsed by their belated offspring.

That was not the end for *Masque*, however. From deepest South Africa, Harry Alan Towers returned with his own version, *The Masque of the Red Death* (with 'the' in front of the title to differentiate it from Corman's) later that same year. Incredibly, he, Alan Birkinshaw and screenwriter Michael J Murray turned Poe's tale of death, decay and poetry into a routine slasher movie.

Filmed in Johannesburg, this version stars Frank Stallone (brother of Sylvester); Oscar-nominated (for *Once Is Not Enough*, 1975) actress Brenda Vaccaro and genre stalwart Herbert Lom (Hammer's *Phantom of the Opera*, 1962). The updated version concerns photographer Rebecca Stephens (Michele McBride), who forges an invitation to a castle in Bavaria for a 'Masque of the Red Death' party hosted by an aristocrat called Ludwig (Lom). One by one, the guests are done away with by a masked killer utilising various devices from Poe stories, including a pendulum.

It's faint praise, indeed, but at least Birkinshaw's *Masque* is superior to his *House of Usher*, largely because of its visuals. Although cinematographer Jossi Wein had also photographed *Usher*, his camerawork here is far superior, in part because of some beautiful locations which look more Alpine than African. The costumes for the masque, designed by Melissa Ferreira and Patti Putter, are far more imaginative and colourful than those used in Corman's production of the same year, and the interior sets, although some were recycled from *Usher*, are well lit and lush-looking.

Michael J Murray's script is as bad as it was for *Usher*, but the incidents are livelier and the actors seem to be having a better time. Vaccaro looks as though she's enjoying herself playing the floozy actress, spitting out vulgar lines with machine-gun timing. Lom, an old hand at this sort of thing, once again rises above the material to create an actual character, while McBride floats through the proceedings looking lovely and screaming occasionally, which is all that is required of her. Stallone isn't as bad as one might expect, so we'll just leave it at that.

The Grand Guignol moment in this one occurs about three-quarters of the way through the film, when an unfortunate woman loses her head after the killer traps her within a grandfather clock which contains a razor-sharp pendulum. The sequence is cleverly conceived and extremely gruesome.

Birkinshaw's *The Masque of the Red Death* is at least livelier than Larry Brand's version for Corman, and, while it may not be terribly Poesque, it has enough to satisfy the ghoulish appetites of slasher fans. Poe's name is exploited once again to attract those who have probably never actually read any of his works.

The following year, 1990, saw Corman producing another Poe feature through his Concorde/New Horizons company. Once again, it was a new take on a story he had previously directed, in this case 'Morella,' which had composed one-third of his *Tales of Terror*. Retitling it *The Haunting of Morella*, he gave the directing assignment to his protégé Jim Wynorski.

Wynorski had moved up quickly in the ranks for Corman. He had been hired by the mogul several years previously to cut coming attractions trailers for Concorde/New Horizons before he had directed his first feature (for another company) called *The Lost Empire* (1984). On the basis of that feature, and to reward him for his continuing work for Corman which by that time included writing assignments, Wynorski was asked to helm *Chopping Mall* (1986), the first of many directorial assignments for Corman's company. As a writer/director, Wynorski is something of a cross between Corman and sexploitation filmmaker Russ Meyer (*Beyond the Valley of the Dolls*, 1970) in the sense that he specialises in casting sexy and busty actresses in his films, which often feature plenty of nudity. In 1988, Corman asked him to remake his own 1956 feature *Not of this Earth*, replacing the original film's star Beverly Garland with former porn actress Traci Lords, essentially remaking the original film shot for shot, but with added nudity and gore.

As was the case with *Not of this Earth*, *The Haunting of Morella* was produced mainly for the exploding home video market. With a screenplay by R J Robertson (*The Adventures of Buckaroo Banzai Across the 8th Dimension*, 1984), the film top-lined David McCallum, best known as the character 'Illya Kuryakin' in the 1960s television series *The Man from UNCLE*. The dual role of Morella/Lenora was taken by Nicole Eggert, who was currently popular due to her continuing role on television's *Baywatch*.

Nicole Eggert in *The Haunting of Morella* (1990)

Lana Clarkson in *The Haunting of Morella* (1990)

*The Haunting of Morella* (1990)

David McCallum in *The Haunting of Morella* (1990)

One sexy actress was not enough for a Wynorski film, so *Morella* also included the statuesque Lana Clarkson (*Barbarian Queen*, 1985) as Lenora's governess, Coel; Maria Ford (*Dance of the Damned*, 1989) as Diane; and Gail Harris (*nee* Thackeray, *Sorority House Massacre II*, 1990)) as Ilsa. All three actresses were Corman/Wynorski regulars. Filmed back to back with *Transylvania Twist* (also directed by Wynorski), *The Haunting of Morella* was shot at the Concorde/New Horizons studios in California.

Interviewed during the summer of 2018 for this book, Wynorski recalled the genesis of *Morella*: 'He (Corman) had asked me my thoughts on doing a Poe picture, so I consulted with my late writing partner R J Robertson. R J and I decided we wanted to adapt 'Morella' (which had been part of an earlier Corman anthology) into a full-length movie. Roger was certainly familiar with the story and saw the possibilities for making the tale full-length. He said move forward, so R J started writing the script. I provided my input after every ten pages or so.'

The opening scene of the film is an obvious tribute to Mario Bava's *Black Sunday*. Wynorski noted, "I like a lot of his (Bava's) work, *Danger: Diabolik* being my favourite.'

Wynorski was very keen to work with one of his idols on the film: 'I'd always been a fan of *The Man from UNCLE* TV show, so I went to Robert Vaughn and David McCallum respectively on *Transylvania Twist* and *The Haunting of Morella*, which were shot back to back on nearly the same sets. McCallum was a treat… giving 100% of his talent. Vaughn was just as nice in his own way.'

As for Clarkson, Wynorski said, 'She did a nice job, but we weren't fans of each other off-screen. No animosity, mind you, but I found her rather cold and unfriendly. Yet, I'm still sorry her life was cut short so tragically by Phil Spector.'

Wynorski was referring to Clarkson's murder by record producer Phil Spector in the early hours of 3 February 2003. The actress, currently working at the House of Blues in Los Angeles, had met Spector at the nightclub, and he had driven her to his mansion afterwards. His driver heard a gunshot while he waited outside in the car about an hour after he had dropped them off, and saw Spector run outside holding a gun. He was tried for second degree murder on 20 October 2008 and was convicted of murdering Clarkson. He was sentenced to 19 years to life in state prison.

One of the 'controversies' involving *Morella* was, fortunately, of a much lighter nature. In a scene toward the end of the film, Clarkson's character has a lesbian tryst near a waterfall with Maria Ford's character, and the two women wear very out-of-period underclothes (in Ford's case, a thong). I asked Wynorski if that scene was intentionally anachronistic or if the actresses had refused to do 'the full monty.' His response: 'Lana had been in a skiing accident which put her on crutches prior to shooting. She felt she was overweight and requested the panties. I told her I didn't think the panties would hide anything, but she insisted. I had no choice but to allow them. I told Maria Ford (who had no problem with full nudity) to also wear panties so it wouldn't look as obvious.'

Wynorski said it was a fast shoot, although he has done faster ones: 'The film was shot over a 14-day schedule at Corman's studio in Venice, California and also Malibu State Park (formerly owned by 20th Century-Fox). It's where the majority of the *Planet of the Apes* films were shot, along with other features like *Our Man Flint* and *Von Ryan's Express.*'

I pointed out to Wynorski that there are visual homages in *Morella*, not only to Corman's Poe pictures, but to various Hammer films (especially *Lust for a Vampire*, 1970) and to the aforementioned Bava film. I asked Wynorski if he were a fan of all those types of films: 'I was brought up on those early Poe pictures – and, of course, all the Hammer films. Who wouldn't be affected?'

*The Haunting of Morella* was quite successful on home video, and I asked Wynorski why Corman produced no more Poe pictures after that. His tongue-in-cheek answer: 'He felt he could never top mine!' On a more serious note, Wynorski replied that, 'Yes, of course' he would be interested in directing another gothic horror film should the opportunity arise.

Full disclosure; *The Haunting of Morella* is a not-so-guilty pleasure for your humble author, a sexy gothic horror treat that could easily have been made by Hammer (or AIP) in the early 1970s. The atmospheric cinematography by Zoran Hochstatter (Wynorski's *Not of this Earth*) creates a hypnotic mood, which is complemented nicely by the musical score by Chuck Cirino and Fredric Ensign Teetsel. Although the budget is low, the production design by Gary Randall makes the film look more expensive than it is, and Sandra Araya Jensen's costume design (except for the out-of-period underwear in the waterfall scene) is quite elegant.

McCallum does well in a role that would have been played by Vincent Price in Corman's original Poe cycle and Halstead is an appropriately stalwart leading man. Eggert is a bit out of her depth in a dual role, although she doesn't embarrass herself, and Clarkson is suitably evil (and seductive) as the duplicitous Coel.

Wynorski directs with a sure hand, making the film a visual feast that holds the interest throughout. *The Haunting of Morella* is a retro delight, perhaps the most perfectly realised 'Poesploitation' movie, giving the fans everything they could ask for with its classically styled gothic flavour updated to the 1990s adding nudity, sex and gore. Wynorski has made a great many films over the years, but I find *The Haunting of Morella* to be his most enjoyable.

After this pleasant Poe-esque romp, it was back to South Africa and Harry Alan Towers' Breton Film Productions for another addition to their own Poe cycle. This time, it was derived from *Premature Burial* and was called *Buried Alive* (1990). With a screenplay by Jake Chesi and Stuart Lee, *Buried Alive* was directed by French porn filmmaker Gerard Kikoine (*The Tale of Tiffany Lust*, 1979), who was attempting to break into the mainstream and had just directed an adaptation of *Dr Jekyll and Mr Hyde* for Towers in 1989 called *Edge of Sanity*, which had starred Anthony Perkins.

*Buried Alive* top-lined another American star, Robert Vaughn, best known at the time as 'Napoleon Solo' in the TV spy series *The Man from UNCLE*. Vaughn had garnered an Academy Award nomination for his role in *The Young Philadelphians* (1960), but was a long time away from those heady days here.

The supporting cast is an interesting and eclectic one. Donald Pleasence returned to work for Towers as Dr Scheaffer in the film; former *Playboy* Playmate Karen Witter played Janet, the female lead; Hollywood veteran John Carradine appeared in his final film role as Jacob; and Ginger Lynn Allen, a porn star (*New Wave Hookers*, 1985) who was also looking for a mainstream career were all featured in the film. And so *Buried Alive* became a mainstream horror film based loosely on the works of Edgar Allan Poe, directed by a porn filmmaker, featuring a porn star alongside Vaughn, Pleasence and Carradine!

Needless to say, the plot has nothing to do with Poe: A young woman (Witter) goes to teach at the Ravenscroft Institute, an old gothic girls' school that just happens to be staffed by former mental patients. Several students have disappeared, and it transpires that they have been assaulted by a man wearing a Richard Nixon mask who places them into darkened crypts where they are entombed alive.

As was the case with Towers' other two Poe pictures, the basic idea is taken from Poe and tarted up with elements from various slasher films. Poor Poe would have barely recognised his own work here, not that much of it remains.

Most of *Buried Alive* is simply dreadful, one of the worst so-called Poe adaptations ever to hit the screen. The biggest problem is the script, which is muddled, to say the least, and makes no dramatic sense. The other problem is the acting; Witter is not an actress and walks through her role as though she is, in fact, buried alive. Unfortunately, that has nothing to do with her character, who is supposed to be riddled with anxiety but seems more riddled with somnambulism.

For the first two-thirds of the film, Vaughn acts as though he'd rather be in Philadelphia; by the time the third act rolls around and it is revealed that (spoiler alert!) he's the one kidnapping the girls and walling them up, he goes way over the top. Vaughn probably did the film because a) he needed the work and b) he got the chance to play a psychopath, but he relishes the chance a bit too much at the crazy climax, in which it is also revealed that his father (Carradine) has been imprisoned in the basement for God knows how many years. Suffice it to say that the two of them come to a supposedly bad end, although there is a cheap coda just before the end credits in which it appears they're still among the living.

Pleasence is wasted in a thankless role and, ironically, the liveliest performance in the film is that of Allen, who is obviously relishing the opportunity to go mainstream. Her career outside of porn never really took off, however, and she soon found herself back in the saddle in the likes of *New Wave Hookers* 6 (2000).

Incredibly, there had been plans for a sequel, but *Buried Alive*'s failure at both the box office and the home video market put paid to that idea. It seems apropos that Poe's middle name is once again misspelled in the opening credits, as he must have been revolving in his own grave at immense speed at this atrocity. What a shame it had to be Carradine's final film.

The sudden rush to make Poe 'exploitable' led to another version of 'Premature Burial' being produced that same year for the home video market. Directed and written (under the nom de plume Sherman Scott) by maverick filmmaker Fred Olen Ray on a shoestring budget of roughly $115,000, *Haunting Fear* (which sounds more like a Lovecraft title than Poe) features a cast every bit as eclectic as the one for the Harry Alan Towers version. Top-lined by B-movie scream queen Brinke Stevens (*Sorority Babes in the Slimeball Bowl-O-Rama*, 1988), the film also features Jan-Michael Vincent (*White Line Fever*, 1975), former *Penthouse* pet Delia Sheppard, Oscar-nominated actress Karen Black (*Five Easy Pieces*, 1970) B-movie veteran Robert Clarke (*The Hideous Sun Demon*, 1958), AIP horror star Robert Quarry (*Count Yorga, Vampire*, 1970) and 1970's horror icon Michael Berryman (*The Hills Have Eyes*, 1976).

Ray is an interesting study: a lifelong horror fan born in Florida, he moved to Hollywood after making a few ultra-low budget horror films with such titles as *The Brain Leeches* (1978) and *The Alien Dead* (1980) in his home state. In Hollywood, he directed features made for the home video market, including *The Tomb* (1986) *Hollywood Chainsaw Hookers* (1988) and *Beverly Hills Vamp* (1989). Few of his films have ever been made for more than $500,000 and he's still working today, directing such low-budget fare as *Fiancée Killer* (2018). Ray enjoys casting many of the actors he grew up with in his films, hence the appearances of Clarke, Quarry and Berryman in *Haunting Fear*.

Writing under the name of Sherman Scott, Ray's take on 'Premature Burial' is at least livelier, if you'll pardon the pun, than *Buried Alive*. Constructed more like an erotic thriller than anything conceived by Poe, the story concerns Victoria Munroe (Stevens), who has recurring nightmares of being buried alive. Her husband Terry (Jay Richardson) convinces her to go to Dr Carlton (Clarke), toward whom Victoria harbours resentment about her father's death. Carlton sends her to a hypnotist (Black) to get to the root of her problem. Meanwhile, Terry is having an affair with his voluptuous secretary (Sheppard) while attempting to pay off a gambling debt to a gangster (Quarry). He and his secretary cook up a scheme to 'dispose' of Victoria so they can get their greedy hands on her money. Needless to say, things go awry...

The production is threadbare and looks it, although Gary Graver's cinematography is often nicely lit, with just enough shadows to give the film a more polished look than one might expect. Chuck Cirino's low-key score gives the proceedings a noirish touch, but the film is let down by some stiff performances, especially that of Vincent, who looks as though he's suffering from a whiskey hangover through the entire film. Stevens doesn't come to life, ironically, until she's buried alive, and then seems to be having fun enacting revenge on her would-be-murderers.

The script has some problems as well, especially in a dream sequence in which Terry's affair with his secretary is a key point – but at this stage of the plot, Victoria doesn't know of the affair, so how could she have dreamed about it? There are other loose ends, Black looks embarrassed to be in the film and only Richardson and Sheppard bring any life to their performances, although their frequent sex scenes are awkwardly directed by Ray.

*Haunting Fear* is rock-bottom 'Poespoitation,' throwing in as much nudity, sex and gore as possible without a great deal of care shown in production or direction. It does, however, have more of Poe in it than the execrable *Buried Alive*, and Stevens at least attempts to capture the horror of being prematurely interred in the latter stages of the film. The ending, however, is shamelessly cribbed from the final shots of John Carpenter's *Halloween*, proving once again that Poe and slashers don't mix.

The next Poe picture in the very busy year of 1990 was far more ambitious. *Two Evil Eyes* began life as a proposed cable TV series to be produced by Italian horror icon Dario Argento (*Suspiria*, 1977), based upon Poe's works. George A Romero (*Night of the Living Dead*, 1968) signed on to direct the pilot, 'The Facts in the Case of M Valdemar,' although his first choice had been 'The Masque of the Red Death.' That story was proposed instead for Italian filmmaker Michele Soavi (*The Church*, 1989). Richard Stanley (*Hardware*, 1990) was suggested to direct 'The Cask of Amontillado,' with Michael Gambon (*The Cook, the Thief, His Wife & Her Lover*, 1989) as Fortunato and Jonathan Pryce (*Something Wicked This Way Comes*, 1983) as Montressor. Unfortunately, funding was not forthcoming for the TV project, so it was turned into a two-story feature film with Romero directing 'Valdemar' and Argento contributing 'The Black Cat.'

Previously, Argento's brother Claudio had been one of the producers of Romero's highly influential *Dawn of the Dead* (1979), which Dario had co-edited, so Argento and Romero were not strangers to each other. *Two Evil Eyes* combined their talents in one gruesome package, attracting some top acting talent in the process. Romero's segment featured Adrienne Barbeau (Romero's *Creepshow*, 1982), E G Marshall (another *Creepshow* alumnus best known for Sidney Lumet's *12 Angry Men*, 1957) and Tom Atkins (John Carpenter's *The Fog*, 1980). 'The Black Cat' starred Harvey Keitel (Martin Scorsese's *Taxi Driver*, 1976), Madeleine Potter (James Ivory's *The Bostonians*, 1984) Kim Hunter (*Planet of the Apes*, 1968) and Martin Balsam (Hitchcock's *Psycho*, 1960).

Filmed in Romero's old stomping ground in and around Pittsburgh, Pennsylvania, *Two Evil Eyes* has much to recommend it. The acting in both stories is of a high calibre and the film looks extremely polished, thanks to the cinematography by Peter Reniers, who later became Director of Photography on the acclaimed TV series *Breaking Bad* (2010). Cletus Anderson's production design on *The Black Cat* is also first rate.

Romero's segment is the weaker of the two. His take on *Valdemar*, which he also scripted, has a film noirish flavour: Jessica Valdemar (Barbeau) and her lover Dr Hoffman (Ramy Zeda) hatch a plot to hypnotise her infirm old husband Ernest (Bingo O'Malley) into leaving her all of his money. Hoffman has the old man under his mesmeric influence, but suddenly, Valdemar passes away while under hypnosis and is stuck in limbo, between the world of the living and the world of the dead. Valdemar wants to be released from his trance because other malevolent spirits are surrounding him, but Hoffman finds himself fascinated by this unplanned experiment. Jessica can't take it anymore, however, and shoots Ernest, thinking he will finally expire. That doesn't happen, unfortunately, and Ernest – as well as the other spirits surrounding him – exact revenge on them both.

Compared to Corman's typically economical version of the story, Romero's is slow and the pace drags. The contemporary setting drains the tale of atmosphere, although the ending – when it finally arrives – is quite effective. Barbeau, Zeda, O'Malley and Marshall are all fine in their roles, but Romero's only attempt at adapting a Poe story just misses the mark.

Not so with Argento's *The Black Cat*, a brutal, amped-up, hallucinatory journey into madness that, despite its ultra-modern setting, manages to encapsulate the feeling of Poe quite effectively. As usual, Argento fills his segment with strong colour effects, razor-sharp editing and performances that are just far enough over the top to keep the story compelling, but not enough to turn it into parody.

The script, concocted by Argento and Franco Ferrini, combines elements of 'The Pit and the Pendulum' and 'Berenice,' as well as naming its lead character (Keitel) Roderick Usher…Rod, for short! In Pennsylvania, Usher works as a tabloid photographer who specialises in particularly gruesome crime scenes. Usher has been living for several years with his girlfriend, Annabel (Potter), who teaches the violin. When she brings a stray cat home to their apartment, Rod takes an immediate dislike to the creature. He ends up photographing himself torturing the cat for a book he's putting together; the cat disappears and Annabel happens to see the book in a bookstore. Horrified, she comes to the conclusion that her boyfriend has killed the cat. She threatens to leave him, but Usher finds a stray cat in a bar that is given to him by the bartender (Sally Kirkland). Annabel is preparing to leave the apartment when she finds the cat. After an altercation, Usher ends up murdering her, walling up her body behind a bookshelf. Anyone who knows the story knows the rest, but the karmic coda includes a shock ending in which Usher kills the policemen who have discovered his grisly secret, then tries to hang one of the bodies outside his window, but ends up hanging himself instead.

Argento's take on Poe is everything that Romero's wasn't; it's grand, it's grisly and it's bizarre. There is a dream sequence that's almost beyond description in its pure weirdness involving Usher, his girlfriend, the black cat and a group of cultists. Keitel goes mad nicely, although he seems slightly bonkers to begin with, somewhat akin to Jack Nicholson's character in Stanley Kubrick's version of Stephen King's *The Shining* (1980). Potter is appropriately off-kilter as his fragile girlfriend, and the appearance of Balsam as a neighbour gives the latter half of the story a somewhat Hitchcockian flavour.

*Two Evil Eyes* is obviously a mixed bag, although its soundtrack is consistently excellent thanks to the score by Pino Donaggio (*Carrie*, 1976). While Romero's segment is just average, Argento's is a tour-de-force of style, mood and characterisation that ranks with some of his best work. *Two Evil Eyes* is one of the finest films in the 'Poesploitation' cycle because of his superior segment. Argento's take almost lives up to the plaque on Poe's house in Baltimore that opens the film. It reads: 'Edgar Allan Poe 1809-1849: Dreaming dreams no mortal ever dared to dream before.'

Full Moon Productions was a company formed in the late 1980's by B-movie veteran producer Charles Band, who had previously run Empire Pictures, the company that had released Stuart Gordon's game-changing gore-fest, *Herbert West – Re-Animator* in 1985. When Empire Pictures went out of business, Band created Full Moon Productions, essentially the 1990's answer to American International Pictures. As AIP had released its output to drive-in theatres, Full Moon released its own variable product to the venue that had replaced the drive-ins, the home video market.

Full Moon teamed up with Paramount Pictures and Pioneer Home Entertainment to release films to VHS and laserdisc, and the first production from the company, *Puppet Master* (1989), turned out to be a direct-to-video hit that spawned a series of sequels. Full Moon specialised in franchises, including the sci-fi series that had begun with Empire's *Trancers* (1984) and a vampire series that began with *Subspecies* (1991). In 1990, with the 'Poesploitation' fad in full swing, Stuart Gordon hoped to film *The Pit and the Pendulum*, set during the period of the Spanish Inquisition, starring Peter O'Toole as Torquemada and featuring Sherilyn Fenn (who had just starred in Full Moon's *Meridian* that same year) and Billy Dee Williams (*Star Wars Episode V: The Empire Strikes Back*, 1980), but O'Toole turned down the role. Producer Albert Band (Charles' father) then sought Anthony Perkins for the part, but he also turned it down.

That incarnation of the project was cancelled, as were plans to film in England and then Romania. Finally, financing was raised to shoot the film in Italy, and Lance Henriksen (*Aliens*, 1986) was cast as Torquemada. Henriksen, an intense actor, seemed right for the role as written by Denis Paoli (*Re-Animator*) in which the Grand Inquisitor falls in love with the innocent young Maria (Rona De Ricci), who has spoken out against the Inquisition and is therefore arrested and accused of being a witch. Torquemada has 'plans' for the girl, however, and attempts to seduce her, but is impotent. To ensure that she never tells anyone, he cuts out her tongue. Her husband Antonio (Jonathan Fuller) breaks into Torquemada's castle to rescue his wife, but is captured and imprisoned. The Grand Inquisitor tests out his new torture device, a pendulum, upon poor Antonio. The story also includes elements from 'The Cask of Amontillado.'

Also in the cast were Frances Bay (*The Grifters*, 1990), Jeffrey Combs (Herbert West himself), Mark Margolis (*Scarface*, 1983), Tom Towles (*Henry: Portrait of a Serial Killer*, 1986) and none other than Oliver Reed as the Cardinal. Stuart Gordon's *The Pit and the Pendulum* was filmed over a three and a half week period from 17 September 1990 to 12 October 1990 in and around Castello di Giove in Italy.

By all accounts, Henriksen's behaviour on the set was problematic. A method actor, he prepared for the part by eating and drinking only bread and water during filming. Taking a great deal of time to study the history of the Inquisition and the true character of Torquemada, he remained in character even between takes, which was somewhat unsettling to both cast and crew. He and Gordon frequently clashed, with Henriksen stating his opposition to Gordon's trademark black humour, which was peppered throughout the film. Ultimately Gordon threw up his hands and told Henriksen he could do whatever he pleased with the character.

Although his role is just a glorified cameo, Reed was around the set enough to lighten the mood, drinking wine (no surprise there) with Henriksen between takes. Ultimately, by the end of shooting, Henriksen and Gordon

Lance Henriksen and Mark Margolis in
*The Pit and the Pendulum* (1990)

*Chapter Seven – THE EXPLOITABLE POE*

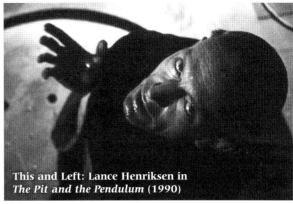

This and Left: Lance Henriksen in
*The Pit and the Pendulum* (1990)

Tom Towles and Rona De
Ricci in *The Pit and the
Pendulum* (1990)

made peace with each other and the result is probably Henriksen's finest performance and Full Moon's greatest production.

The plot is very different from Corman's version, as is the mood. Whereas the 1961 telling concentrated on gothic atmosphere, Gordon's version opens up full throttle with the exhumation of a skeleton and its subsequent whipping and dismemberment (the man in question was deemed to be a heretic) in front of his widow and child. After this horrific sequence, the title credits roll, accompanied by Richard Band's impressive musical score. The story proper actually has similarities to that of Corman's *The Masque of the Red Death*, in that the hero (Fuller) breaks into the castle to rescue his lady love (De Ricci).

Gordon, of course, goes much further in his depiction of gore and sex than did Corman, but Paoli's screenplay is consistently intelligent and never veers into sexploitation or blood for the sake of blood. The film is most effective in its depiction of religious hypocrisy, with Gordon's black humour often nailing the point home, so to speak. Torquemada's assistant Gomez (Stephen Lee) gets many of the wittiest lines, such as when Dr Heusos (William Norris) admonishes him and the other lackeys for (so he thinks) tearing out Maria's tongue: 'You idiots, why did you tear out her tongue?' to which Gomez replies, 'We didn't! We don't do tongues!'

Although Henriksen's complaints about the film's humour are understandable from the actor's point of view, it works in the context of the film, which is, like most of Gordon's work, operatic in its intensity. When an accused witch (Bay) goes to the stake for burning, she consumes several scoops of gunpowder, and when the fire reaches her, she explodes, causing a few fatalities in the sadistic crowd. The scene is horrific and wickedly funny at once.

Henriksen's powerful performance dominates the proceedings; he could easily have played Torquemada as evil incarnate, such as Price's Prospero in *Masque*, but he gives the character several shades of grey and manages to make the Grand Inquisitor as psychologically tortured as his victims are physically tortured. While the actor's eccentricities may have caused problems – one anecdote has it that, still in character as Torquemada while visiting the Vatican, he leapt out of a cab to pursue a random stranger up the street while yelling obscenities at him – there are no issues with his performance. The fact that he sleeps under a suspended 'sword of Damocles' to prove how fragile life can be (an inspired touch by Paoli) gives Torquemada unexpected depth, and, while he tries to fight his feelings for Maria, his lust for her is matched only by his inability to perform.

The other characters are not as well drawn, although De Ricci, who has only one other screen credit to her name, shines as the long-suffering Maria. Combs comes close to stealing the show at times with his quietly effective, surprisingly compassionate scribe commenting on the gruesome action. When the prisoners are released at the end of the film, one character says to him, 'What about the others?' Combs succinctly sums up the Inquisition by noting, 'There will always be others.'

Reed's appearance as a cardinal who likes to drink is something of an in-joke, but it's also an interesting take on 'The Cask of Amontillado.' In this case, he is walled up by Torquemada himself, and the exchange in which he pleads, 'For the love of God,' to which Torquemada responds, 'Yes, for the love of God,' takes on additional meaning.

Although *The Pit and the Pendulum* has all the elements of 'Poesploitation,' including sex, nudity and gore, it also has elegant costumes, authentic locations, eloquent writing and fluid direction. It is perhaps the finest film in the late 1980's/early 90's Poe cycle and is ripe for rediscovery.

The final nail in the coffin of the 'Poesploitation' cycle arrived in 1993, courtesy of – no surprise here – producer Harry Alan Towers. Supposedly intended for director Ken Russell (*The Devils*, 1971), which would have been very interesting, the project was instead turned over to veteran TV and film director Gerry O' Hara, who had cut his teeth on such British TV series

Tony Curtis and Leslie Hardy in *The Mummy Lives* (1993)

BOUND BY DESTINY... CONSUMED BY SIN... HIS VENGEANCE IS ETERNAL.

THE MUMMY LIVES

as *The Avengers* (two episodes in 1965 and 1966) and Hammer's *Journey to the Unknown* (1968). The screenplay by Nelson Gidding (*The Haunting*, 1963) was, as the opening credits read, 'suggested by "Some Words With a Mummy" by Edgar Allan Poe.' In the film, a mummy is restored to life and becomes obsessed with a woman who he believes to be the reincarnation of his lost love – in other words, it had the same plot as just about every other 'mummy' movie ever made.

Originally, Anthony Perkins had been slated to star, but he passed away before production began. Christopher Lee was also asked to take over the top role, but he turned it down at the last moment. Instead, Hollywood star Tony Curtis (*Some Like It Hot*, 1959) was chosen to portray the dual role of Aziru/Dr Mohassid, the 'mummy' of the title. Towers later said that it was a mistake to place Curtis in the role, as he was miscast. He couldn't have been more correct in that assessment, but more on that later.

The other dual role, that of Sandra Barnes/Kia (Aziru's lost love) was given to young actress Leslie Hardy, later to make a name for herself in such American television series as *Nash Bridges* (1997-1999). As the production was filmed in Egypt and Israel, most of the supporting roles were filled by local actors, with the exception of young American TV actor Greg Wrangler, who played the stalwart Dr Carey Williams.

There is virtually nothing to recommend *The Mummy Lives*. Curtis is indeed wildly miscast, his accent sounding more like the Bronx than ancient Egypt. The fact that Poe's story was actually a satire of the Egyptian craze that was taking place in the 19th Century has completely escaped the filmmakers, and Curtis plays the dual role without a shred of humour, wit or intelligence. If the mummy lives, he isn't really awake; Curtis sleepwalks through the role.

The other actors are no better, and some of the Israeli and Egyptian performers are poorly dubbed, which doesn't help. There are a few shots of PG-13 rated gore, but there is very little action, eroticism or anything else to keep the viewer awake. The Egyptian locations are attractive, but the interiors, murkily shot by Avi Koren, are drab and dark. The entire enterprise is deadly dull, making its 97-minute running time seem much longer than it is.

And so, the 'Poesploitation' cycle ended not with a bang, but with a whimper. Poe became quiescent in film – even made-for-video film – once again, except for the odd short adaptation, only picking up steam on television. In the early 2000s, the cycle came round again – which brings us to our next and final chapter.

# CHAPTER EIGHT
# THE 21ST CENTURY POE

*'It was night, and the rain fell; and falling, it was rain, but, having fallen, it was blood.'*

**Silence**, *A Fable*

It has become something of a cliché to say that 9/11/01 changed everything, but, in many respects, it's the truth. When one thinks of life, especially in the United States before that terrible day and life afterwards, it seems as though we're dealing with two completely different realities. Before 9/11, American society was generally open and welcoming. After, 'Give us your tired, your poor…' suddenly transformed into, 'We don't want you here,' and, echoing the McCarthy era of the 1950s, American life became closed, paranoid and suspicious.

There were some pundits who felt that, after the real horrors of 9/11, horror movies would become a thing of the past. The fact that those pundits were completely wrong should not surprise us; as we have seen, audiences tend to flock to films featuring shock, horror and terror when reality is at its worst, whether it be the Great Depression, World War II or, indeed, the war on terror.

Halloween 2001 was perhaps a bit lower-key than usual – but there was a horror film called *Thirteen Ghosts*, a semi-remake of a 1960 William Castle production of that title, released on that spooky holiday, and it made millions at the box office, proving that horror was still a popular commodity even in these dark times.

It was in the very next year, 2002, that Poe returned courtesy of a major filmmaker: None other than Ken Russell wrote, directed and produced the rather remarkably titled *The Fall of the Louse of Usher: A Gothic Tale for the 21st Century*, loosely based on several Poe stories including 'Usher.' A comedy/musical/horror film, it tells the bizarre story of rock star Roddy Usher, whose wife is murdered, causing him such grief that he is sent to a lunatic asylum where the therapy is straight out of 'The System of Dr Tarr and Professor Fether.'

Southampton-born Russell was known for his flamboyant, experimental approach to filmmaking, beginning with his work for the BBC in the 1960's. He was best known for his Oscar-winning adaptation of D H Lawrence's *Women in Love* (1969), his shocking *The Devils* (1971), *Tommy* (1975) and *Altered States* (1980). His over-the-top biopics of famous composers included *The Music Lovers* (1970), starring Richard Chamberlain as Tchaikovsky; *Mahler* (1974), with Robert Powell in the title role; and *Lisztomania* (1975), starring The Who's Roger Daltrey as Franz Liszt.

By the late 1990's, Russell's career seemed to flounder, although his earlier high-energy, highly-sexualized movies were still well-regarded. The Hollywood studios had pretty much abandoned him in favour of less controversial, more commercial directors such as Steven Spielberg, Tim Burton and George Lucas, however. In 2000, he put his own money into a low budget production called *The Lion's Mouth*, which went nowhere; undeterred, he produced, wrote and directed *The Fall of the Louse of Usher* the following year, shot on his own estate (much of it in his garage) with a digital camcorder. Always keen to embrace new technology, Russell essentially made a glorified home movie in his own inimitable style, casting friends, neighbours, and himself in the leading roles.

Composer/actor James Johnston plays Roddy Usher as well as a character called Gory the Gorilla; Lisi Tribble, who was Russell's fourth wife, was cast in several roles, including Madeline Usher, Masked Mary, a mummy and Dr Wells; writer/actress Marie Findley portrays the dual role of Nurse ABC Smith and Dream Woman; and Russell himself plays the head of the lunatic asylum, Dr Calahari (an obvious spoof of Dr Caligari – Russell was rarely subtle).

Released directly to video in 2002, *The Fall of the Louse of Usher* is bizarre even by Russell's self-indulgent style. With interiors shot mostly in his garage/studio, the movie obviously lacks the gloss of his studio-financed productions, but Russell attempts to make up for the lack of money with a lot of ingenious, creative improvisation. As it is, to some extent, a musical

Scenes from *The Fall of the Louse of Usher* (2002)

**Mark Redfield as Poe in *The Death of Poe* (2006)**

comedy, it helps that the score is quite good, with Poe's words set to music in such songs as 'Tolling of the Bells' and 'Annabelle Lee,' and references to the author flying so fast and furiously that it's difficult to keep up.

The framework is loosely based on 'Dr Tarr and Professor Fether,' combined with elements of 'Usher,' 'The Black Cat,' 'The Pit and the Pendulum,' 'The Tell Tale Heart, ' 'The Facts in the Case of M Valdemar' and 'Murders in the Rue Morgue.' Russell himself wildly overacts as Dr Calahari, with Johnston and Tribble not far behind. Findley seems to be having a good time as the nurse and the dream woman, while Peter Mastin plays Ernest Valdemar in gooey fashion; Russell's son Alex is one of four actors playing Gory the Gorilla, the others being Johnston, Barry Lowe and Roger Wilkes.

At its best, *Louse of Usher* conveys the joy of filmmaking with friends, family and neighbours on a basic level. The movie runs the gamut from charming to irritating, but it's hard to dislike a production that depicts the fall of the house of Usher itself as the destruction of a child's 'bouncy house.' As with all of Russell's films, *The Fall of the Louse of Usher* is an acquired taste: it's excessive, at times quite funny, at other times quite unfunny, full of sex, nudity and gore that's so over the top that it's impossible not to laugh at it. Yet it is undeniably made by the same hand and demented brain that crafted such films as *Lair of the White Worm* (1988) in its self-referential cinematic and carnal delights. It's anybody's guess as to what Poe would have thought of it, but one suspects that if he were drunk enough, he would have found it quite amusing.

Multi-talented Poe aficionado Mark Redfield hails from the author's old stomping ground of Baltimore; an actor, writer, filmmaker and artist, Redfield specialises in making ambitious films on tiny budgets. One of his best-known productions is *The Death of Poe* (2006), a fictionalised account of the final weeks in Poe's tortured life, offering up possible reasons for his untimely death in 1849 Baltimore. As every Poe follower is aware, he was planning a trip to New York City, vanished for a few days in Baltimore and was found a few days later in a gutter, alive but incoherent. He was hospitalised for three days, where he lay in a delirious stupor, dying on the third day. The cause of his untimely death remains a mystery.

*The Death of Poe* combines factual recreations of Poe's final days with gothic imagery from his stories and poems. Redfield directed the project and plays Poe as well. Also in the cast are New York actor Kevin G Shinnick as Dr John Moran, Kimberly Hannold as Virginia Clemm, George Stover as brothers Thadeus and Zachariah Wainwright, and Debra Murphy as Maria Clemm.

Interviewed for this book, Redfield revealed his lifetime love of Poe, his working methods and his plans for the future. I have included the entire interview here:

**Q. How long have you been fascinated by Poe? What was the first story by him that you read?**
**A:** Since my early teenage years, certainly. Sometime around my twelfth or thirteenth year Poe came loudly rapping at my chamber door. I think the first Poe story I ever read was in a large-format Warren magazine, perhaps

Mark Redfield as Poe in *The Death of Poe* (2006)

an adaptation of "The Black Cat" in *Creepy* or *Eerie* magazine.

The first story that I'm certain I read, from an anthology of horror short stories, was "The Tell-Tale Heart". It's the perfect short story, by Poe's own definition. It creates a strong emotion in the reader, isn't sharply defined by detail of the characters, but gives just enough flesh to the old man with the "vulture eye" and the (unreliable) first-person narrator for us to believe in them fully. Currently my favourite Poe tale is "Hop Frog", a wonderfully grotesque fairy tale. I want to make a movie of that.

**Q: What is actually known about how Poe died?**
**A:** Nothing. Except the day and date of his death. Medicine was primitive in 1849, and he was misdiagnosed when he was discovered and eventually brought to the hospital in Baltimore where he died. The attending physician, Dr Moran, was vague about the exact cause of death because he just didn't know. And then, later in his life, when Dr Moran wanted to make a buck off of Poe and lectured at Temperance Society meetings about the evils and immorality of alcohol, he changed much of his story to paint Poe as a victim of alcoholism, and that the "demon drink" was what killed him. The obituary that his arch-enemy wrote, Rufus Griswold, helped cement the myth that Poe died drunk, friendless and alone. Nothing could be farther from the truth.

I think that Poe suffered from some sort of malignant brain tumour, and that something traumatic, like a blow to the head, exacerbated the pre-existing malady and created a situation that doctors of the day were not able to handle.

Every crackpot theory that's been floated out there over the last thirty years or so has been well debunked. Rabies is the most hilarious and was instantly dismissed when it was introduced into the scholarship in the 1990s. But misinformation peskily persists.

There is the "cooping" theory, however, and I lean toward that as a possible instigator of violence that may have been visited upon Poe. Political gangs in the rough and tumble 1800s would round up the homeless and indigent, the drunks, sailors and travellers, and hold them in rooms, cellars or stables (hence "coop" them up) and ply them with lots of alcohol so they'd do their bidding by voting for their candidate. Over and over and over until they passed out or dropped dead.

While Poe was traveling from Richmond to New York, raising money for a new publishing venture, getting ready to marry a childhood sweetheart, had sworn off alcohol and was happy and clean and sober, he stopped in Baltimore to change from the steamboat to the train. There was an election in Baltimore. It's a well-known fact that political gangs would stuff the ballot boxes with ballots for their candidates with votes from the homeless and indigent. And these political gangs were ruthless. They were paid by the campaigns to get as many votes as possible, and so they made the poor saps they "shanghaied" into voting over and over, until they dropped dead or unconscious from exhaustion and the amount of liquor they were kept lubricated with. There's a fantastic sequence dramatising this "cooping" method in Martin Scorsese's "Gangs of New York".

**Q: I got the impression that some of the sets in the movie were actual historic houses in Baltimore. Was that the case?**
A: Yes. Some were, but the majority were sets we built in the studio. Unfortunately, none of the locations were actual places Poe had been during the last week of his life, as all of those buildings and places have long since been demolished.

I wanted the hospital and many of the places Poe "lived in" during the week the film depicts to be somewhat artificial, not "real; To feel dreamlike, and specifically like being in a box. In a coffin. In a dream. So, intentionally, many of the rooms in the various places are the same set, just subtly re-dressed to be a different place, but look like many other places in the course of events in the film.

I would have loved to have shot in the actual hospital where Poe died, which is still standing, and is still a working nurses teaching school and residency, but the interiors have completely modernized and are nothing like what they were in 1849. It's called Church Home and Hospital now. No longer in operation, and was in recent years an elderly care facility and a nurses quarters. It was called Washington Medical College in Poe's day.

**Q: What kind of research was involved for your interpretation of Poe? Was it based on biographies and/or historical anecdotes?**
A: I'd read every biography written up to that point, and had access to many of Poe's letters before The Poe Society of Baltimore published them. Some were at the Enoch Pratt Library. But in the end, it was actor instinct that informed certain choices. In the film, I don't use any touch of a southern, or Northern Virginia accent, although in some recordings I've made as Poe since, I lean toward giving him a flavour of The Southern Gentleman, which he so wanted to project to people.

**Q: How difficult is it to both direct a film and play the leading role?**
A: It's not difficult for me at all on film. A little trickier on stage. Making films, I prepare very well as a director and plan and storyboard the shots out with the camera-person well in advance, and discuss where the camera will go and how a sequence will cut when we location-scout or go over my set designs. All that preparation allows room for improvisation and changing camera placement or movement. Nothing is completely locked in, as an actor might do something surprising and you should accommodate him, if you can.

And I have a great team on my films who run the machine. A good production manager and a good assistant director keep the crew and schedule together. And it's invaluable to have a camera-person who has a crack crew. They in and of themselves are often autonomous and their professionalism

*The Death of Poe* (2006)

keeps the whole production moving forward. Because one never has enough time. As an actor I always make sure that I have a good person who I trust to watch my performance and advise me to re-take or modulate something. For *The Death of Poe*, I had Tom Brandau on set, who is a fine director and someone I trust. I rarely do many takes when I'm in front of the camera.

**Q: When was the movie filmed and how long did it take in total?**
A: We had a 12-day schedule for *The Death of Poe* with a couple of days of pick-ups and things. Three of my other films had strict 18-day schedules.

**Q: If you don't want to reveal the movie's cost, I'll understand, but I'd love to know!**
A: Not enough and too much. I couldn't afford myself, but everybody else got paid. It made its money back after many years on DVD.

**Q: You obtained solid performances from all the actors, with my personal favourites being George Stover and Kevin G. Shinnick. You implied that you wrote the roles for them. How long have you known each other?**
A: Yes, once I cast them I shaped the roles for them.

I've known George since I was 14. I went to 16mm film screenings around Baltimore and we'd sometimes go to George's house to watch something from his collection. I've worked with George a number of times over the years, and wanted to be the first filmmaker to have two George Stovers on screen at the same time. The idea of the twins came first. George playing the twins was something I couldn't resist.

Kevin was a friend for a number of years and I knew I needed a good actor to anchor the film once the focus was taken away from Poe, as Poe spends the second half of the film thrashing about or comatose in bed. I'd also always wanted Moran to have an Irish brogue, and Kevin does the accent effortlessly. Fine actors, both.

Conrad Brooks was almost in the movie, and I'm sad that it didn't work out. He was going to play another unfortunate soul, a drunk who gets shanghaied into the forced voting pool that Poe finds himself in. Conrad's character was to have a dialogue scene with Poe, and for Poe to watch him die, but I felt it was all too "on the nose" and cut the scene before shooting. There really wasn't anything else for Conrad to do as the other roles were filled.

**Q: What is your favourite movie based on an Edgar Allan Poe story (or stories)?**
A: It shifts as moods shift, but I'll go with Corman's *House of Usher* for AIP.

**Q: What is your opinion of the Corman Poe cycle?**
A: Oh! I love his films, and those in particular!

I don't have much truck with people who complain that adaptations "aren't faithful" to the literary source material. That's the whole point of an adaptation, to make something new from the material! "Inspired by," "adapted from," I don't care – give me your take on the material! The original literary work is still there, it still exists for people to read and enjoy! It's not been harmed or destroyed in any way!

**Q: You have made me envious by appearing in Larry Blamire's *Dark and Stormy Night*. How did that come about?**
A: Larry and I met soon after our first films hit the festival circuits and after a few lunches and yap-sessions about films and fund-raising and things, Larry called and said he had a part for me. A lovely set to be on, and I love working for Larry and playing his material. He gave me a fun character in *Dark and Stormy Night* that people seem to like. I look forward to when we can work together again!

Also interviewed for this book, Shinnick (who also played Dracula onstage in a New York production in 2017) explained how he ended up in the role of Dr Moran, a genuine historical figure: 'Mark Redfield had done one of the best cinematic adaptations of *Dr Jekyll and Mr Hyde* (2002) and I was pleased to get to know him at several horror conventions. We both shared a great love of theatre as well as of classic horror films.

Jennifer Rouse & Kevin G. Shinnick in *The Death of Poe* (2006)

Mark Redfield as Poe in *The Death of Poe* (2006)

'When he offered me the role of Dr John J Moran, I was stunned but accepted readily. When he sent me the script, I was even more pleased, as it followed the known facts about the last days of the author.

'… They had created a studio space and built sets to represent the hospital, bedroom, a bar, etc. What was most astonishing was that they had created them in mere days when some planned locations had fallen through. Almost everyone in the cast and crew wore multiple hats as needed. I felt lazy, as I merely concentrated just upon my character!

'I researched the accent that I used and was pleased that several people noted the accuracy of it; plus, the film allowed me to give a little nod to my acting inspiration, Peter Cushing. In the scene where I amputate the leg… you will notice me "carelessly" wipe the blood upon my clothes. I admit my little lift/ripoff to the great actor.'

I asked Shinnick how it was to work for the triple-threat Redfield: 'Mark as a director was exact, but also graciously allowed me a lot of freedom with my character… The film that was finally finished was a beautiful art house work that seemed at times to be influenced by Poe's fever dreams. Most notable is the truly praiseworthy performance by Mark that drives the story forward, as well as his magnetic personality as the author, that holds it together. When you consider all the other things he was doing off-camera as well, and that he could still give such a focused and exact performance makes me wonder why he is not working on larger projects.'

Indeed, *The Death of Poe*, despite its minuscule budget, is one of the finest movies yet made about Poe. It follows the known facts as related by Dr Moran (although some say his credibility was apparently questionable) and, although the details of what led to Poe's death are, by nature, inconclusive, the story as told here is certainly plausible. There are few embellishments and Redfield's acting is so persuasive that one can easily believe that this is what happened to the author: as many writers have postulated, he was beaten in a tavern, his money was stolen and, severely injured and mostly delirious, he was found by members of a cooping ring.

In *The Death of Poe*, the author is finally released by the cooping ring and left in the street, where he is found by a local tavern owner who then contacts Poe's uncle (Wayne Shipley) and a doctor (Sean Paul Murphy). He is finally transported to Washington College Hospital, where he is tended to by Dr Moran, who is unable to save him. Poe dies three days later.

Shot on video, mostly in black and white with occasional colour sequences, *The Death of Poe* never lets its stylistic directorial flourishes get in the way of the story, which is quite straightforward. There are several hallucinatory sequences, but as Poe's last few days were apparently filled with delirium, they are entirely appropriate. The film is dominated by Redfield's performance; more than perhaps any other actor who attempted the role before him, Redfield *is* Poe, both dramatically and physically. Shinnick is also absolutely first-rate as Moran, who at one point admits to his wife in frustration, that he doesn't want to be known 'as the physician who killed Edgar Allan Poe.' While the rest of the performances are variable, Redfield and Shinnick anchor the production in reality, and, although it is almost relentlessly grim (how could it be otherwise?), it is an exceptional tribute to Poe the man.

*The Death of Poe* received its world premiere at the Festival of Fantastic Films in Manchester, England on 20 September 2006, with the US premiere at the Charles Theatre in Baltimore on 11 October 2006. The production deserves to be far more widely known (it is available in the US on DVD) and no aficionado of Poe should miss it.

**John Cusack in *The Raven* (2012)**

Redfield wanted to do more adaptations with Shinnick that have not yet come to fruition: 'We have spoken over the years about working on other projects. The biggest disappointments to me were *The Tell-Tale Heart*, which would have starred Mark, Jennifer (Rouse), Robert Quarry, Ingrid Pitt, Debbie Rochon and myself; and the as of yet unmade Sherlock Holmes project with Mark as the great detective and myself as his Boswell, Dr Watson. Still, hope springs eternal, and even if I am not in those projects, I would be the first to line up to see them.'

The next major Poe picture was released under the hoary old title of *The Raven* in 2012, although it has nothing to do with Poe's poem and little to do with Poe himself, despite the fact that he's the central character. Written by Hannah Shakespeare (presumably no relation to William) and Ben Livingston, the film is about a madman who commits horrifying crimes inspired by Poe's poems and stories. A young detective in Baltimore (Luke Evans) teams up with Poe (John Cusack) to track down the killer.

Directed by James McTeague (*V for Vendetta*, 2005), *The Raven* attempts to bring Poe to the Attention Deficit Disorder generation with such stars as Cusack (*Grosse Pointe Blank*, 1997), Evans (*Clash of the Titans*, 2010), Alice Eve (*Sex and the City 2*, 2010) and Brendan Gleeson (Martin Scorsese's *Gangs of New York*, 2002). The results are decidedly mixed.

Although set in Baltimore, the film was actually produced in Hungary and Serbia with a mainly British cast, all playing Americans. Ewan McGregor was originally slated to portray Poe but dropped out. Sylvester Stallone had tried to set up a rival Poe picture with Robert Downey Jr as Poe, but that project fell through – perhaps mercifully.

Like Redfield's *The Death of Poe*, *The Raven* purports to dramatise Poe's last days in Baltimore, but far more fancifully. With a much larger budget of around $26,000,000 and given a wide release in the USA by Relativity Media on 27 April 2012, *The Raven* is handsomely mounted, but in its attempt to appeal to the broadest possible audience, the film is not all it could have been,

First of all, it's full of anachronisms, especially in the dialogue. A typesetter named Ivan (Sam Hazeldine) tells Poe that he is his 'biggest fan.' The word 'fan' (short for fanatic) was not used in this sense until forty years after the events in the film took place. Phrases such as 'straight razor' (used by one of the detectives) would have been redundant, as they were the only types of razor in existence at the time. Ivan also mentions Jules Verne, but Verne was not well known until at least fourteen years after Poe's death. Perhaps most egregious of all, the words 'A SERIAL KILLER' are emblazoned across the front page of a newspaper; the term was not in common usage until the 1970's. In a rather nice touch, however, it is hinted that Poe himself came up with the phrase.

As portrayed by Cusack, Poe is unaccountably encumbered with a goatee rather than the neatly trimmed moustache he actually wore. On the plus side, Cusack is quite good, hitting the right notes (if rather broadly because of the script), making the most of such lines as, 'Her innocence was the

The Raven (2012)

John Cusack in *The Raven* (2012)

first part of her soul to die,' and, 'I often thought I could hear the sound of darkness as it stole across the horizon, rushing towards me. But here I was overwhelmed by a sorrow so poignant… Once she finally died I felt in all candour a great release, but it was soon supplanted by the dark and morbid melancholy that has followed me like a black dog all my life.'

The production is handsomely mounted, but the characters are not well rounded, nor, with the exception of Poe himself, even developed. Evans and Eve are given little to do but go through the motions, while Cusack dominates the proceedings. The murders are gruesome enough; within the first fifteen minutes, we see murders (or their gory aftermaths) based on 'Murders in the Rue Morgue' and 'The Pit and the Pendulum.' Later, there's an attempted premature burial and a fair amount of frenzied carnage.

Rated R for its violence and gore, *The Raven* received mostly poor reviews, with Mick LaSalle of the San Francisco Chronicle writing, '*The Raven* has John Cusack and it has Edgar Allan Poe. It has other things not quite as good. The story has its moments, and yet there is something about this tale of a serial killer's patterning his crimes on Poe's most gruesome works that doesn't completely satisfy.' At the box office, the film made a small profit, grossing $29.65 million worldwide – not bad, but not enough to begin a new Poe pictures cycle at the multiplex.

'The System of Dr Tarr and Professor Fether' was once again adapted for the screen in 2014 under the title *Stonehearst Asylum*. Filmed under the title of *Eliza Graves*, the production featured an A–list cast: Kate Beckinsale (*The Aviator*, 2004), Jim Sturgess (*The Other Boleyn Girl*, 2008), David Thewlis (*Harry Potter and the Prisoner of Azkaban*, 2004), Ben Kingsley (*Gandhi*, 1982) and Michael Caine (*Alfie*, 1966). The director was Brad Anderson (*The Machinist*, 2004) and the film was produced in Bulgaria by Icon Films and Sobini Films from a screenplay by Joseph Gangemi. The substantial production budget was obviously given to the production because of its plot similarities to the

**Kate Beckinsale in *Stonehearst Asylum* (2014)**

highly successful Martin Scorsese movie *Shutter Island* (2010), in which Ben Kingsley had played a similar role of an asylum doctor.

The story follows the bare bones of Poe: Edward Newgate (Sturgess) takes up residence at Stonehearst Asylum, a forbidding structure in an isolated location, where he discovers that the 'revolutionary' treatments given to the inmates are cruel and twisted, and ultimately finds that the inmates are, in fact, running the asylum and are torturing their former 'captors.'

Beckinsale plays Eliza Graves, a woman imprisoned in the asylum with whom Newgate falls in love. Much of the film's running time is taken up with this star-crossed romance, although Anderson also has an eye for Gothic imagery, as the asylum is depicted as a cold and forbidding place straight out of a Hammer horror movie. Unfortunately, that's about as close as the film gets to actual horror, although the mental torture that the inmates are forced to go through is pretty gruelling. The pacing is slow, however, and the script has none of the dark wit that Poe's story possessed.

The acting is uniformly good, with Kingsley taking the honours as the appropriately chilly doctor who runs the asylum. Thewlis is downright creepy as his weird assistant, a role that probably would have been played by Dwight Frye in the Universal days. Beckinsale and Sturgess have a good chemistry together, but Caine is mostly wasted in a role with which he can do little.

The final twist of *Stonehearst Asylum* (which will not be revealed here) comes as a genuine surprise, but, again, it's too obviously modelled on that of *Shutter Island*. Released just before Halloween 2014 in the US, *Stonehearst Asylum* disappointed both horror fans and filmgoers who were expecting

Ben Kingsley and Jim Sturgess in *Stonehearst Asylum* (2014)

Sophie Kennedy Clark and Kate Beckinsale in *Stonehearst Asylum* (2014)

something more from the A-list cast. It remains a pretty but plodding failure, a diversion for a rainy Sunday afternoon perhaps, but nothing more.

The only film to feature the participation of both Christopher Lee and Bela Lugosi, the screen's two most iconic portrayers of Dracula, *Extraordinary Tales* (2015) lives up to its title. Presented by Oscar-winning fantasist Guillermo del Toro (*Pan's Labyrinth*, 2006), the animated anthology film, written and directed by Raul Garcia, features the Poe stories 'The Fall of the House of Usher' (narrated by Lee), 'The Tell Tale Heart' (narrated by Lugosi), 'The Facts in the Case of M Valdemar' (narrated by Julian Sands), 'The Pit and the Pendulum' (narrated by del Toro) and 'The Masque of the Red Death' (which is presented entirely visually with no narration).

Produced by Melusine Productions Luxembourg, *Extraordinary Tales* features a variety of digital animation styles, with each story a different type of visual delight. The film opens with its framing device, in which a raven who is actually Poe himself (voiced by Stephen Hughes) has a conversation with Death (voiced by Cornelia Funke), who is represented as a statue in a cemetery.

The dialogue itself is very Poesque, with Death beginning: 'You have devoted so many pages to my name, caressing my face with your poems, kissing my lips with your prose. All veiled love letters addressed to me. You fear me and yet you are insatiably attracted. Come with me. It's time.'

Poe responds: 'No, it cannot be. I don't want to be forgotten. I was buried in a common grave. My writings were forgotten for years."

Death: 'You are already dead. How could you remember your own death…unless you have succumbed to my embrace? Your life is not worth living anymore. It is time…'

Raven: 'Sometimes I think the only thing that kept me from you was my beating heart.'

The first story is 'Usher,' told in a very stylised type of animation, floridly Gothic yet somehow modern. Narrated with Lee's deep basso voice, who actually intones some of Poe's words in this all-too-brief encapsulation, it captures Poe's mood of death, decay and madness perfectly, and is one of the few versions to suggest that Madeline may not, in fact, have been buried alive, but that Usher only believes she was, and is driven to madness by his own guilt.

The next story is 'The Tell Tale Heart,' featuring a somewhat scratchy recording of Lugosi's own mellifluous voice, his heavy Hungarian accent giving the tale, which is Poe almost word for word, an oddly otherworldly feeling, aided and abetted by Garcia's choice of using black and white images, with an occasional splash of red to accent the final horror. When Lugosi intones, 'It is the beating of his hideous heart!' it's as if Poe just met Bram Stoker in Transylvania.

'The Facts in the Case of M Valdemar' features a mesmerist who looks exactly like Vincent Price and a Valdemar who ends up looking exactly like the 'oozing liquid putrescence' at the chilling climax. Sands doesn't have quite the gravitas of Lee or Lugosi, but he does a yeoman's job as narrator and the sequence is one of the more effective versions of the tale.

'The Pit and the Pendulum' features del Toro's narration, quite fitting as it's set during the Spanish Inquisition. This sequence features a far more realistic form of computer-generated animation and maintains a highly

This page scenes from *Extraordinary Tales* (2015)

effective sense of claustrophobia and impending doom throughout. As the only story with a 'happy' ending, the viewer feels a sense of relief when the protagonist is rescued from a fate truly worse than death.

The final story is 'Masque,' and it's told completely visually, with no narration whatsoever. The sequence doesn't hesitate to show the debauchery of Prince Prospero and his companions, and, in an inspired touch, the only words in the story are uttered by Prince Prospero when the Red Death enters the ballroom: 'Who dares insult us with this blasphemous mockery?' The inside joke is that Prospero is voiced by none other than Roger Corman!

The framing story ends when Poe finally realises that Death is his ultimate fate: 'Come now, you love me. You've been a corpse walking among the living for a long time, Edgar. It must have been a strain.'

'Maybe you're right,' Poe says with resignation.

The ending is marred somewhat by a misquote on Poe's tombstone: It reads 'Quot the Raven, "Nevermore" rather than 'Quoth the Raven...' By the time the film's short (73 minutes) running time is over, however, this 'typo' doesn't diminish the power of what we have seen before. *Extraordinary Tales* is one of the rare Poe pictures to give viewers a sense of the author's poetry, mood and dark power. Heightened by the music of Sergio de la Puente and Javier Lopez de Guerena, the film is a loving homage to both Poe the writer and Poe the man.

The 21st Century remains a dark time, replete with terrorism, bigotry, hatred and, above all, fear. As long as there is fear, however, Poe's stories will resonate. Although there have been numerous short films and 'no-budget' indie features based on Poe's work that have been made since, *Extraordinary Tales* is to date, the most recent major feature film based on his writings. It will certainly not be the last. With its homages to Corman's Poe cycle, *Extraordinary Tales* points the way to the future of Poe pictures while gazing through the prism of the past. And who is looking back at us through that prism?

None other than Edgar Allan Poe himself.

# INDEX OF FILM AND TELEVISION TITLES

Battle of the Worlds (1961) 134

Baywatch (1989-2001) 198

Beach Blanket Bingo (1965) 115

Beast of Hollow Mountain, The (1956) 158

Becket (1964) 105

Berenice (1959) 128

Betrayal, The (1957) 131

Beverly Hills Vamp (1989) 201

Beware! The Blob (1972) 189

Beyond, The (1981) 152

Beyond the Valley of the Dolls (1970) 196

Beyond Re-Animator (2003) 175

Bicycle Thief, The (1948)

Biggest Battle, The (1978) 148

Bionic Woman, The (1976-1978) 161

Bird of Paradise (1951) 93

Birth of a Nation (1914) 14

Bitter Rice (1949) 64

Black and White (1931) 28

Black Cat, The (aka The House of Doom, 1934) 35-40, 45

Black Cat, The (1941) 47-48

Black Cat, The (1966) 186,187

Black Cat, The (1981) 151-153

Black Raven, The (1943)

Black Room, The (1935) 37

Black Sabbath (1963) 137, 146

Black Sleep, The (1956) 77

Black Sunday (UK: Revenge of the Vampire, 1960) 82, 132, 134, 141, 189, 198

Black Torment, The (1964) 116

Blade of the Ripper (1971) 148

Blood and Black Lace (1964) 148

Blood and Roses (1960) 145

Blood and Sand (1941) 49

Blood Beast Terror, The (1967) 118

Blood Drinkers, The (1966) 186

Blood Feast (1963) 185

Blood of the Vampire (1958) 75, 115, 127

Bloody Judge, The (1970) 192

Bloody Pit of Horror (1965) 138

Blow-Up (1966) 138

Body and Soul (1947) 125

Born Yesterday (1950) 49

Bostonians, The (1984) 202

Brain Leeches, The (1978) 201

Brainwashed (1960) 34

Breakfast Club, The (1985) 166

Breaking Bad (2008-2013) 204

Bride of Frankenstein (1935) 37

Bride of Re-Animator (1989) 175

Brides of Dracula, The (1960) 114

Brute Force (1947) 46

Bucket of Blood, A (1959) 113

Bullwinkle Show, The (1959-1964) 61

Buried Alive (1990) 199-201

Burning Hills, The (1956) 113

But Not for Me (1959) 125

Bwana Devil (1952) 60


C

Cabinet of Dr Caligari, The (1919) 20, 21, 25

Captain Clegg (US: Night Creatures, 1962) 108, 111

Captain from Castile (1947) 191

Carrie (1976) 205

Cash on Demand (1961) 111

Castle Freak (1995) 175

Castle of Blood (aka Danza Macabre, 1964) 134-137, 145, 146

Castle of Fu Manchu, the (1969) 125

Cat People (1942) 49, 86, 113

Charlie Chan at Monte Carlo (1937) 158

Charlie Chan in Rio (1941) 49

Sorry, Wrong Number (1948) 70

South Pacific (1958) 82

Space: 1999 (1975-1977) 173

Spectre of Edgar Allan Poe, The (1974) 189-
191

Sphinx, The (1933) 53

Spider Baby (1967) 98

Spirits of the Dead (aka, Histories
Extraordinaires, 1969) 120,143-

Spooks Run Wild (1941) 53

Stand, The (1994) 194

Star Wars (1977) 126

Star Wars Episode V: The Empire Strikes Back
(1980) 205

Stonehearst Asylum (2016) 222-224

Strange Vice of Mrs Wardh, The (1971) 148

Strangler of Blackmoor Castle, The (1963) 139

Straw Dogs (1971) 125, 172

Strip Nude for Your Killer (1975) 148

Student Prince in Old Heidelberg, The (1927)
37

Study in Terror, A (1965) 116

Subspecies (1991) 205

Sudden Fear (1952) 142

Summer With Monika (1953) 64

Suspiria (1977) 202


T

Take the High Ground! (1953) 67

Tale of Tiffany Lust, The (1979) 199

Tales of Mystery and Imagination (1995) 171

Tales of Mystery and Imagination: The Fall of
the House of Usher (1995) 171-172

Tales of Mystery and Imagination: The Oval
Portrait (1995) 172

Tales of Mystery and Imagination: Berenice
(1995) 172

Tales of Mystery and Imagination: The Black
Cat (1995) 172

Tales of Mystery and Imagination: Ligeia
(1995) 173

Tales of Mystery and Imagination: The Cask of
Amontillado (1995) 173

Tales of Mystery and Imagination: Mr
Valdemar (1995) 173

Tales of Mystery and Imagination: The Tell
Tail Heart (sic, 1995) 173-174

Tales of Mystery and Imagination: Morella
(1995) 174

Tales of Mystery and Imagination: The Pit and
the Pendulum (1995) 174

Tales of Mystery and Imagination: The Masque
of the Red Death (1995) 174-175

Tales of Mystery and Imagination:
Biographical Portrait (1995) 175

Tales of Terror (1962) 89-94, 196

Taras Bulba (1962) 124

Tarzan the Fearless (1933) 37

Tarzan's Magic Fountain (1949) 139

Taste the Blood of Dracula (1969) 56

Taxi Driver (1976) 202

Tea and Sympathy (1956) 82

Teenage Caveman (1958) 74

Tell Tale Heart, The (1928) 25, 26

Tell-Tale Heart, The (aka Bucket of Blood,
1934) 34-35, 127

Tell-Tale Heart, The (1941) 45-47

Tell-Tale Heart, The (US, 1953) 61-62

Tell Tale Heart, The (UK, 1953) 62

Tell-Tale Heart, The (1960) 129-132

Ten Commandments, The (1923) 29

Ten Little Indians (1974) 192

Tenant, The (1976) 168

Terror, The (1963) 97-99

Village of the Damned (1960) 111

Von Ryan's Express (1965) 124, 199

Voodoo Island (1957) 77

Voyage to the Bottom of the Sea (1961) 113

**W**

Walking Down Broadway (aka *Hello Sister!*, 1933) 41

War of the Worlds (1953) 69

War-Gods of the Deep (aka *City in the Sea,The*, 1965) 113–116

Web of the Spider (aka *Nella Streta Morsa del Ragno*, 1971) 145–147

Weird  Science (1985) 167

Werewolf of London (1935) 37

White Line Fever (1975) 201

Wicked Lady, The (1945) 61

Wild Angels, The (1966) 113

Wild Wild West, The (1965-1969) 125

Will & Liz (2018) 183

William Tell (1958-1959) 131

Winter Carnival (1939) 50

Witchfinder General (US: *The Conqueror Worm*, 1968) 116–119, 120, 122, 141

Wizard, The (1927) 32

Wolf Man, The (1941) 37

Woman Below the Cross (1937) 124

Women In Love (1969) 116, 212

Woman of Mystery, A (1958) 131

**X**

X: The Man with the X-ray Eyes (1963) 89

**Y**

Yesterday, Today and Tomorrow (1963) 137

You Only Live Twice (1967) 139, 192

Your Vice is a Locked Room and Only I Have the Key (1972) 148–149

Young Philadelphians, The (1960) 200

Young Racers, The (1963) 104, 134

Yum Yum Girls, The (1976) 149

**Z**

Zombi 2 (US: *Zombie*, 1979) 151, 152, 153

Zorro (1959) 158

Zulu (1964) 62